RUSSIA AND THE ARTS

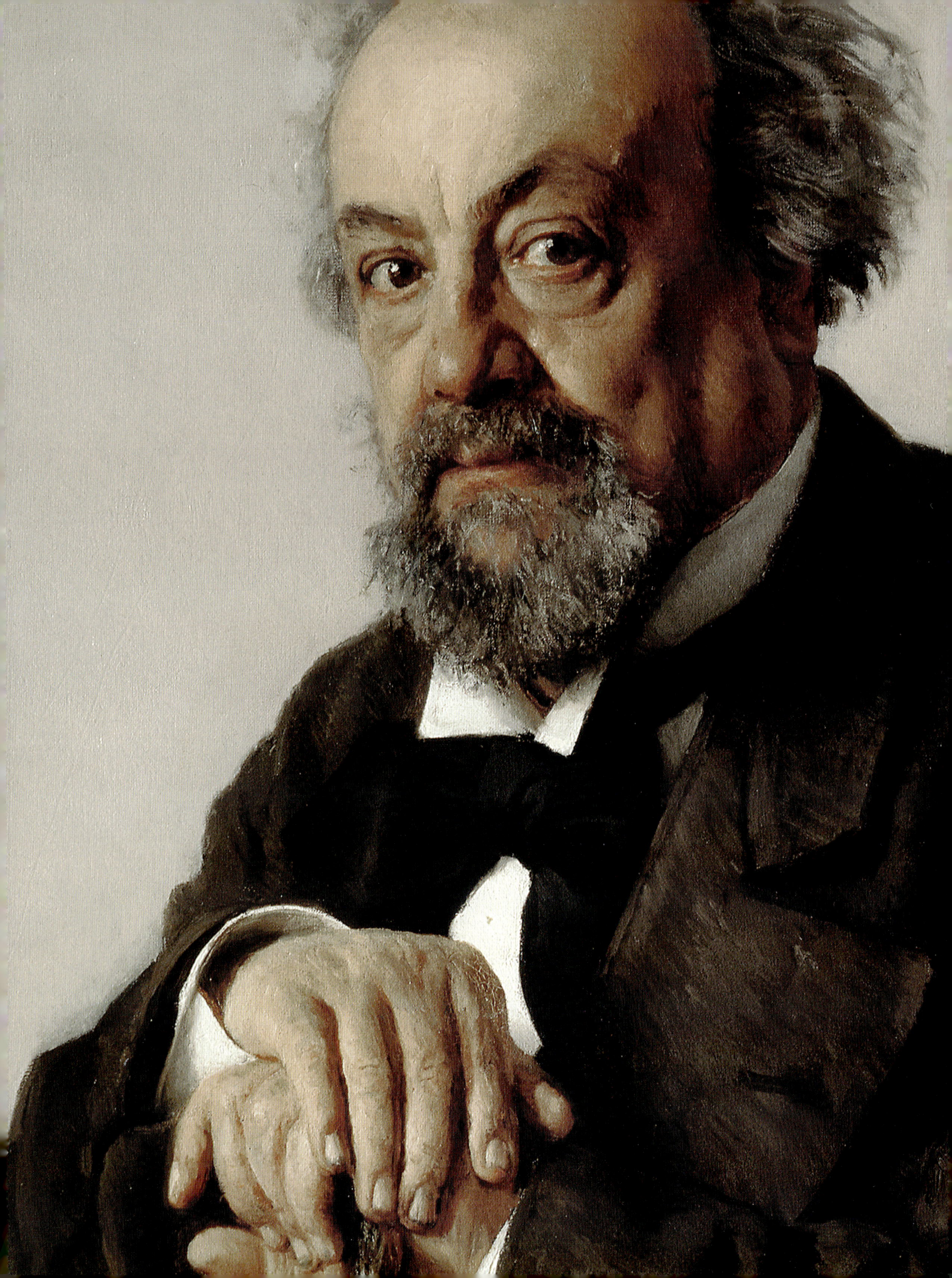

RUSSIA AND THE ARTS

THE AGE OF TOLSTOY AND TCHAIKOVSKY

ROSALIND P. BLAKESLEY

NATIONAL PORTRAIT GALLERY, LONDON

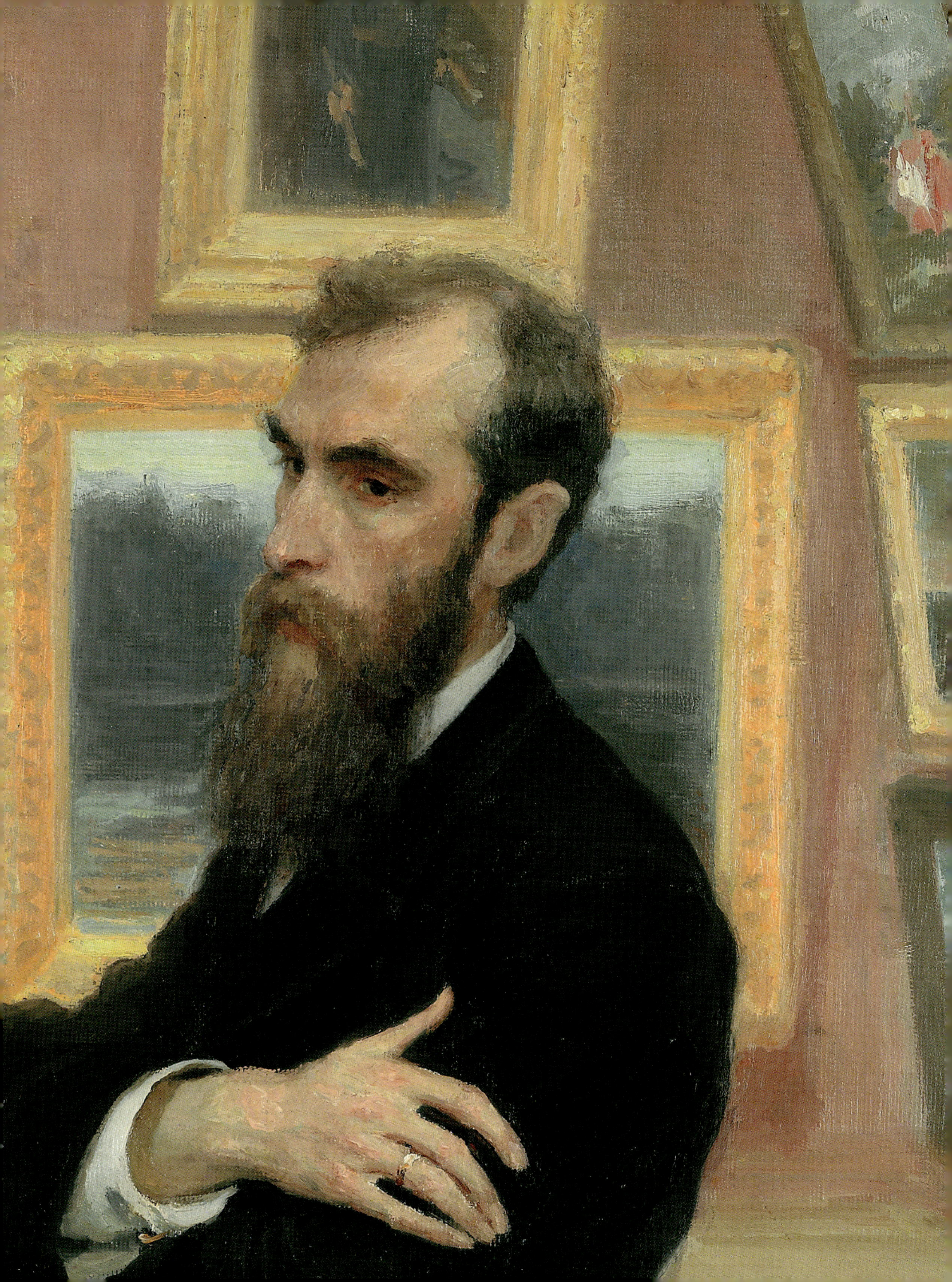

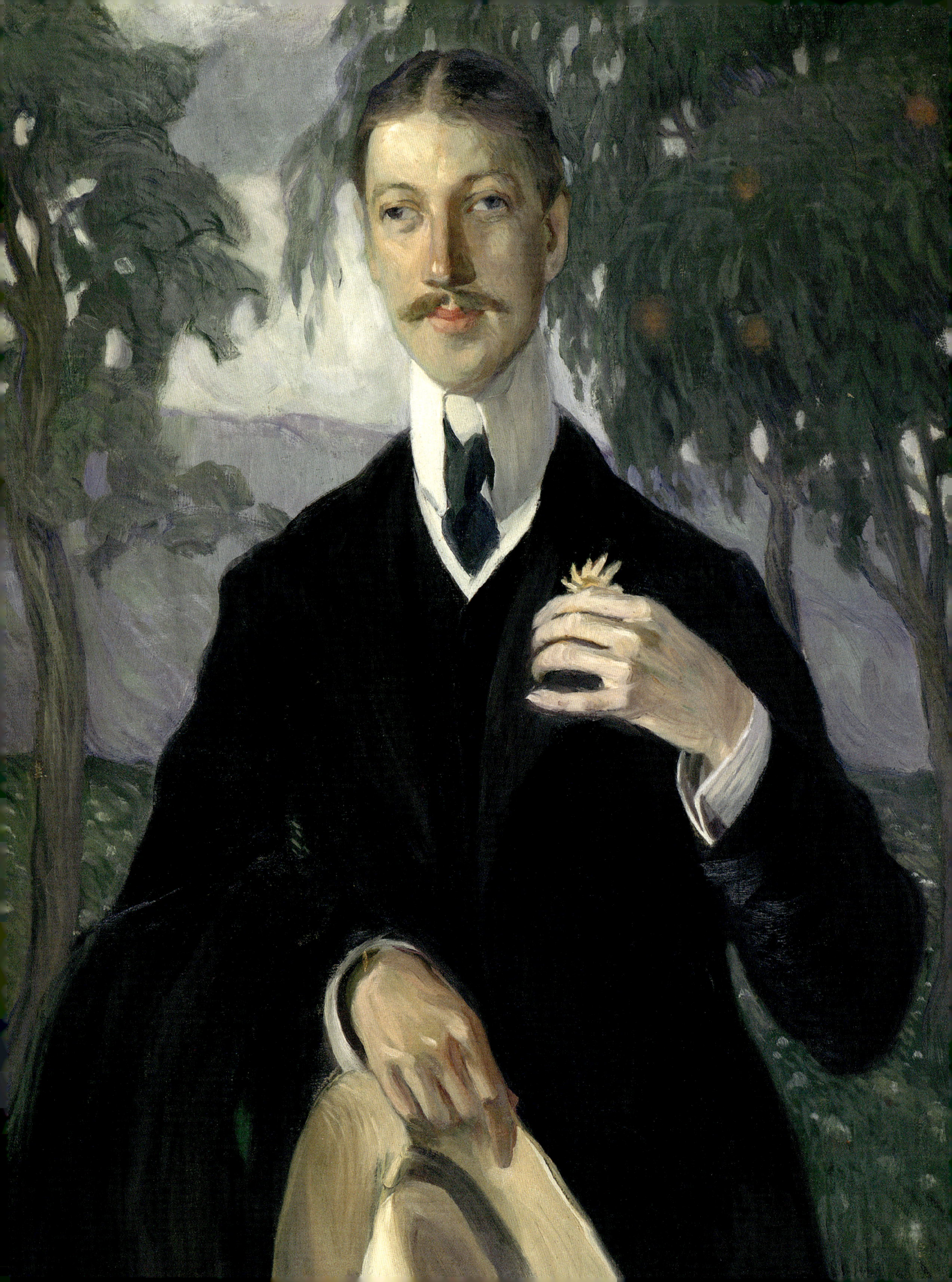

CONTENTS

Forewords   13

1. FROM HUMBLE ORIGINS TO FAVOUR AT COURT   16

2. A COMING OF AGE   35

3. THE QUEST FOR RUSSIAN DISTINCTION   60

4. ENGAGING WITH MODERNISM   94

5. A COUNTRY IN CRISIS   118

THE PORTRAIT GALLERY OF PAVEL TRETYAKOV   145
Tatiana Karpova

The State Tretyakov Gallery   162
Acknowledgements   163
Bibliography   164
Picture credits   166
Index   170

PLATES

1 *Alexander Herzen* Nikolai Ge, 1867

2 *Alexander Ostrovsky* Vasily Perov, 1871

3 *Vladimir Dal* Vasily Perov, 1872

4 *Fedor Dostoevsky* Vasily Perov, 1872

5 *Ivan Turgenev* Ilia Repin, 1874

6 *Alexei Pisemsky* Ilia Repin, 1880

7 *Modest Mussorgsky* Ilia Repin, 1881

8 *Anton Rubinstein* Ilia Repin, 1881

9 *The Actor Alexander Lensky as Petruchio in Shakespeare's* **The Taming of the Shrew** Ivan Kramskoy, 1883

10 *Pelageia Strepetova* Nikolai Iaroshenko, 1884

11 *Leo Tolstoy* Nikolai Ge, 1884

12 *Vladimir Stasov at His Dacha in the Village of Starozhilovka near Pargolovo* Ilia Repin, 1889–90

13 *Sophie Menter* Ilia Repin, 1887

14 *Baroness Varvara Ikskul von Hildenbandt* Ilia Repin, 1889

15 *Petr Tchaikovsky* Nikolai Kuznetsov, 1893

16 *In the Summer* Valentin Serov, 1895

17 *Nikolai Rimsky-Korsakov* Valentin Serov, 1898

18 *Anton Chekhov* Iosif Braz, 1898

19 *Pavel Tretyakov* Ilia Repin, 1901

20 *Savva Mamontov* Mikhail Vrubel, 1897

21 *Nadezhda Zabela-Vrubel* Mikhail Vrubel, 1898

22 *Fedor Shaliapin* Konstantin Korovin, 1905

23 *Maria Ermolova* Valentin Serov, 1905

24 *Ivan Morozov* Valentin Serov, 1910

25 *Nikolai Gumilev* Olga Della-Vos-Kardovskaia, 1909

26 *Anna Akhmatova* Olga Della-Vos-Kardovskaia, 1914

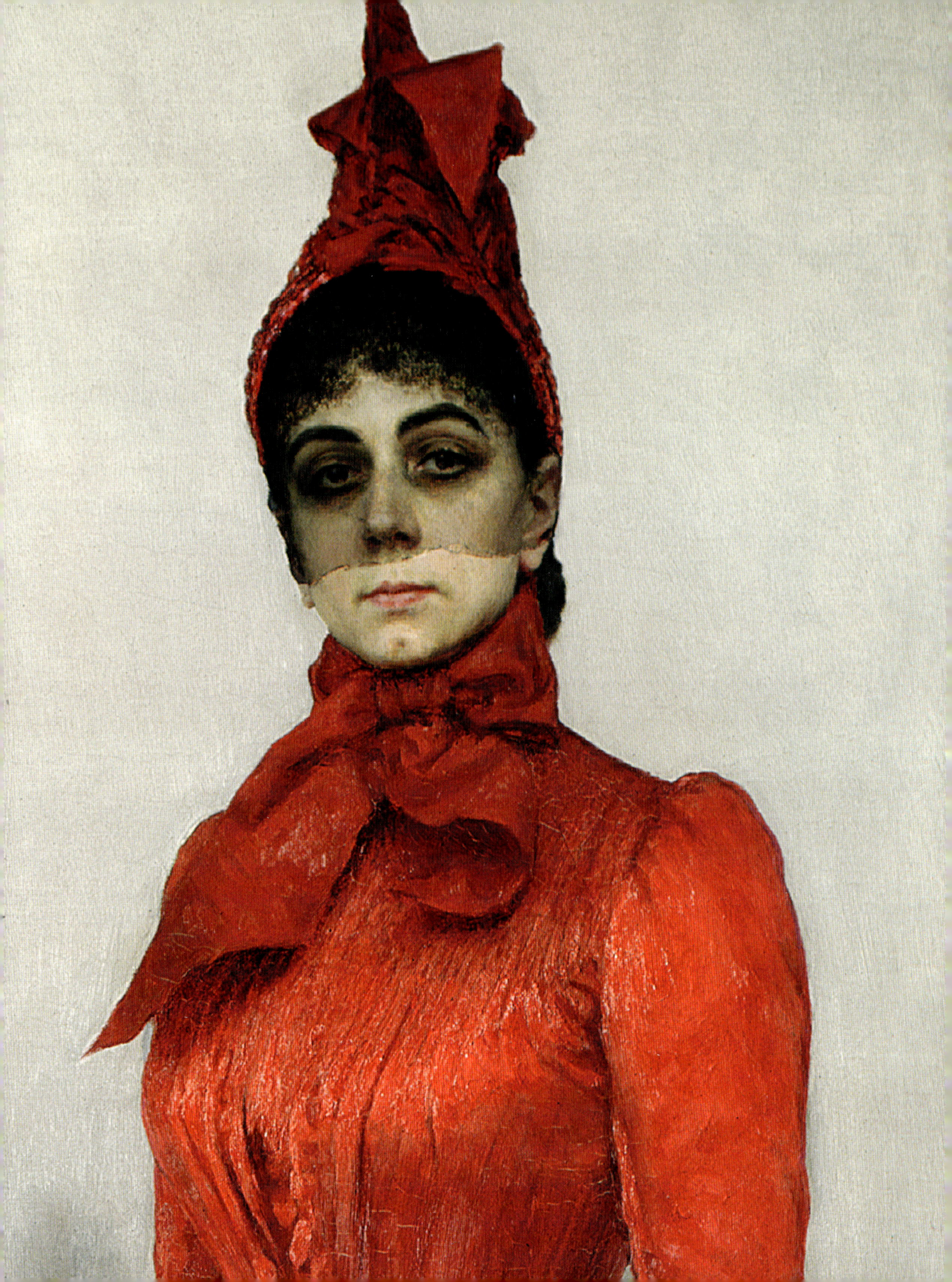

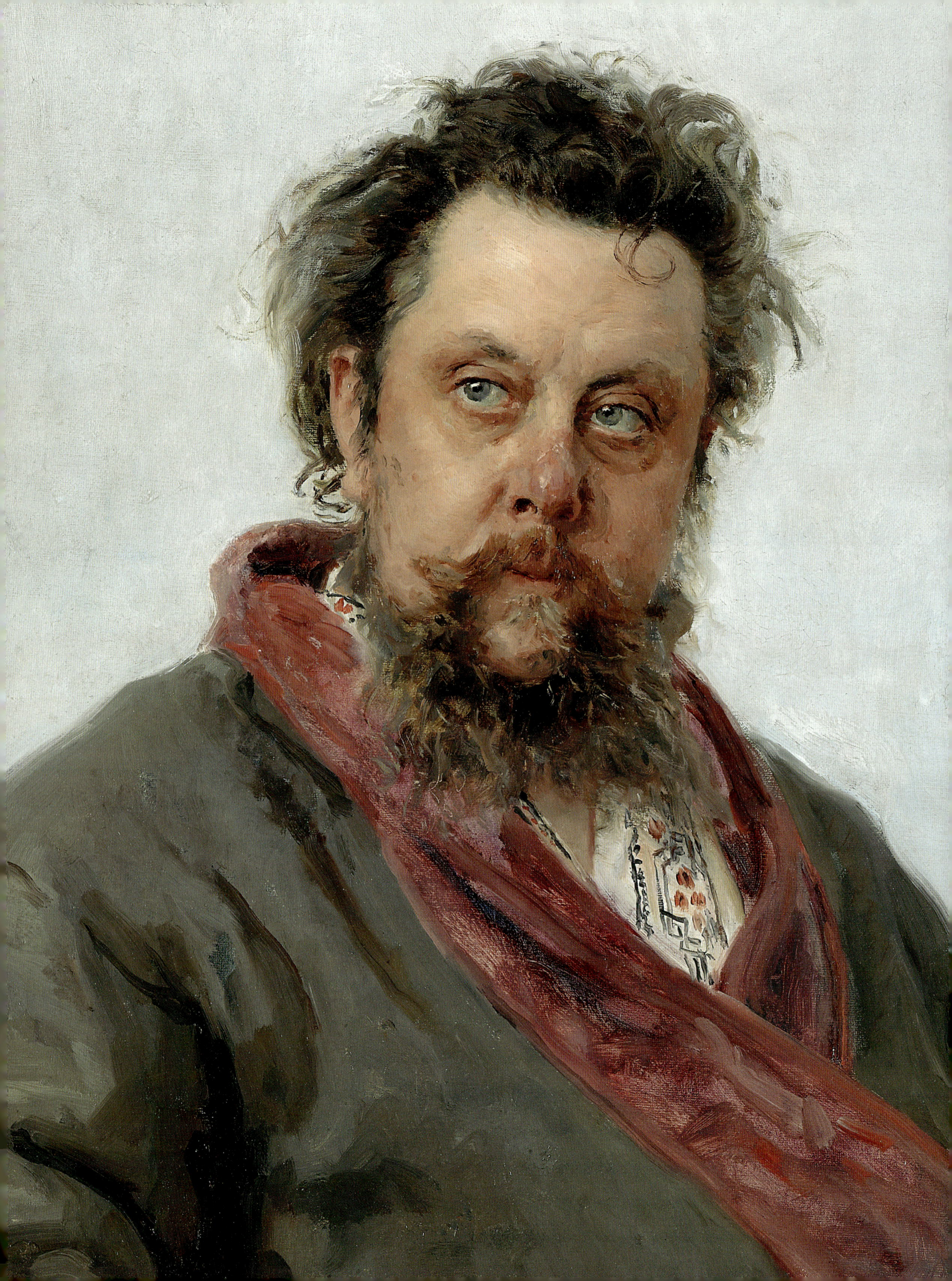

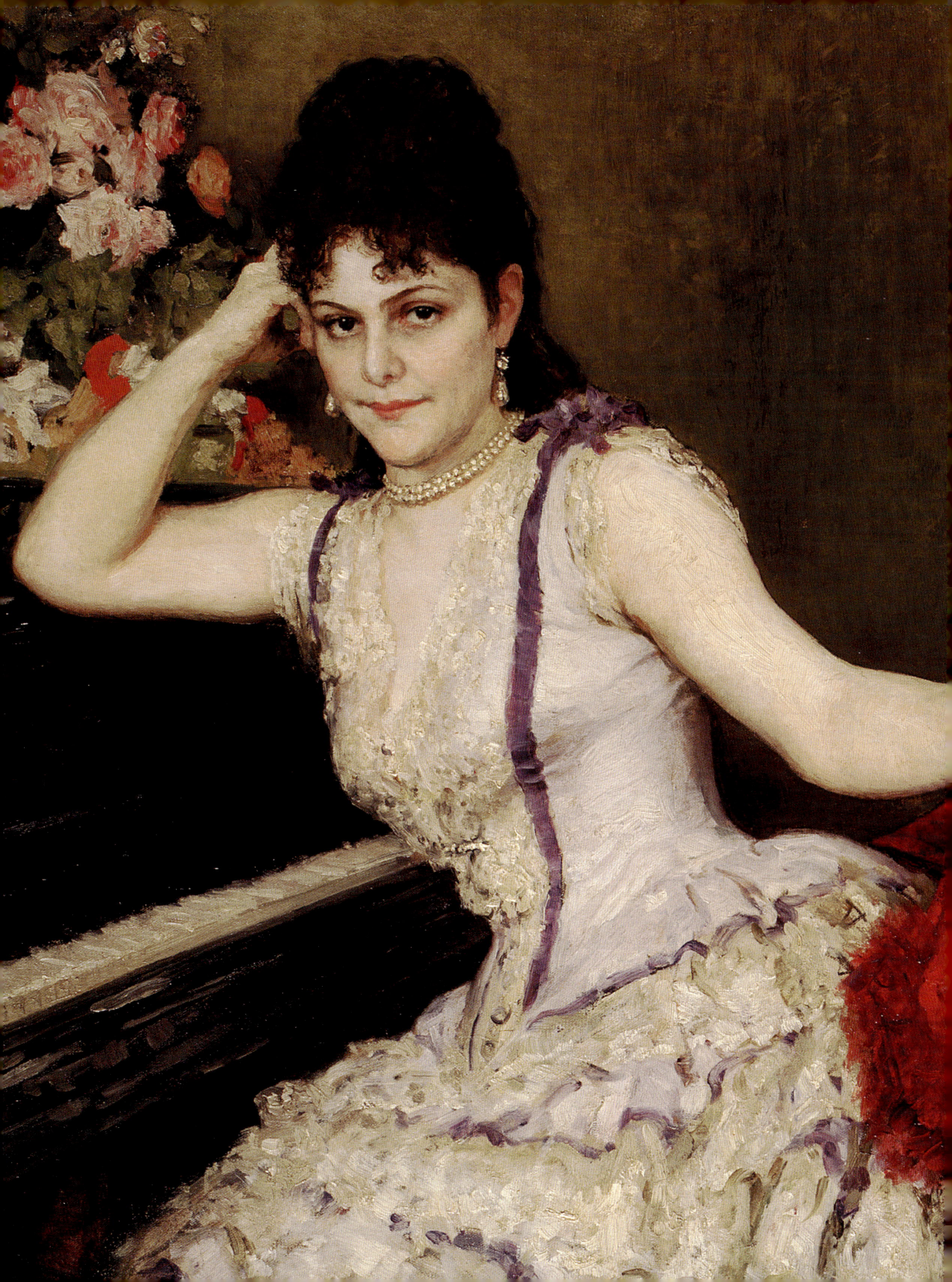

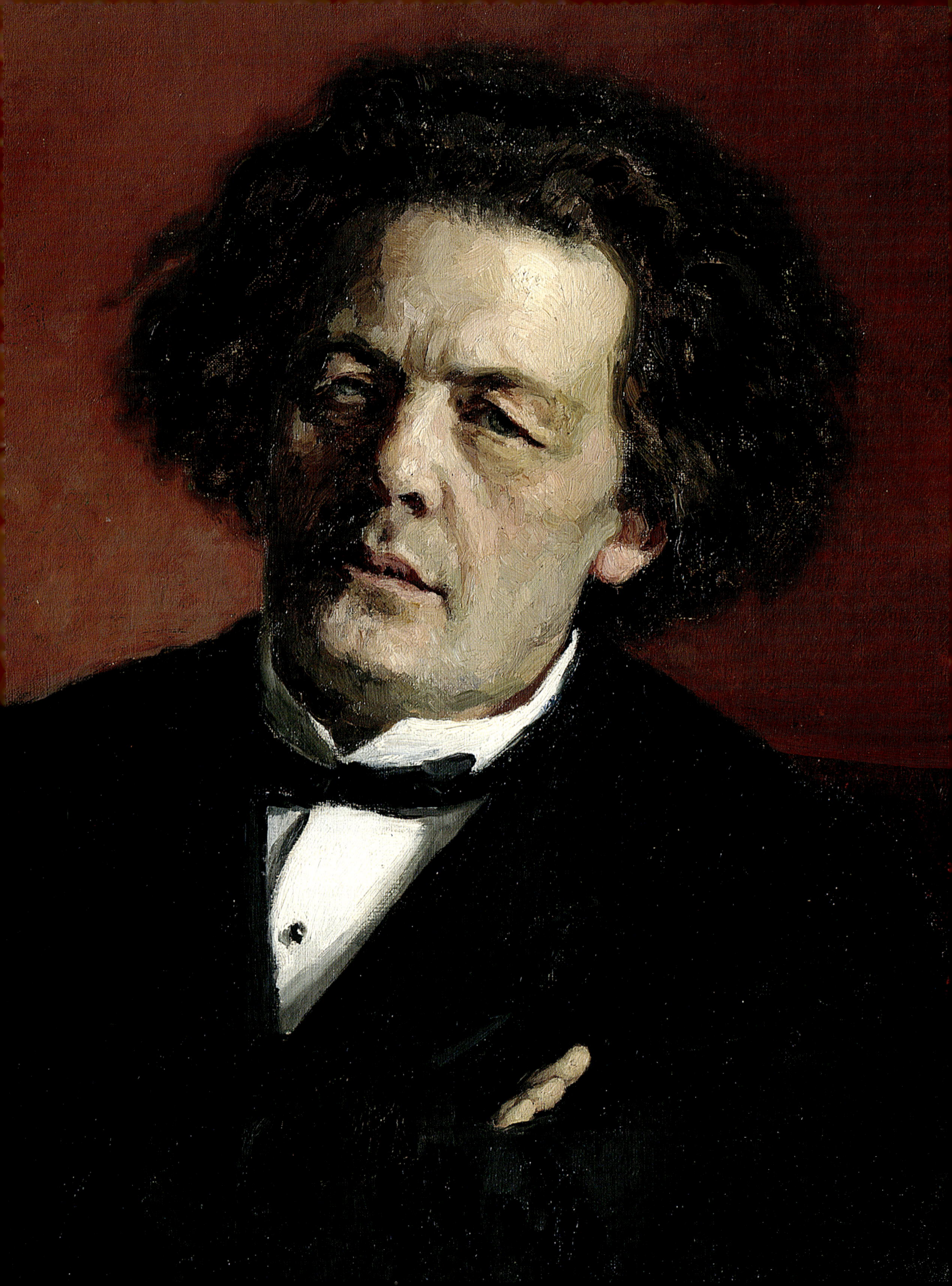

DIRECTOR'S FOREWORD

In 1856, two galleries in two quite different countries were founded. The first of these was that of Pavel Tretyakov, which would later become the State Tretyakov Gallery, Russia's national gallery in Moscow. Part of its remit was to put together a collection of portraits of the country's most eminent and influential figures, including writers, scientists, artists, actors, composers and musicians. In London that very same year the National Portrait Gallery was founded by, among others, Philip Henry Stanhope, 5th Earl Stanhope, Thomas Babington Macaulay, Benjamin Disraeli and Thomas Carlyle. It therefore seems a particularly fitting way to celebrate both institutions' 160th anniversaries that the first picture to enter the National Portrait Gallery's Collection – the so-called 'Chandos' portrait of William Shakespeare – will travel to the State Tretyakov Gallery along with more than forty other key portraits from our Collection. These portraits will comprise the exhibition *From Elizabeth to Victoria: British Portraits from the Collection of the National Portrait Gallery*, which opens at the same time as *Russia and the Arts: The Age of Tolstoy and Tchaikovsky* at the National Portrait Gallery. These two exhibitions, staged simultaneously in London and Moscow, form an important act of cultural exchange for both institutions.

The exhibition in London surveys an extraordinary period of vibrancy in Russia's cultural life during the late nineteenth century – one that is justly world famous. Names such as Dostoevsky, Tolstoy and Tchaikovsky need no introduction, although the parallel developments in the visual arts and the artists who painted the portraits of such figures could be better known in the UK, and bringing them to the public's attention is one of the chief aims of this exhibition. The twenty-six portraits of writers, composers, musicians and actors, together with a couple of their more flamboyant patrons, celebrate their achievements in the most ambitious exhibition of Russian portraiture ever to take place in a British museum. Painted by outstanding artists of the period, these commissions constitute Russia's first and most significant national portrait collection. Our foremost thanks therefore go to our colleagues at the State Tretyakov Gallery for making this important collaboration and exchange possible. First of all

we would like to thank Zelfira Tregulova, Director; Tatiana L. Karpova, Deputy Director General on Scientific Affairs; Tatiana Gubanova, Head of International Exhibitions; and Maria Shelkova, Exhibitions Coordinator.

At the National Portrait Gallery, profound thanks go to Rosalind P. Blakesley, Reader in Russian and European Art at the University of Cambridge and a Fellow of Pembroke College, Cambridge, for originating and curating such a beautiful and thought-provoking exhibition. Foremost among Gallery colleagues with whom she worked in close collaboration are Peter Funnell, Curator of Nineteenth-Century Portraits and Head of Research Programmes; Rosie Wilson, Head of Exhibitions; Michelle Greaves, Exhibitions Manager; Ulrike Wachsmann, Exhibitions Assistant; and Jude Simmons for designing the layout of the exhibition. I would also like to thank Pim Baxter, Nick Budden, Robert Carr-Archer, Naomi Conway, Tarnya Cooper, Joanna Down, Andrea Easey, Neil Evans, David McNeff, Nicola Saunders, Fiona Smith, Liz Smith, Christopher Tinker, Sarah Tinsley, Denise Vogelsang and Helen Whiteoak. Sincere thanks are also due to the Blavatnik Family Foundation for their generous support of the exhibition, and to those individuals within the Exhibition Supporters Group.

The exhibition is accompanied by this wonderful publication, so our sincere thanks go again to Rosalind P. Blakesley for her engaging and rigorous text, and all the team in our Publications Department for their sterling work – Andrew Roff, Editor, Ruth Müller-Wirth, Production Manager and Kathleen Bloomfield, Editorial and Production Assistant – and designer Will Webb for creating such a handsome volume.

Nicholas Cullinan
Director, National Portrait Gallery, London

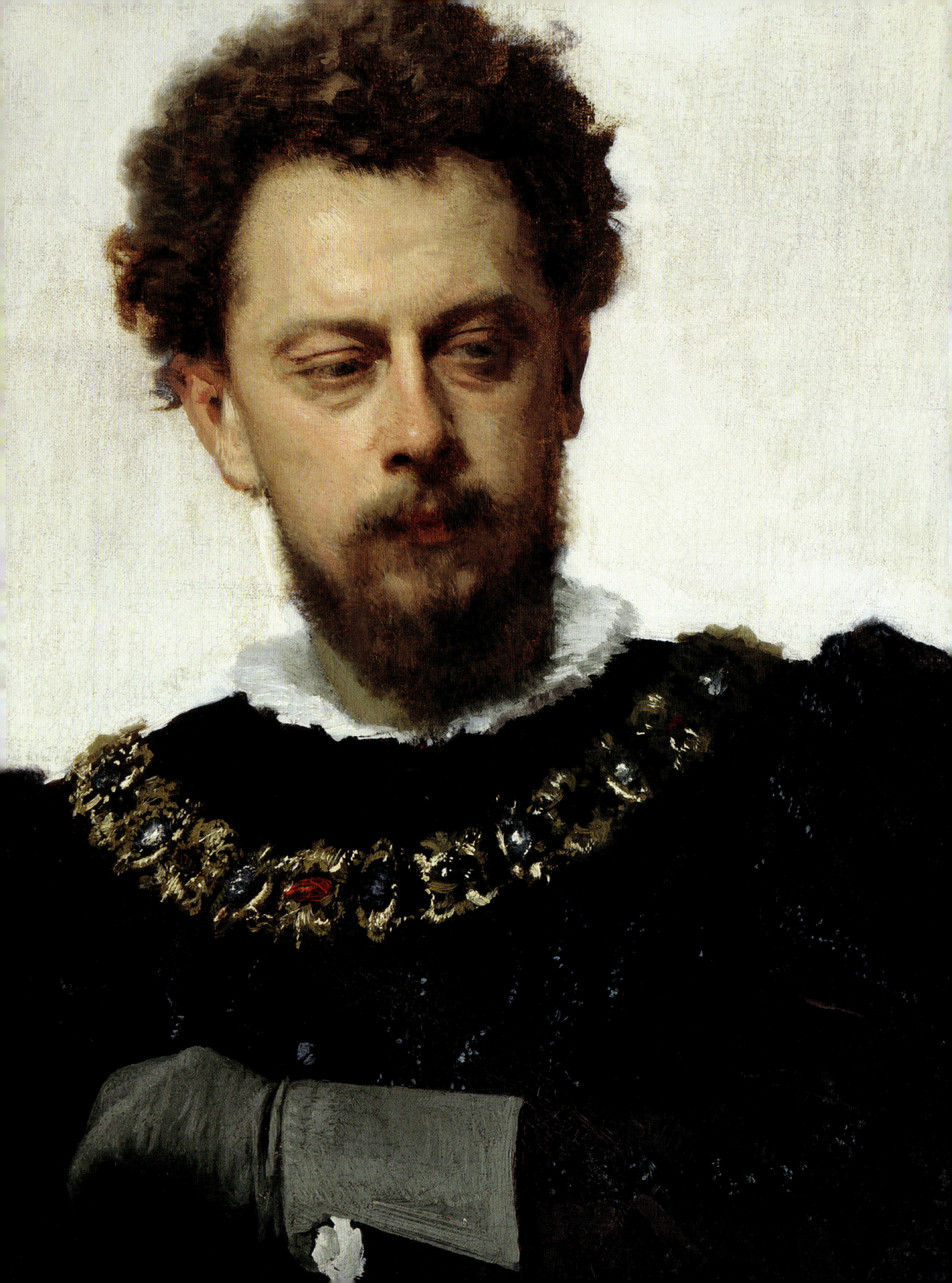

TRETYAKOV GALLERY DIRECTOR'S FOREWORD

Russia and the Arts: The Age of Tolstoy and Tchaikovsky is the first collaboration between the State Tretyakov Gallery in Moscow and the National Portrait Gallery in London. This project will give British audiences the opportunity to view a golden age of Russian culture at close quarters. The writers Chekhov, Dostoevsky, Tolstoy and Turgenev, composers Mussorgsky, Rimsky-Korsakov and Tchaikovsky, actors and singers Ermolova, Shaliapin and Strepetova, and patrons and collectors Baroness Ikskul von Hildenbandt, Mamontov and Morozov will be on display in twenty-six portraits painted by the greatest Russian artists of the second half of the nineteenth and early twentieth centuries, including Nikolai Ge, Ivan Kramskoy, Vasily Perov, Ilia Repin, Valentin Serov and Mikhail Vrubel.

The exhibition features works that are the pride of the Tretyakov Gallery and an integral part of the permanent display, rarely if ever leaving its walls. They are in their own way icons of Russian culture. The portrait of Dostoevsky, for example, is a work of exceptional historic and artistic value – the only portrait of the writer painted during his lifetime. That of Herzen, the radical political exile, was painted in Florence and smuggled into Russia by the artist Nikolai Ge, who covered it with a thin sheet of paper depicting the prophet Moses. The portrait of Tolstoy presents the writer in the study of his Moscow home at work on the manuscript of his philosophical treatise *What I Believe*. Indeed, the writing desk depicted in the portrait has been preserved and can still be seen at the L.N. Tolstoy House Museum. The portrait of Mussorgsky was painted just a few days before his death in a military hospital.

Other undeniable highlights of the exhibition are the monumental and emotionally charged portrait of the dramatic actress Maria Ermolova, painted by Serov over the course of thirty-two sittings, and a portrait of the brilliant and independent host of a literary salon, Baroness Ikskul von Hildenbandt, by Repin.

The majority of the portraits on display in the exhibition were bought or commissioned directly from the artists by Pavel Tretyakov, a merchant, philanthropist and the founder of our museum. His portrait by Repin is a fitting opener to the exhibition. Tretyakov conceived his portrait collection as 'a museum within a museum' – a portrait gallery as part of a national art gallery. There is strong evidence to suggest that in his collection of portraits of 'individuals whom the nation holds dear' Tretyakov, who often visited London on business matters, drew not only on the opinions of Russian historians, writers and philosophers, but on his experience of the National Portrait Gallery, which opened in London in 1856, and on the work of one of its founders, Thomas Carlyle.

A portrait of Ivan Morozov, a Russian merchant, successful entrepreneur and passionate collector of French painting, completes the panoramic view of extraordinary individuals in Russian culture. Serov painted Morozov against the backdrop of Matisse's *Fruit and Bronze*, a work that now belongs to the collection of the Pushkin Museum of Fine Arts in Moscow.

The British school of painting has always enjoyed great affection and attention in Russia, but unfortunately British paintings are not well represented in the collections of Russian museums. Recently, a series of exhibitions in Moscow, including those as part of the UK–Russia Year of Culture in 2014, featuring works from a variety of museums in Great Britain, has gone some way to filling this void.

Continuing and extending this relationship between Russian and British museums, the Tretyakov Gallery is planning an exhibition of works from the Collection of the National Portrait Gallery for April 2016, titled *From Elizabeth to Victoria*. It will be the Russian public's first encounter with this wonderful institution. The famous portrait of Shakespeare from *c*.1600–10, the first item to be acquired by the National Portrait Gallery, will be the opening object on display as part of this exhibition.

Russia and the Arts in London and *From Elizabeth to Victoria* in Moscow are two parts of a joint Russian–British project that signal the start of a bright new chapter in the history of cultural cooperation between our two countries. We are certain that our projects with the National Portrait Gallery will form the basis of a long-standing relationship, and that we will have the opportunity to broaden the perceptions of both British and Russian audiences about the character of 'individuals whom the nation holds dear'.

Zelfira Tregulova
General Director of the
State Tretyakov Gallery, Moscow

1
FROM HUMBLE ORIGINS TO FAVOUR AT COURT

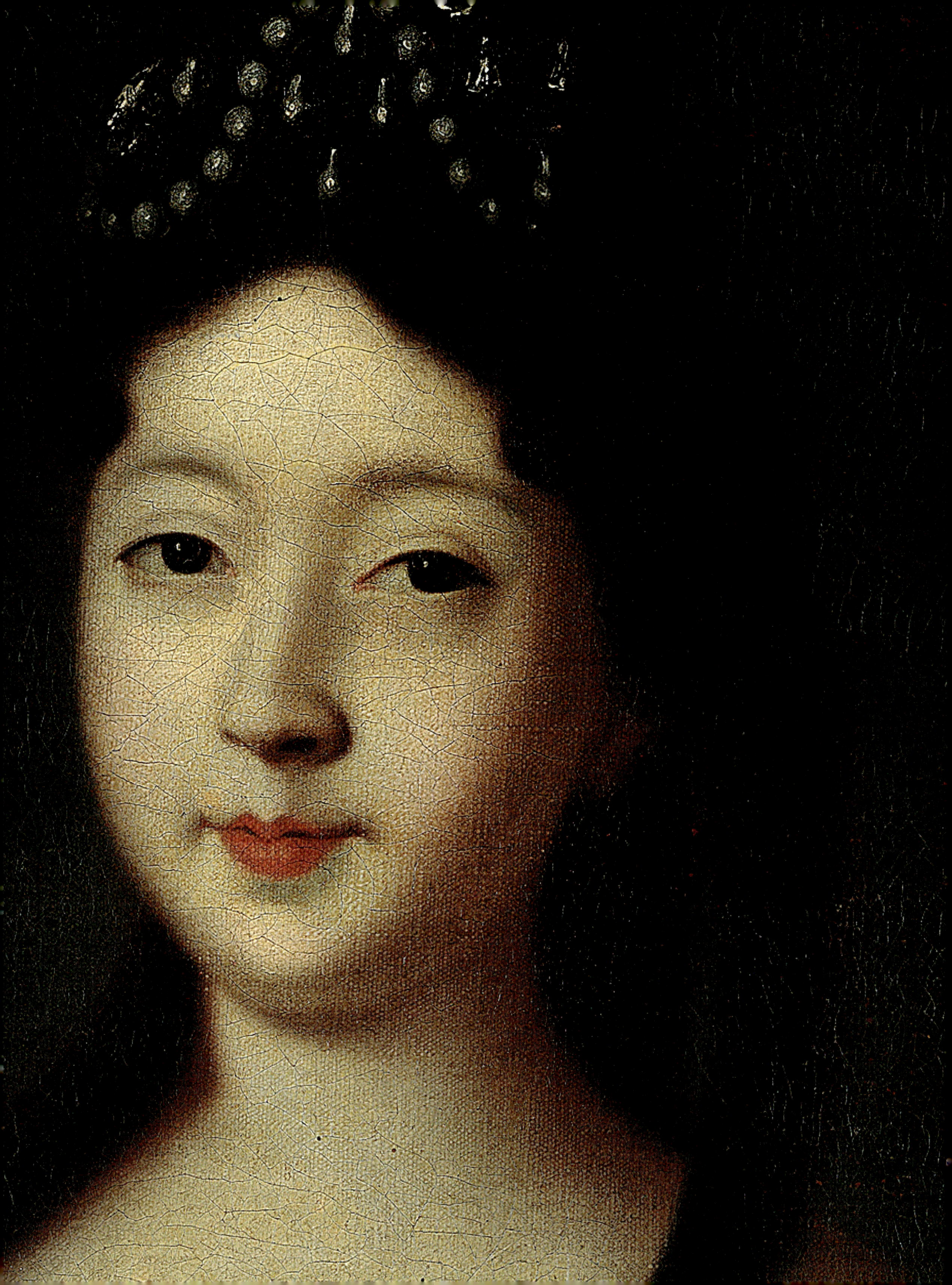

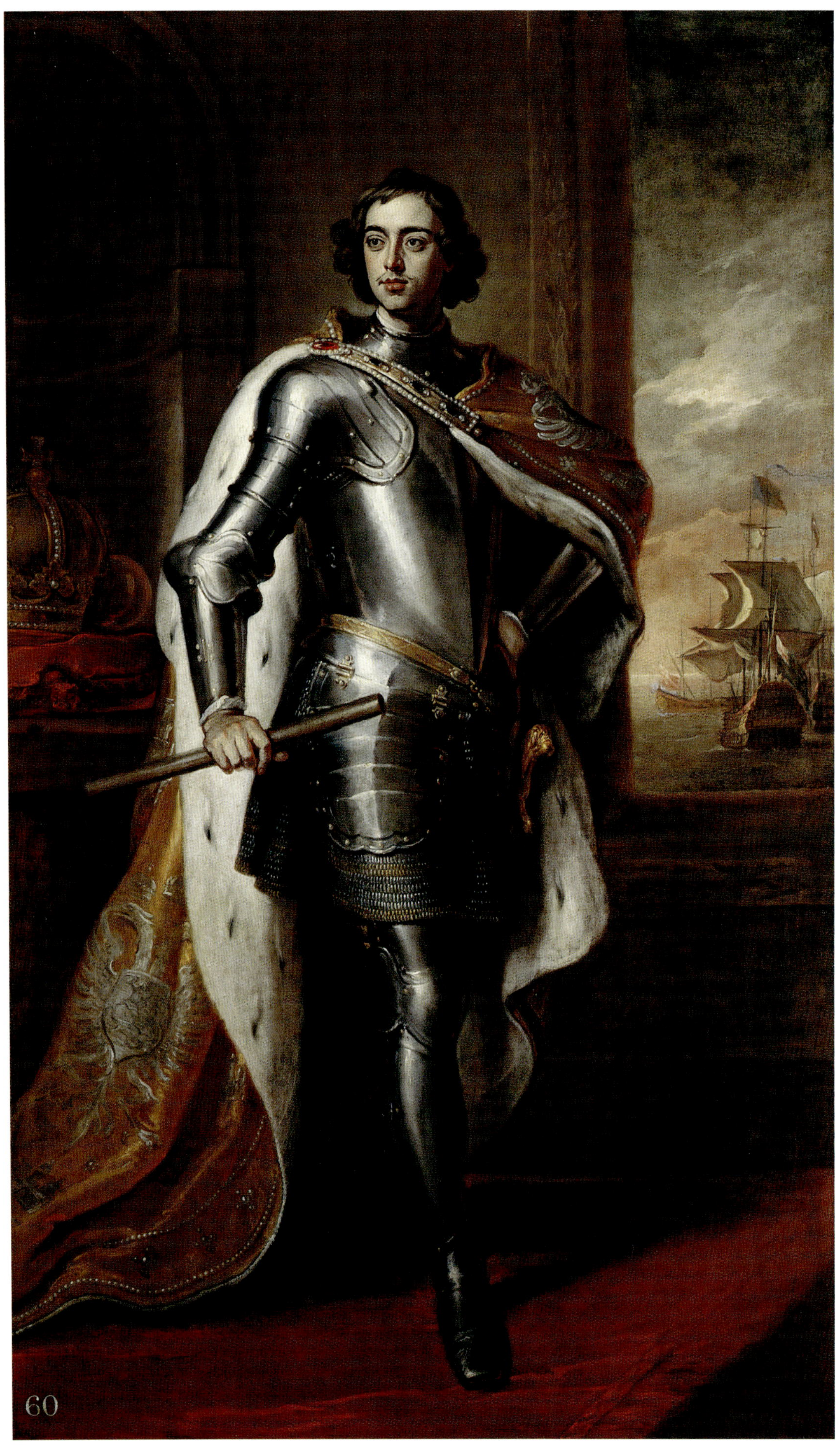

60

I N 1697, PETER THE GREAT (1672–1725), that most statuesque of Russian tsars, embarked on his first 'Grand Embassy' to Europe. He had high hopes of travelling incognito, the better to observe European civilisation undisturbed. Frustratingly for Peter, his cover tended to be blown the moment he stepped ashore. At over two metres tall, fond of a party, and with a wide-eyed and rowdy retinue that included four dwarfs, the tsar was hard to miss. 'People run after every Muscovite thinking that it's His Majesty,' one witness wryly observed.[1] Yet for all these distractions, Peter eagerly embraced the educational opportunities that foreign travel presented, hungry for commercial and technological knowledge that would help him in his quest to modernise life at home.

The tsar spent a full four months studying shipbuilding in the East India Company Docks in Holland, with an eye to improving the Russian navy that he had founded a couple of years previously. Curiously, he then learnt to extract teeth, which became one of his less welcome party tricks. He maintained his fascination in matters naval and maritime in Greenwich and Deptford, where he saw a Royal Navy Fleet Review, and wrecked the home of the diarist John Evelyn during some riotous drinking bouts. In all this noble self-improvement and ignoble revelry, the tsar also made time for the quieter pursuit of sitting for a portrait. At some stage during his stay in London from January to April 1698, Peter was painted by Sir Godfrey Kneller (Fig. 1.1). He presented the result to King William III of England just before his return home.

Kneller portrayed Peter as young and virile, the encumbrance of armour failing to disguise his shapely leg and lanky frame. The tsar's status is conveyed by the crown in the alcove and the cloak embroidered in silver thread with the double-headed eagle of Russia's coat of arms. These are balanced compositionally by a view of ships on exercise, which alludes to Peter's investment in the Russian navy and the strength that this was bringing to his reign. The visual arts were not a priority for the tsar at this stage, but he was not immune to the impact that a judiciously painted portrait could make. It provided the prototype for an entirely new

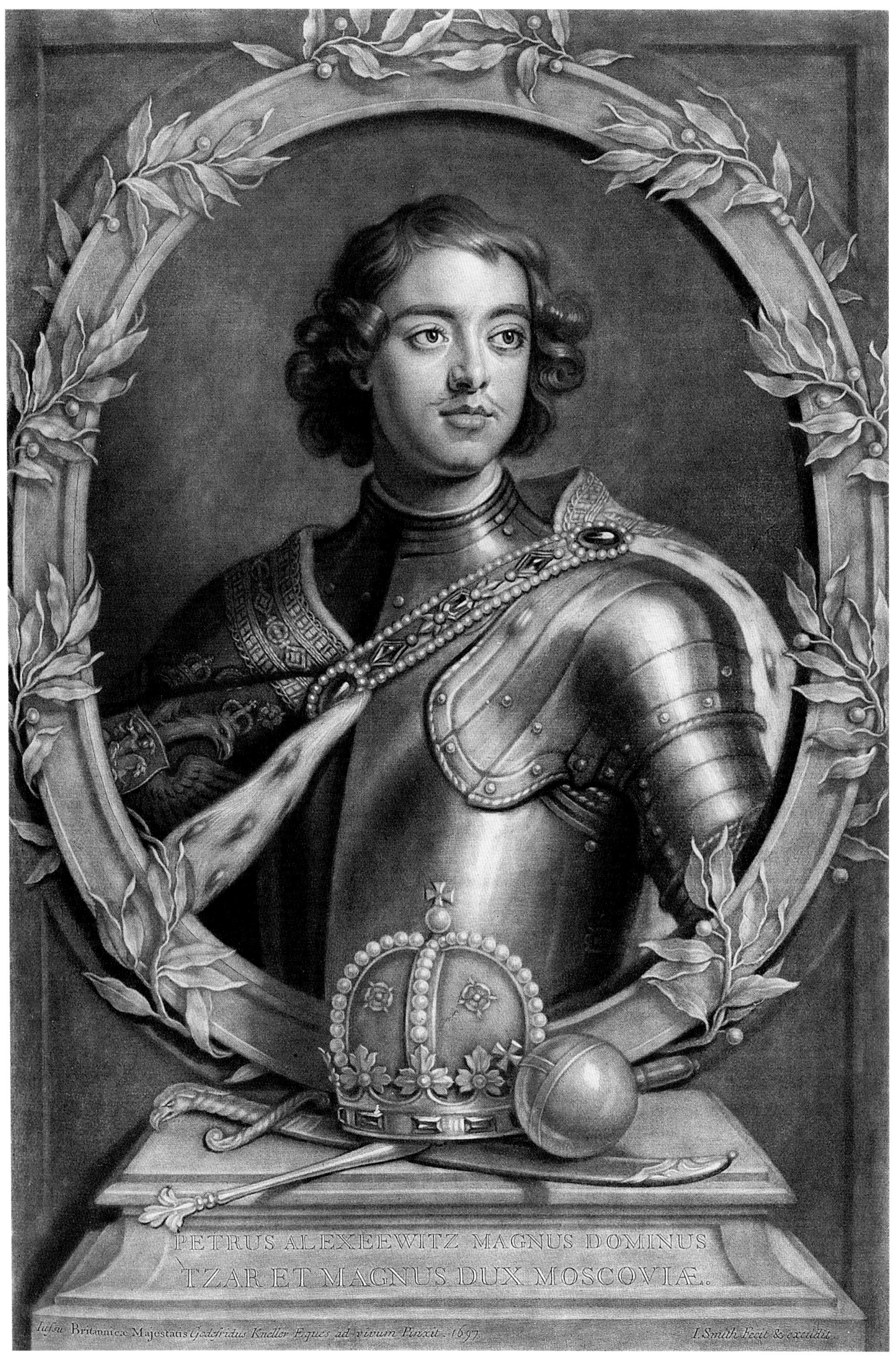
PETRUS ALEXEEWITZ MAGNUS DOMINUS
TZAR ET MAGNUS DUX MOSCOVIÆ.
Iusu Britannicæ Majestatis Godefridus Kneller Eques ad vivum Pinxit. 1697.   I. Smith Fecit & excudit.

iconography of the tsar, inspiring a wealth of prints that disseminated the notion of Peter's strategic and visionary rule (Fig. 1.2).

Kneller's painting of Peter was far from the first portrait of a Russian tsar. There had been paintings of many of Peter's predecessors, among them splendid depictions of his father, Alexei. But Kneller's was undoubtedly the most imposing image of a Russian ruler to date, and offers a convenient starting point to consider the rise of Russian portraiture as a particularly versatile and inventive art form.

Portraiture in late seventeenth-century Russia had yet to achieve anything like the distinction that it enjoyed in western Europe. Russia had an unparalleled richesse of icons, but these were seen very much as devotional objects rather than works of art. There was also an idiosyncratic regional form of portraiture known as *parsuna* painting, which had originated in recent decades in Poland and Ukraine. This tended to retain the full-frontal pose, blocks of colour and flatness of icon painting, but modulated these in a more naturalistic style derived from the West. What was notably lacking, though, was a diverse body of trained portraitists whose work was feted and debated in the wider public sphere. Russia had no Rembrandt or Frans Hals to probe the self-image of her prosperous citizens, no Kneller or Van Dyck to glorify her court. The distinction between artist and craftsman had yet to be made.

All of this was to change in the years that followed Peter's return from Europe in 1698. The tsar's most pressing concern was to quell a troublesome insurrection, for while he had been abroad four regiments of soldiers known as the *streltsy* had marched on Moscow in an attempt to place Peter's half-sister, Sophia, on the throne. The rebels were quickly overcome by troops loyal to the tsar and, following a lengthy trial, over a thousand *streltsy* were tortured and executed across Russia, their rotting bodies left hanging as a stark deterrent to any other critics of Peter's rule. Some were clearly visible from the cells of the Novodevichy Convent in Moscow, where Sophia had been secluded for over a decade. With this brutal suppression, Peter brought to an end a long period of dynastic infighting and political unrest in Russia, and was at last able to focus his attention on the project that had motivated his trip to Europe: the transformation of his country from a benighted, feudal fiefdom to a proud, enlightened European state.

The steps that Peter was prepared to take to achieve this aim knew no bounds. He imported workmen of every persuasion to advance Russia's urban, military and economic expansion. They came in their droves, travelling vast distances to parlay their craft into unimaginable professional and financial rewards in this strange new land. At the same time, Russian subjects were unceremoniously dispatched to study abroad. From merchants and masons to engineers and shipwrights, they ventured to the quarries of Italy and the shipyards of Britain and Holland in search of skills that would help to chisel Russia into shape and steer her new course.

But even this fast and frenetic traffic of expertise was not enough for the tsar, who looked with contempt at the muddy lanes and shambolic dwellings of medieval Moscow. Nothing less than an entirely new city was required to serve the needs of a modern, westernised Russia. Peter duly founded St Petersburg in 1703, and pursued its development with characteristic single-mindedness. No matter that the site he chose in the marshy littoral of the Gulf of Finland caused the foundations of new buildings to flood and collapse. No matter that thousands of men involved in its construction suffered from waterborne diseases and exposure to the elements, or were maimed or killed on unsafe building sites. St Petersburg rose regardless, with masonry construction forbidden elsewhere in Russia so that resources could be concentrated on the new city while it took shape. A vibrant and powerful symbol of modern Russia, it opened a 'window on Europe' and enabled vital new trade routes with the West. Peter's new cosmopolis replaced Moscow as the capital of Russia in 1713, and the tsar designated his country an empire in 1721. His grandiose ambitions for Russia were being realised in both material and rhetorical form.

Fig. 1.2
Peter I (Peter the Great)
John Smith after Sir Godfrey Kneller,
1698

St Petersburg, with its glistening spires and resplendent palaces, its elegant boulevards and sensible radial plan, provided fertile soil for the visual arts. Foreign architects were offered salaries unthinkable in their native countries to come and design its showcase buildings: the Peter and Paul Fortress on its own island in the River Neva; the first Winter and Summer Palaces; Peter's cherished Kunstkamera and Academy of Sciences; and myriad other institutions required to house the increasingly complex apparatus of the state. Newly trained painters strained their necks and eyes to decorate murals and ceilings. Eager young sculptors fashioned lively friezes and bas-reliefs. Precious marble statues, imported from Italy, were installed in the Summer Garden, creating Russia's first public art gallery. This provided a spectacular setting for the social assemblies at which Peter insisted on new modes of behaviour and etiquette. European fashions were introduced, and beards – that perennial signifier of Russian manhood and Orthodox devotion – were proscribed.

There were exciting commissions for portraitists too. The most prestigious of these went to foreign artists, whose superiority over local painters went unchallenged for many decades. Louis Caravaque, for example, was brought over from France to serve as court artist and painted many imperial portraits, among them one of Peter's daughter, Tsarevna Anna Petrovna, whose wasp-waisted gown exemplified the European sophistication that Peter was keen to propagate (Fig. 1.3).

Gradually, though, Russian as well as foreign portraitists began to acquire renown. Key among them was Ivan Nikitin, one of five painters whom Peter sent to study abroad. Returning in 1720, after some three and a half years in Italy, Nikitin was charged with painting Gavriil Golovkin, an astute courtier who occupied positions of great influence during Peter's reign (Fig. 1.4). He had been appointed to the new post of state chancellor in 1709, received the title of count in 1710, and later served as president of the College of Foreign Affairs. Nikitin took care to register the status that these appointments conferred in his meticulous rendition of the orders pinned to his sitter's chest. Golovkin clearly followed Peter's new sartorial edicts, for he poses bewigged and clean-shaven in a richly brocaded waistcoat and frockcoat rather than in traditional Russian attire. The portrait equally stands testament to the impact of Peter's policies on artistic practice, for it is painted with a naturalism and technical finesse that stemmed from Nikitin's time abroad.

The aplomb with which Nikitin appropriated a European style of portraiture led to important commissions in later years, not least that of depicting Peter on his deathbed – a candid image of lifeless flesh and rumpled bedding that seemed to defy the hierarchical and autocratic norms of the period in which it was made. For all Nikitin's success, however, he was as vulnerable as anyone to the vagaries of imperial rule. This was cruelly driven home in 1732, when the painter was arrested, tortured and exiled for maligning a high-placed member of the Holy Synod, the executive organ of the Russian Orthodox Church that Peter had established in 1721. It would take many years before painters would attain the status to escape such arbitrary and heavy-handed treatment, and stake their position as free-thinking professionals. Nonetheless, they had acquired important new patrons and training opportunities during Peter's reign, and began to see their work appreciated for its intellectual insight, rather than for its manual dexterity alone.

On Peter's death in 1725, the crown passed to his wife, Catherine I, marking the beginning of a lengthy period of female rule. The Russian throne would be occupied by women for the best part of the next seventy years. The earliest of these empresses continued to favour foreign portraitists and made no dramatic interventions in Russian artistic life. Peter's niece Anna Ioannovna, for example, turned to that long-standing court favourite Caravaque for a full-length coronation portrait, replete with sceptre, crown and orb, when she was crowned empress in 1730. In 1741, however, Peter's daughter Elizabeth ascended the throne and would preside over developments of great significance for Russian artists.

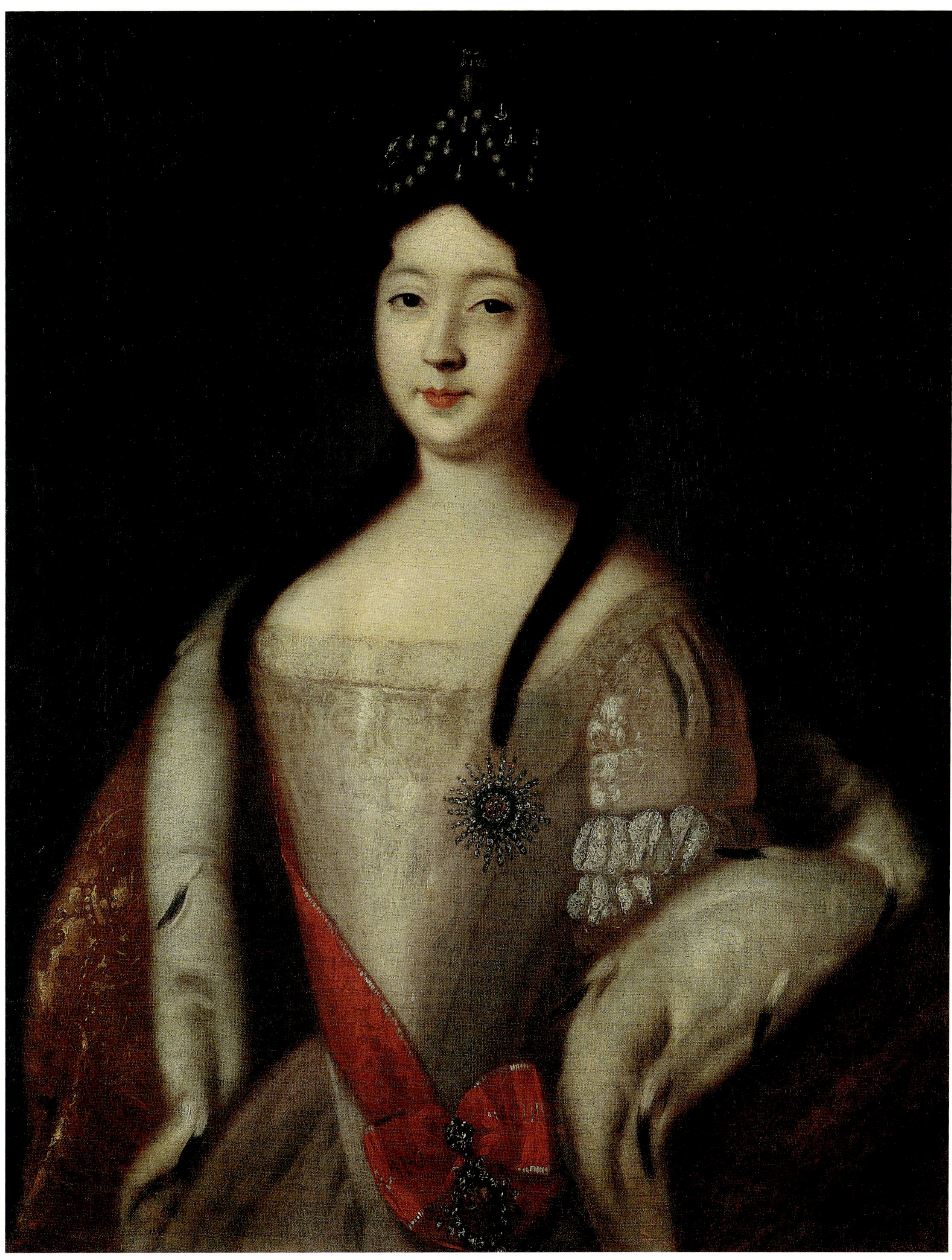

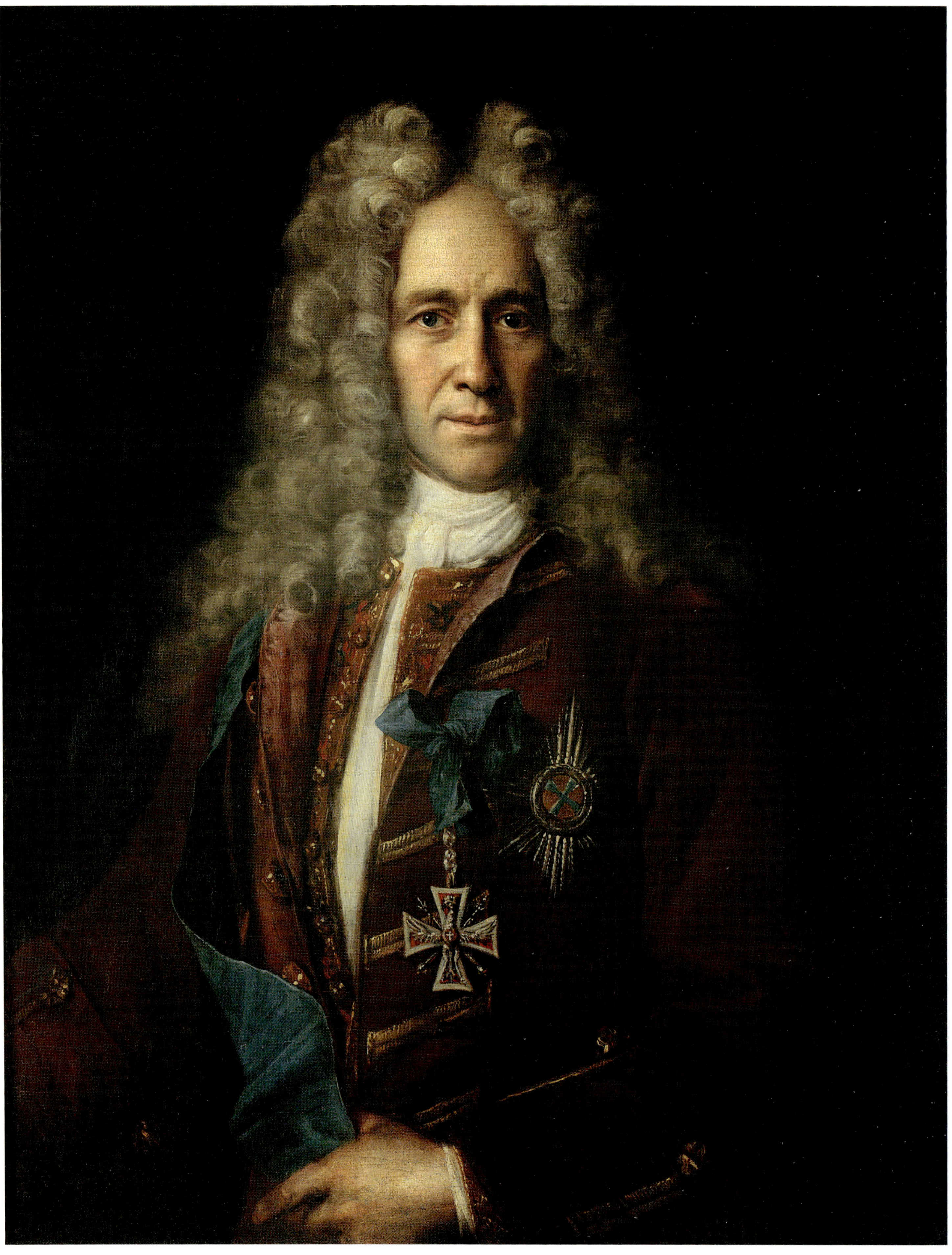

Elizabeth was a woman of wide-ranging appetites, both culinary and intellectual. Renowned for her stamina and voracity at feasts, she valued her chief chef so highly as to make him a brigadier, with a handsome salary of eight hundred roubles a year. At a banquet in 1757, special *contrôleurs de la bouche* (mouth controllers) were employed to enquire of the legion guests what native delicacies they particularly desired.[2] Elizabeth equally delighted in extravagant festivities and decorative effects. Such epicurean proclivities are intimated in a portrait of 1754 by the Austrian artist Georg Caspar von Prenner (Fig. 1.5), in which the voluptuous empress is encircled by a bountiful garland of flowers, creating an overblown effect unlike anything produced in Russia to date.

But Elizabeth was also a woman of shrewd judgement and political nous, and surrounded herself with a phalanx of enterprising intellectuals and courtiers. These included Mikhail Lomonosov, a great polymath, scientist and educationalist, who spearheaded the foundation of Moscow University in 1755; and Count Ivan Shuvalov, one of Elizabeth's most devoted servants and a fervent advocate of the visual arts. Together they campaigned for a new Academy of Arts, which, after a difficult inception, was finally approved by the Russian Senate in late 1757. It opened in Shuvalov's palace in the centre of St Petersburg early the following year.

The Academy's first incarnation was a small but decidedly international affair. Some three dozen students were taught painting, sculpture, printmaking and architectural design by foreign professors who were specially recruited from abroad. As its activities expanded, it moved to adapted premises in other residential buildings and, in 1760, sponsored two students to study abroad for the first time. However, it was not until the reign of Catherine II (1762–96), known for good reason as Catherine the Great, that the Academy became a major operation able to achieve its aim of professionalising the arts.

Catherine's ascent to the Russian throne was an act of astonishing temerity. A Prussian, born Princess Sophia of Anhalt Zerbst, she had married Grand Duke Peter, Elizabeth's nephew and heir, in 1745, and took the name of Catherine Alekseevna on her conversion to the Russian Orthodox faith. On 25 December 1761 Elizabeth died and was duly succeeded by her nephew, who became Peter III (Fig. 1.6). Within six months, however, Catherine launched an audacious *coup d'état* against her husband and was declared empress and sovereign of all the Russias at a barracks on the outskirts of St Petersburg in June 1762. Peter abdicated the throne and died in mysterious circumstances just days later, either by accident or design in an altercation that involved Catherine's lover, Grigory Orlov. A foreign-born woman of just thirty-three now reigned over one of the largest empires the world had yet seen.

Catherine went on to become a formidable and effective ruler, with a passion for the visual arts. Her rapacious and far-sighted patronage led to one of the greatest art collections at any European court, and she became an avid correspondent of those Enlightenment apostles, Diderot and Voltaire. In 1764 she also gave the Academy of Arts its first charter, establishing unparalleled privileges and opportunities for artists. This was followed the next year by the foundation of a magnificent neoclassical building for the Academy on the Neva embankment, into which the institution moved in 1788 (Fig. 1.7). With a carefully structured educational programme, regular exhibitions and sales, and, uniquely among European academies, its own boarding school complete with compulsory uniforms for students and staff, the Academy became the uncontested epicentre of Russia's artistic life.

As was true in academies across Europe, history painting was lionised in the Russian Academy as the supreme form of two-dimensional art, a noble and avowedly intellectual pursuit that required extensive knowledge, imagination and versatility of its practitioners. Yet, as was equally the case in many European academies, it was portraiture that proved the most popular pursuit among painters and patrons alike. More students specialised in portraiture than in any other genre in the early years, and, with rare exceptions, it was portraitists who enjoyed the highest profile.

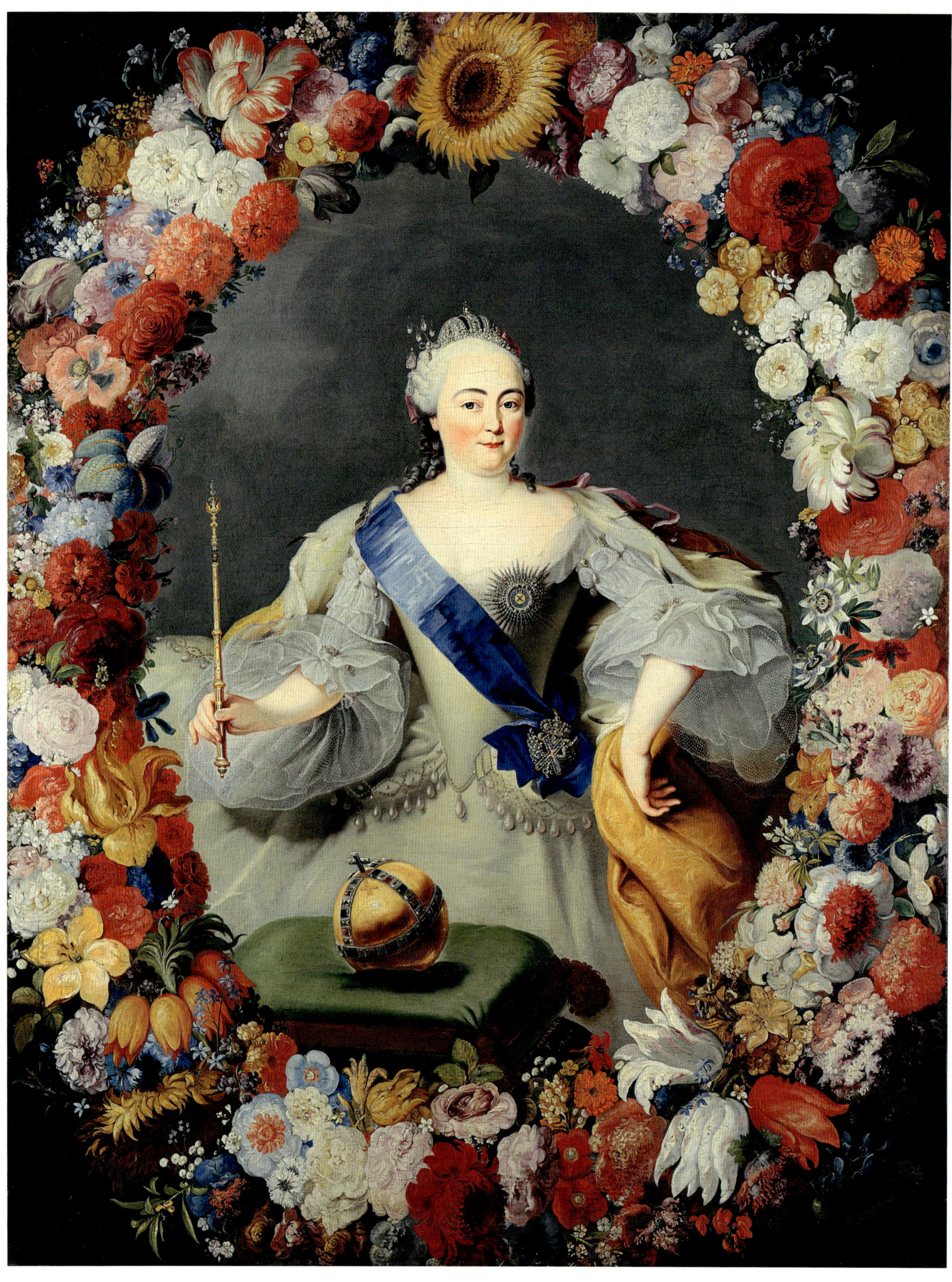

Fig. 1.5 (above)
Empress Elizabeth
Georg Caspar von Prenner, 1754

Fig. 1.6 (opposite)
Peter III
Aleksei Antropov, 1762

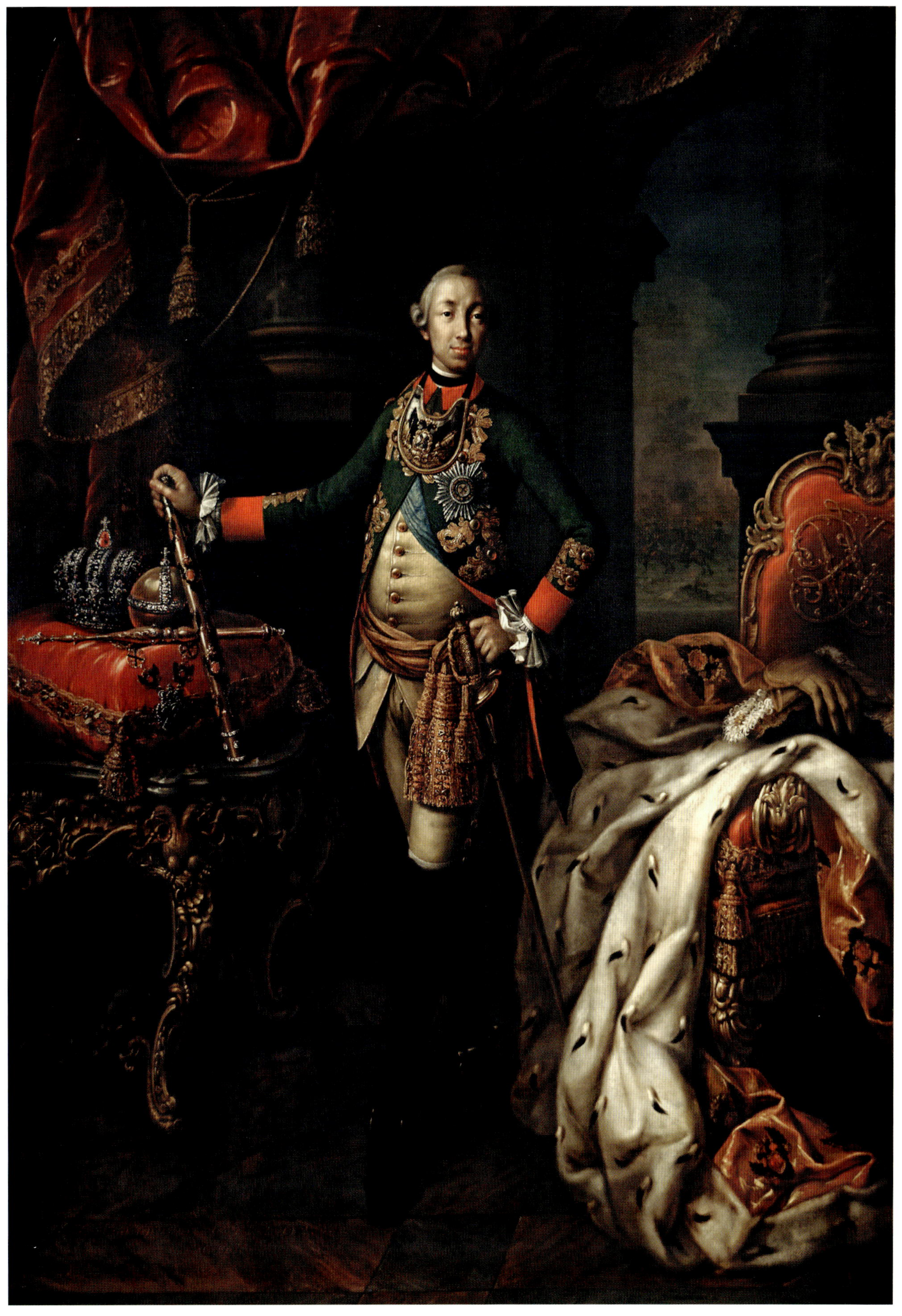

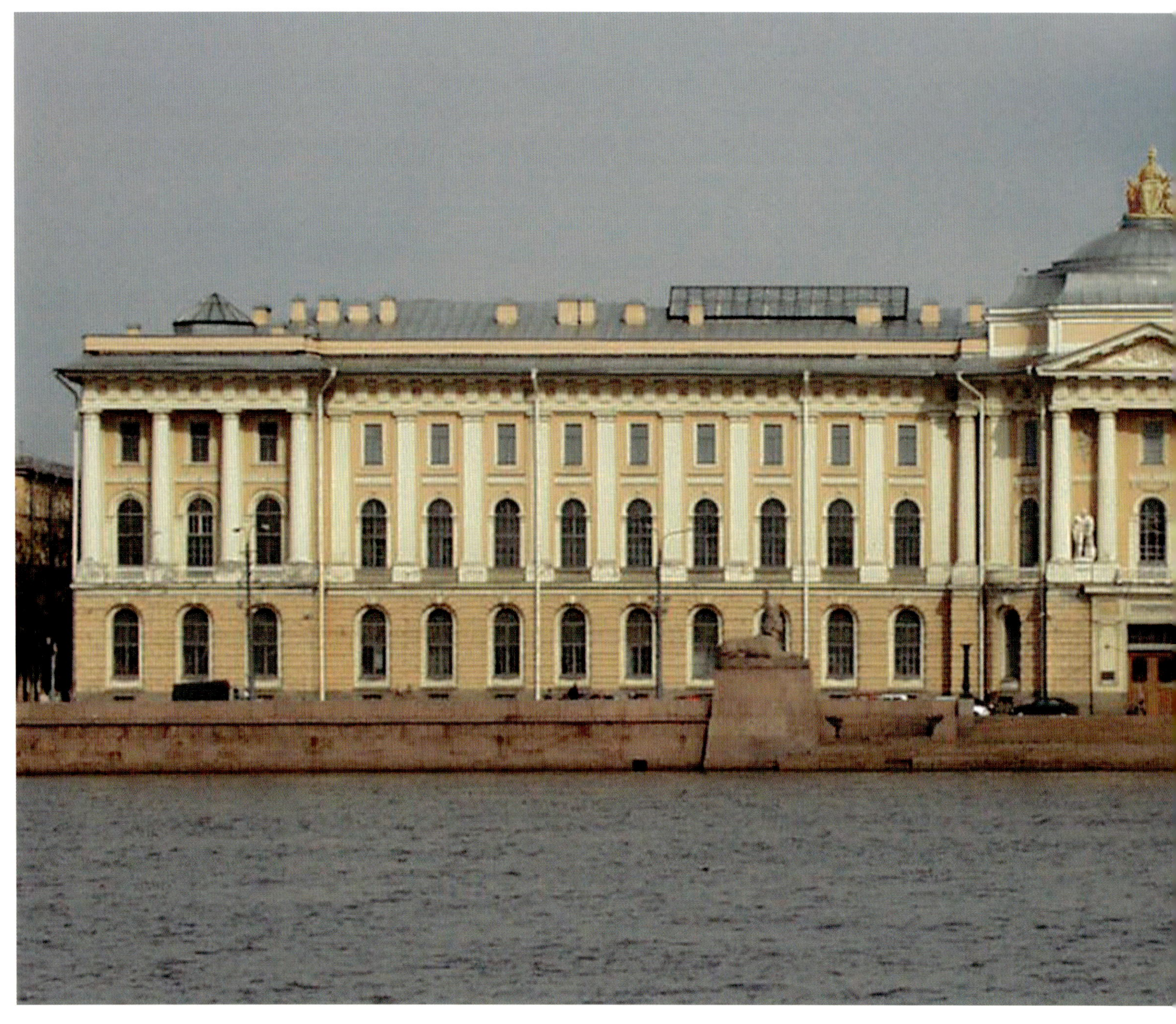

Pre-eminent among them was Dmitry Levitsky (1735–1822), son of a priest and icon painter in Kiev. Like many ambitious Ukrainians, Levitsky moved to St Petersburg to seek his fortune and by the 1770s was running the Academy's portrait class. He soon became the portraitist of choice for Russia's elite, whom he could be relied upon to paint in a suitably dignified and stately mode. In 1772, for example, Levitsky was called upon to portray Prince Alexander Golitsyn, scion of an illustrious noble family who had been appointed ambassador to London in the 1750s and served as Catherine's vice-chancellor after helping to place her on the throne. The prince is depicted before a marble bust of the empress, gesturing to the papers that signify his loyal service to her and wearing the orders that have been his reward (Fig. 1.8).

Levitsky was equally capable of more quixotic portraits, as when he painted Prokofy Demidov in 1773 (Fig. 1.9). Demidov was a major benefactor of the Moscow Foundling Hospital, for which this portrait was commissioned and which appears in the background. He was also a passionate horticulturalist, creating his own botanical garden and lovingly tending

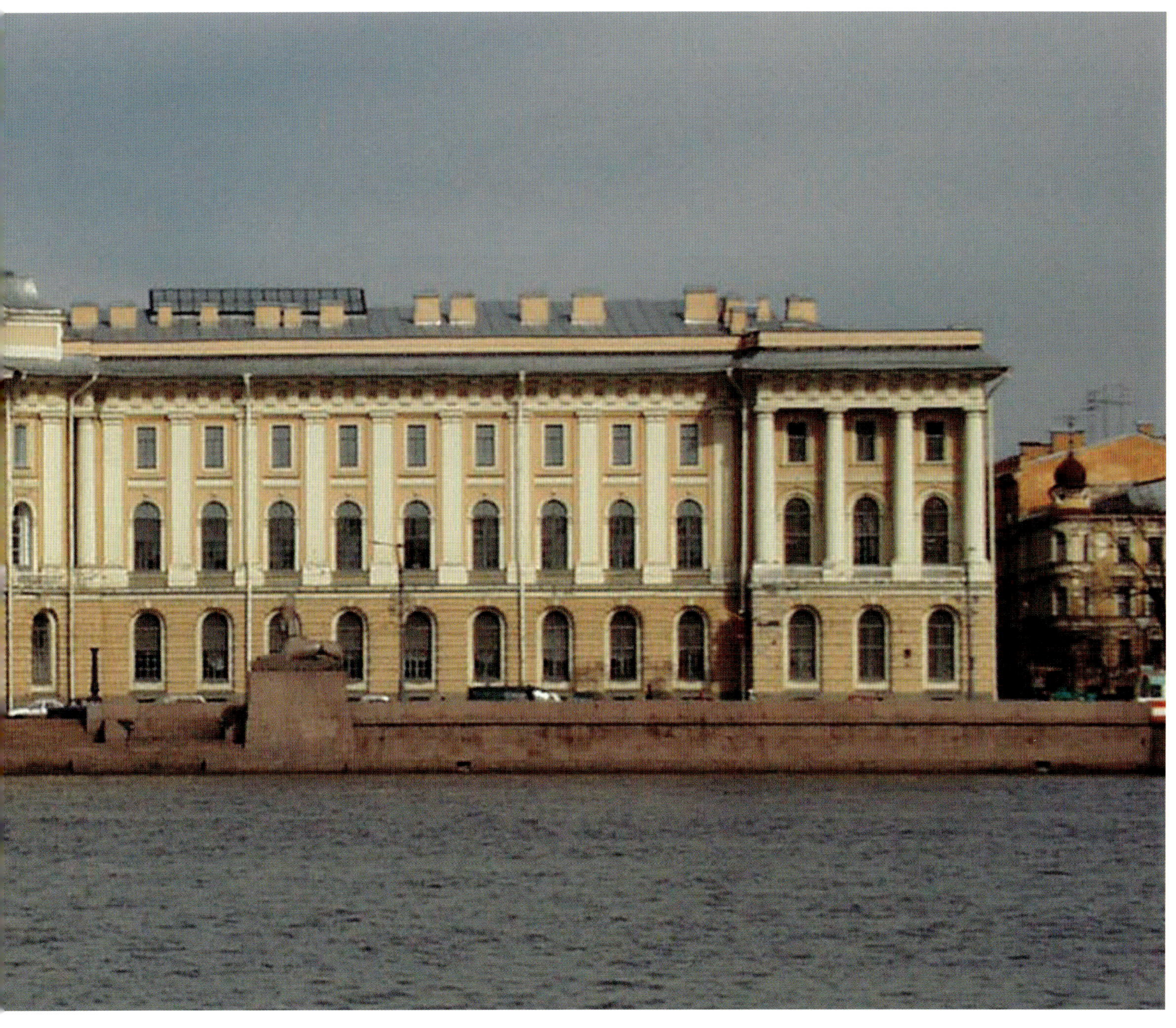

a rare collection of exotic plants. In highlighting these green-fingered activities, Levitsky provides a playful, almost subversive take on the conventional status portrait. Demidov eschews any medals and finery in favour of a jaunty cap and silken gown, with buttons straining as he leans on his trusty watering can and pays homage not to any beneficent patron, but to his beloved shrubs.

If Levitsky flourished as part of the Academy's faculty, other portraitists thrived outside its walls during Catherine's reign. Most striking of all is Fedor Rokotov (*c*.1735–1808), who was born a serf – the term applied in Russia to the millions of peasants who were held in bondage to noble landowners until their emancipation in the mid nineteenth century. On occasion it was possible for serfs to be manumitted before that time, either through some pecuniary or professional leverage, or through the auspices of an enlightened serf-owner, and Rokotov somehow succeeded in acquiring his freedom at a young age. He promptly relocated from his village outside Moscow to St Petersburg, where he caught the attention of

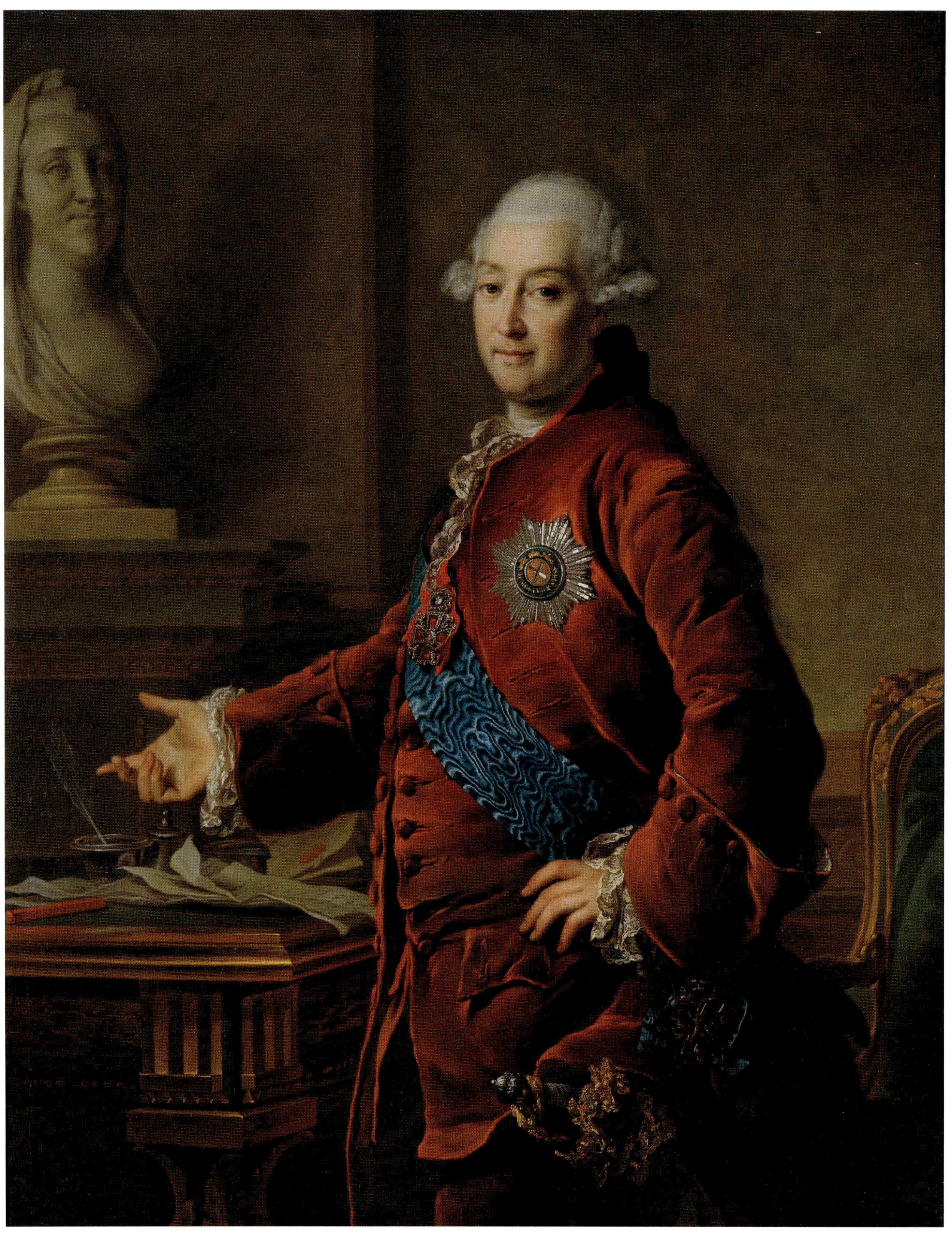

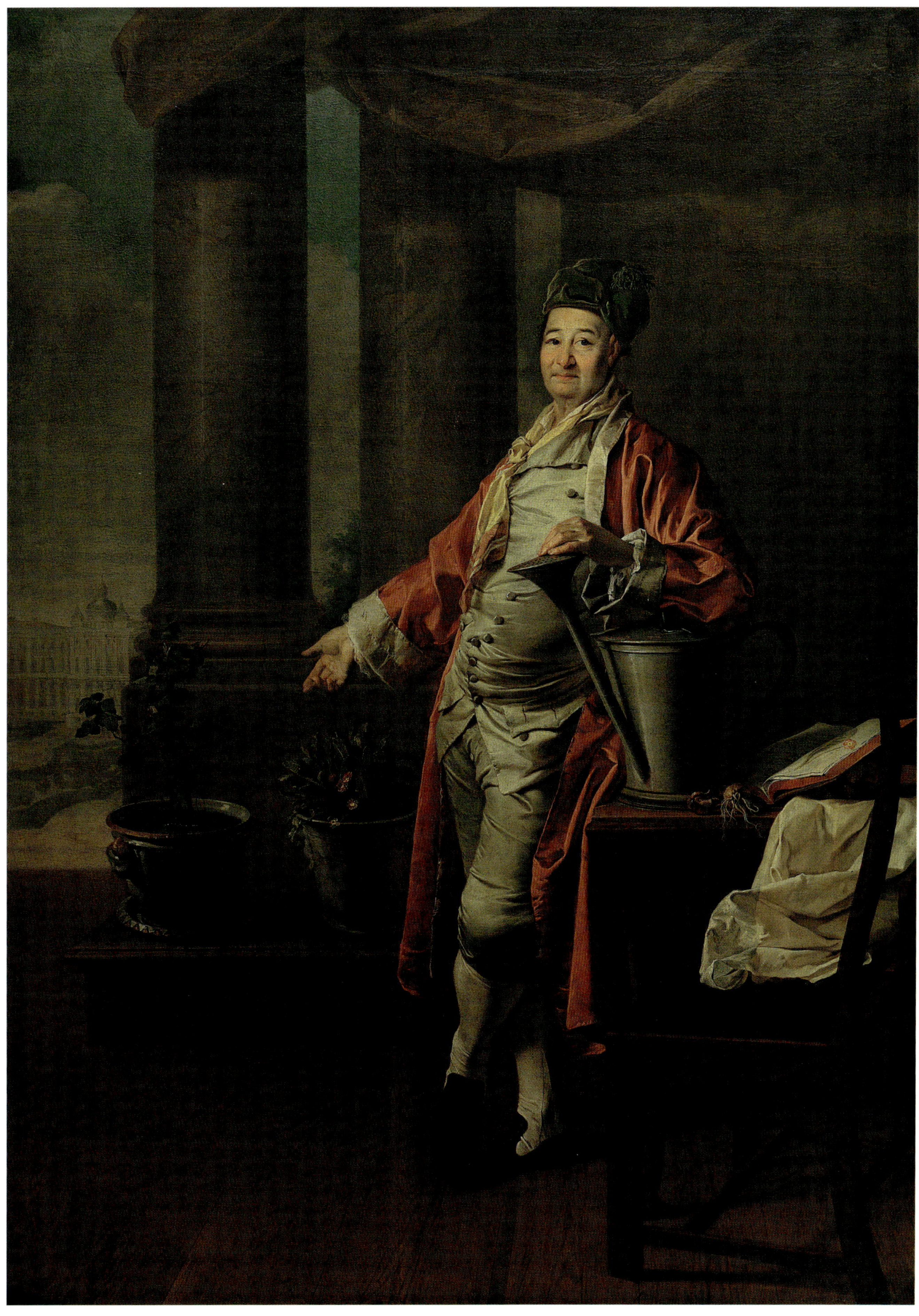

high-ranking supporters and won a place at the Academy. So adroit was his networking and so luminous his talent that within a couple of years he was painting members of the imperial family, including the empress herself.

The only Russian artist to paint Catherine from life, Rokotov was granted just one sitting, in Rostov Veliky, where the empress was travelling. Yet from this single encounter he crafted a majestic image of Catherine that circulated in copies and prints for many years (Fig. 1.10). Rokotov painted the empress in profile, bringing to mind the portraits of Roman emperors on medals and coins. There may be a suggestion too of the bas-relief portraits of cameos, which Catherine collected in their thousands. That an artist of serf origins could paint the Autocrat of all the Russias, as the ruler of imperial Russia was officially styled, calls into question the standard narrative of the country's rigid social stratification. Russia was certainly beset with enforced class divisions, with every subject born a member of a defined social estate. However, the case of Rokotov demonstrates the extraordinary social mobility that was also possible at the time.

By the time of Catherine's death in 1796, the stature of Russian portraitists had changed beyond recognition since the start of her reign. In 1762, local artists had still largely been seen as second-class citizens, labouring in the shadows of foreign virtuosi and rarely winning more than the pickings from their table. By the end of the century, however, they had the benefit of a comprehensive education and a progressive career path through the Academy, and were attracting the attention of Russia's most august patrons. The stage was set for exciting new opportunities for Russian portraitists as a new century dawned.

Fig. 1.10
Catherine II
Fedor Rokotov, 1763

Notes

1   Lindsey Hughes, *Russia in the Age of Peter the Great* (Yale University Press, New Haven and London, 1998), p.24.

2   Christopher Marsden, *Palmyra of the North: The First Days of St Petersburg* (Faber & Faber, London, 1942), pp.130–1.

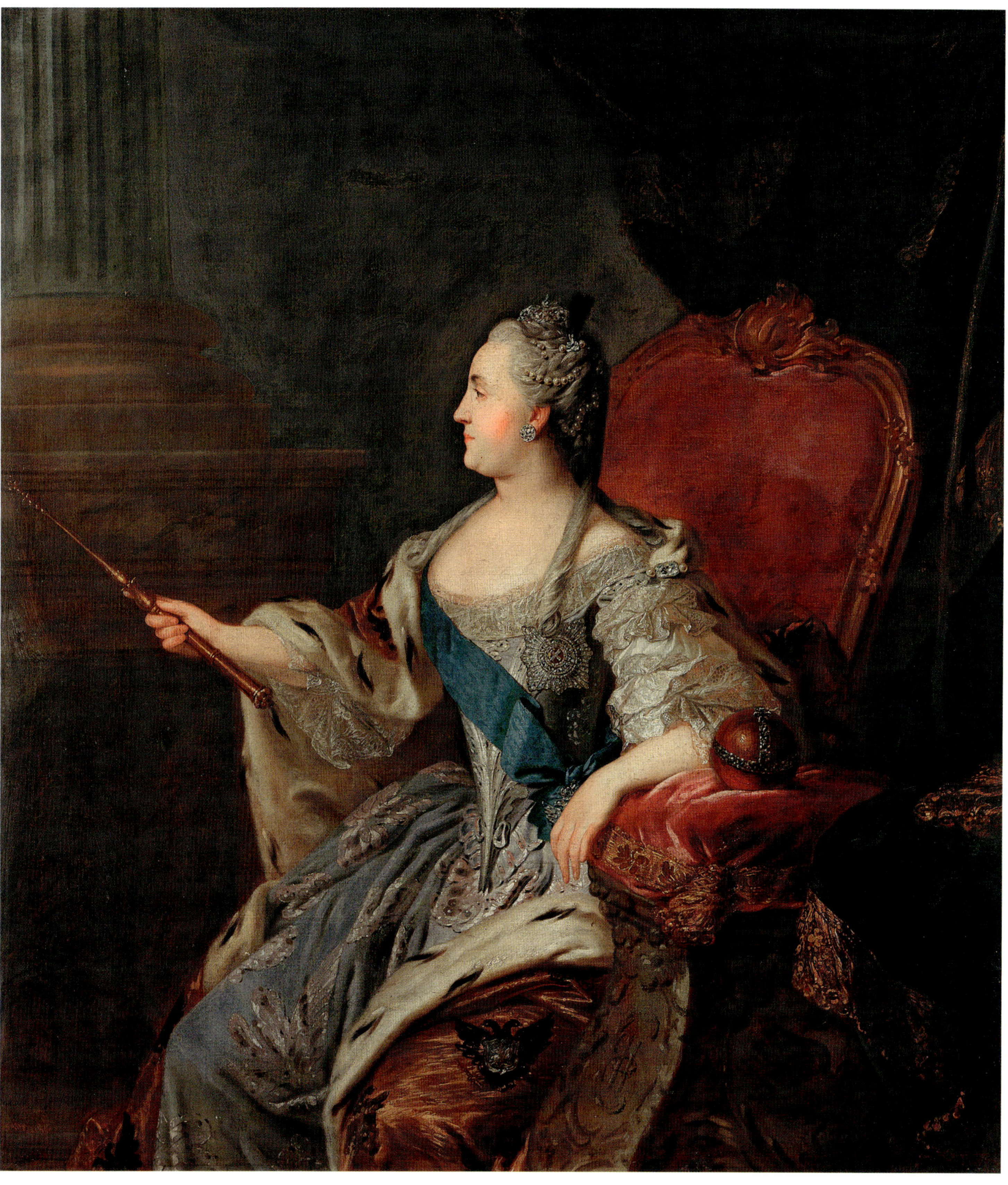

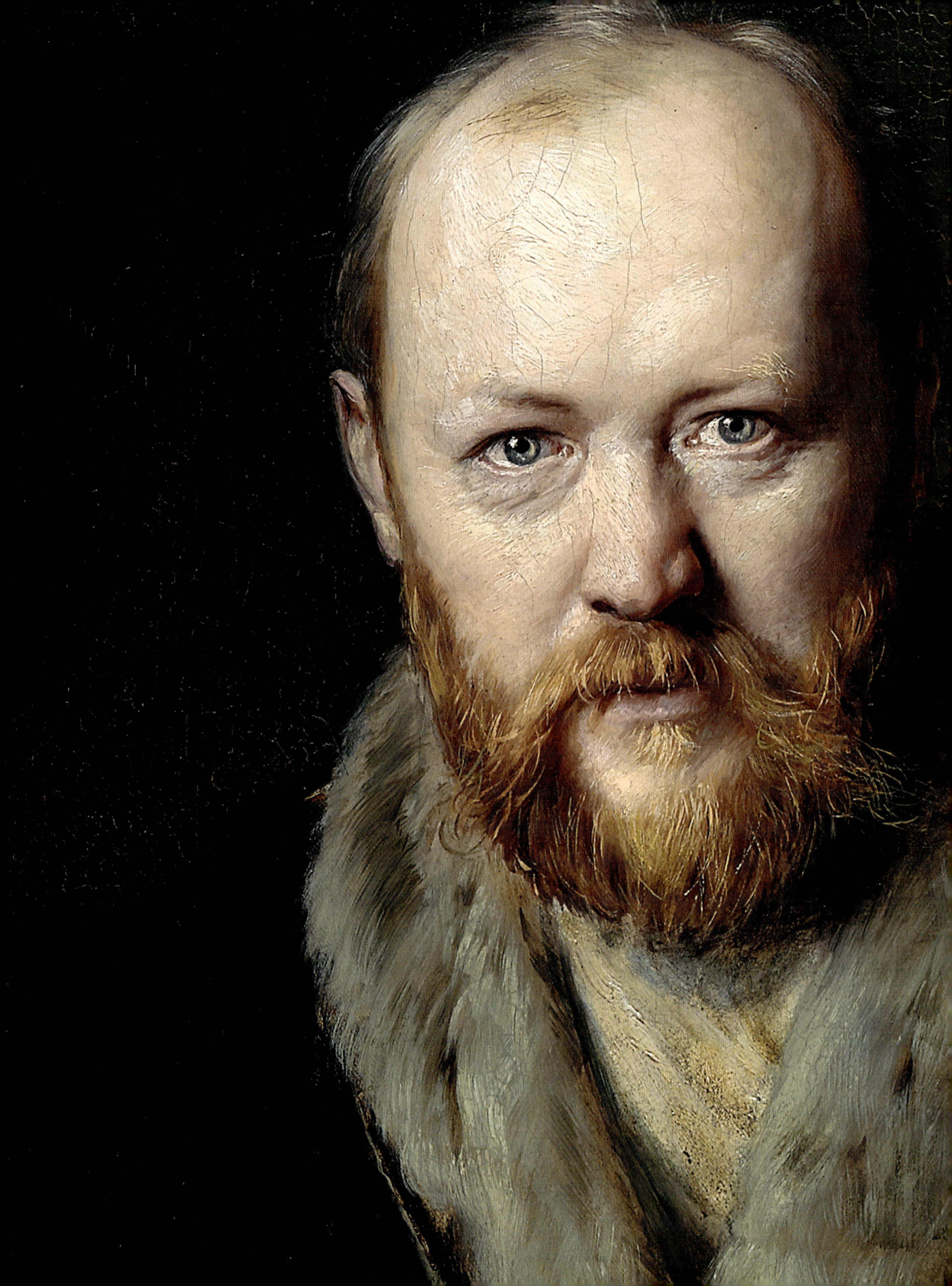

2

A COMING OF AGE

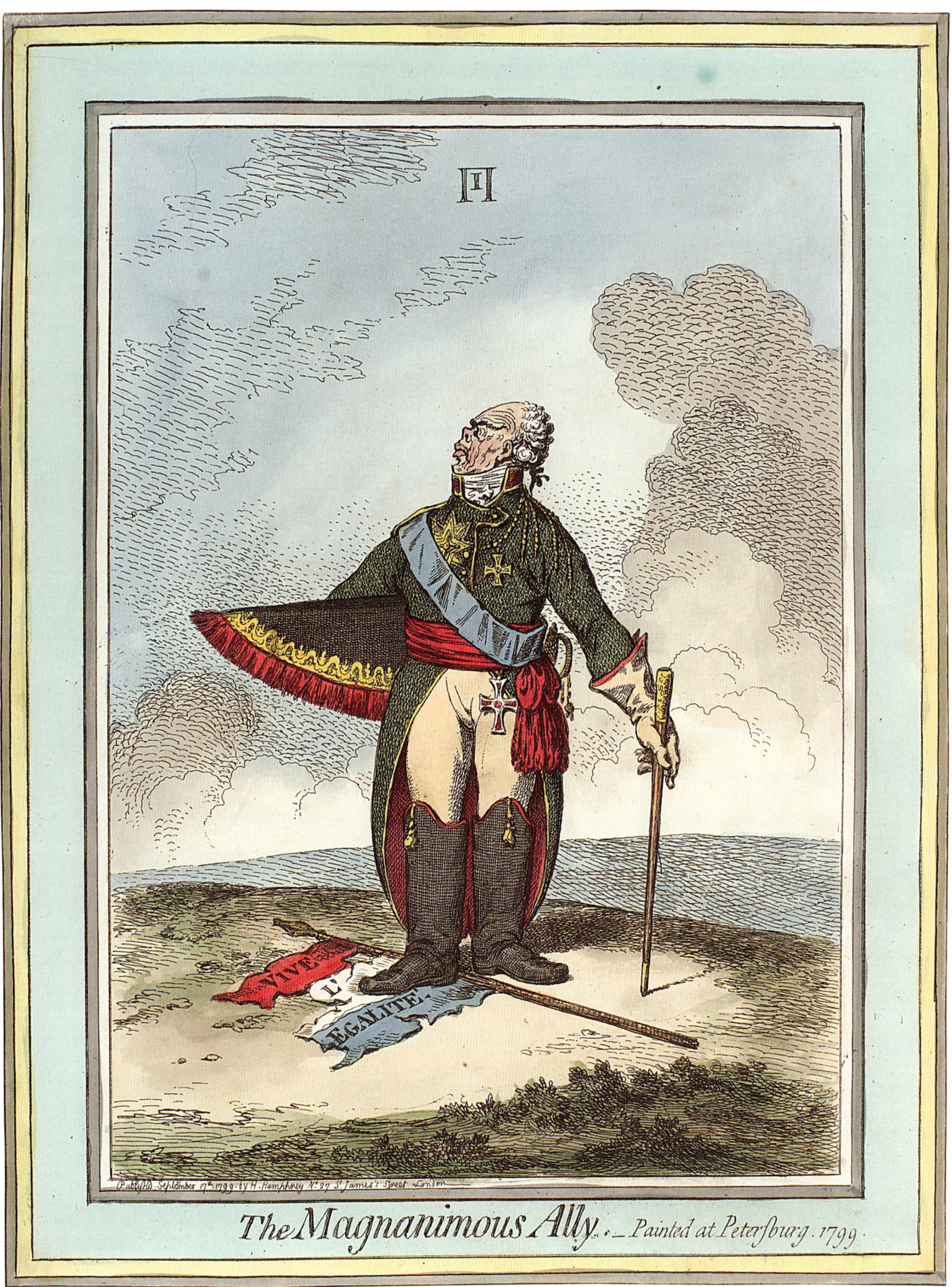

The Magnanimous Ally.__ Painted at Petersburg. 1799

PAUL I, CATHERINE'S SON, was strangled in his bedroom in 1801 by a cabal of disenchanted noblemen and officers who, tired of the tsar's despotism, seamlessly installed his son Alexander on the throne. A testy and mistrustful man so sensitive of his appearance that he banned the Russian word for 'snub nose', Paul would be remembered domestically for his punctilious fixation on military detail. Soldiers trussed in uncomfortable new uniforms lived in fear of making the slightest misstep in interminable daily parades. Internationally, Paul nurtured an implacable loathing of the French that initially prompted an Anglo-Russian alliance. In James Gillray's cartoon *The Magnanimous Ally*, published on 17 September 1799, the stocky and balding tsar adopts a pose parodic of the Apollo Belvedere, and tramples on a tattered French tricolour emblazoned with the words 'Vive l'Egalité' (Fig. 2.1). The Anglo-Russian concord was soon disintegrating, however, leading Prime Minister William Pitt to regret the withdrawal of the emperor's 'magnanimity' in a parliamentary speech the following year.[1]

By contrast the reign of Paul's son, Alexander I, encompassed a quarter century of relative stability at home and rising influence abroad. There was a period of acute tension when Napoleon invaded Russia in 1812, sorely testing the cultured classes' long-standing regard for France. The Russian defeat of Napoleon's troops, aided by the ferocity of a Russian winter that caught the French aggressor unawares, established Alexander as a major player on the international stage.

Alexander chose a foreign artist to commemorate his victory, when in 1818 he commissioned the Englishman and Royal Academician George Dawe to portray every general of Russia's Napoleonic campaign. The tsar was inspired in this respect by George, Prince Regent, who had likewise commissioned Thomas Lawrence to paint portraits of the triumphant leaders of the anti-Napoleonic alliance for the Waterloo Chamber at Windsor Castle. Working in what must have been one of Europe's best-appointed studios in a vast hall of the Winter Palace in St Petersburg, Dawe and his assistants eventually produced well over

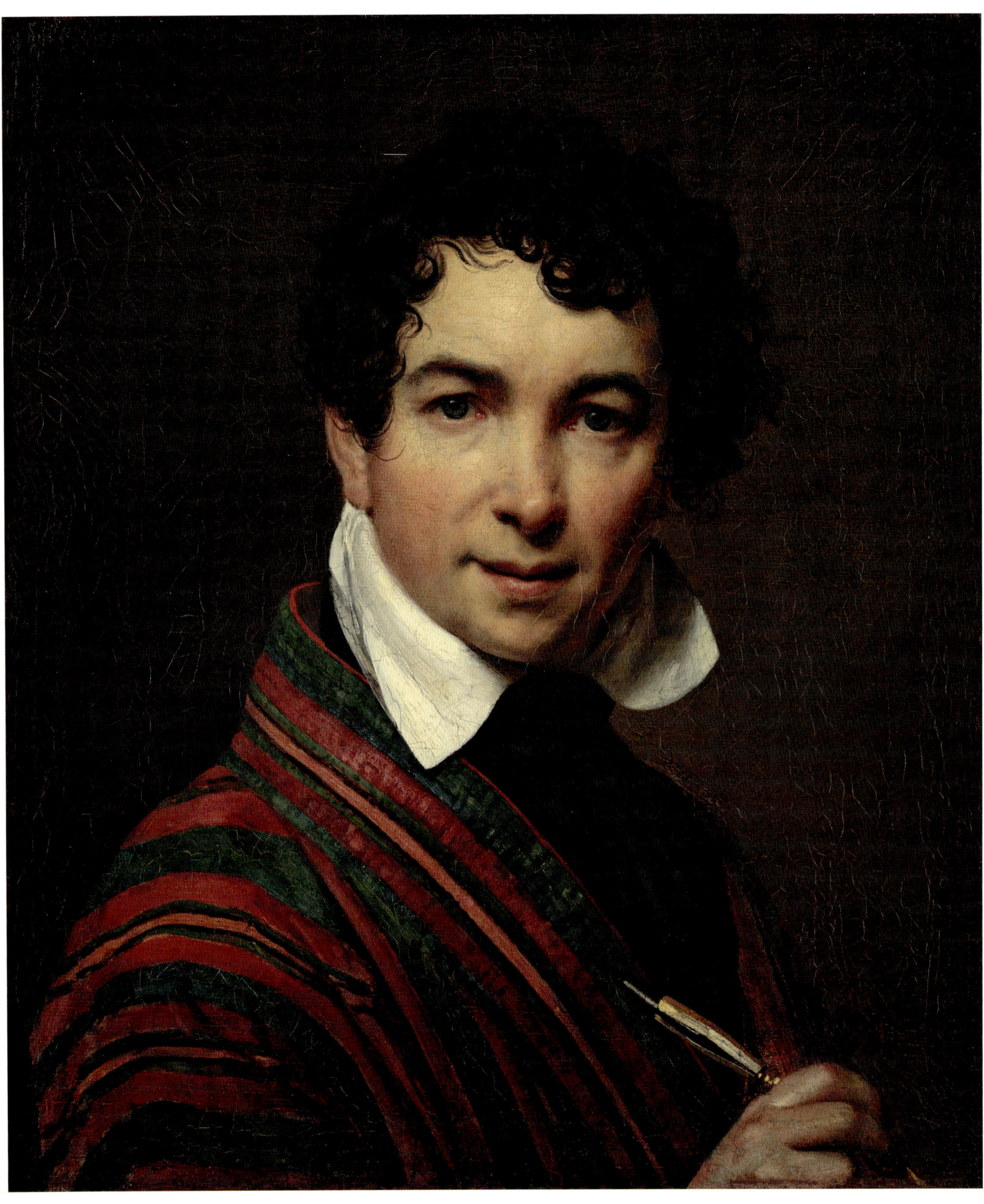

three hundred portraits. These were installed in a purpose-built gallery in the palace, which ambassadors and visiting dignitaries were obliged to visit and admire.

Alexander's bestowal of such a prestigious and lucrative commission on an Englishman suggests that the old habit of valuing foreign artists above locals was dying hard. Criticism of his unpatriotic bias was certainly voiced in the press. But the tsar showed his support of native artists too, for he bought a number of paintings by Russians and in 1825 established a 'gallery of the Russian school' in the Hermitage (the extension to the Winter Palace where Catherine the Great had based her art collection) to display these and other works.

Among the artists to feature in the tsar's new gallery was Orest Kiprensky (1782–1836), the most mercurial portraitist of his generation (Fig. 2.2). The illegitimate son of a landowner and one of his serfs, Kiprensky had an inauspicious start in life. However, his natural father saw to it that Kiprensky's mother was safely married to another serf, and later vouchsafed to liberate the entire family on his death. He also supported Kiprensky's admission to the boarding school of the Academy of Arts at the age of just six, the standard age of recruits to the Academy at this time. The artist graduated with flying colours in 1803, at the age of twenty-one, and in 1816 was sponsored to travel abroad by none other than Empress Elizaveta Alekseevna, Alexander's wife.

Kiprensky's time abroad was productive and controversial in equal measure. He dazzled with an array of history paintings, subject pictures and portraits, and was almost certainly the first Russian artist to have a self-portrait commissioned for the Uffizi Gallery in Florence. Yet he was obliged to curtail his stay in Rome when his model-cum-mistress died in a fire in his studio amid rumours that Kiprensky was engaged in relations with the woman's daughter and had started the fire deliberately.

These allegations drove Kiprensky back to Russia, but did not dampen his career. On the contrary, in 1827 he was commissioned to paint Alexander Pushkin, Russia's greatest writer yet, and responded with an image that tops the canon of Russian portraits (Fig. 2.3). Pushkin is stylish if distracted, his poetic genius suggested by the statue of one of the Muses on the right and his suggestively averted gaze. The brushwork is versatile and assured, deftly negotiating the different textures of tousled hair and polished fingernails, of rakish cravat and tartan scarf. According to Pushkin's father, it was the best-ever likeness of his son, its simultaneous evocation of the writer's panache and reserve delighting those who were busily consecrating him as the nation's foremost literary voice.

By the time of Pushkin's portrait, Russia's artists and writers were entering troubled waters, for the relatively liberal Alexander had died in 1825, to be succeeded by his brother, Nicholas I (Fig. 2.4). An obdurate and militaristic man, Nicholas had been traumatised at the very start of his reign by an ill-fated but significant uprising known as the Decembrist Revolt, when a number of elite army officers had tried to persuade their troops to refuse to take an oath of allegiance to the new tsar. Nicholas responded by hanging the ringleaders, exiling their co-conspirators to Siberia and implementing a serious of repressive measures, including tight censorship of the arts. He personally vetted Pushkin's writing, suppressed progressive publications and discussion circles, and placed the Academy of Arts under his direct control. There the tsar hired and fired professors at will, introduced new statutes that limited the rights of artists and insisted that artworks be altered to suit his personal tastes. With admirable conviction in his own artistic abilities, Nicholas even made modifications to modern and old master paintings himself. By the time he died in 1855, critics of the Academy saw it as little more than an organ of autocratic whim, and many pioneering artists and writers had sought refuge abroad.

By now, that protean body of critical thinkers known collectively as the intelligentsia were subjecting Russia's social and political structures to growing scrutiny. Most contentious of all was the institution of serfdom, which had been condemned as indefensible and unsustainable since at least the reign of Catherine the Great. Recognising the momentum of the campaign

Fig. 2.2
Self-portrait
Orest Kiprensky, 1828

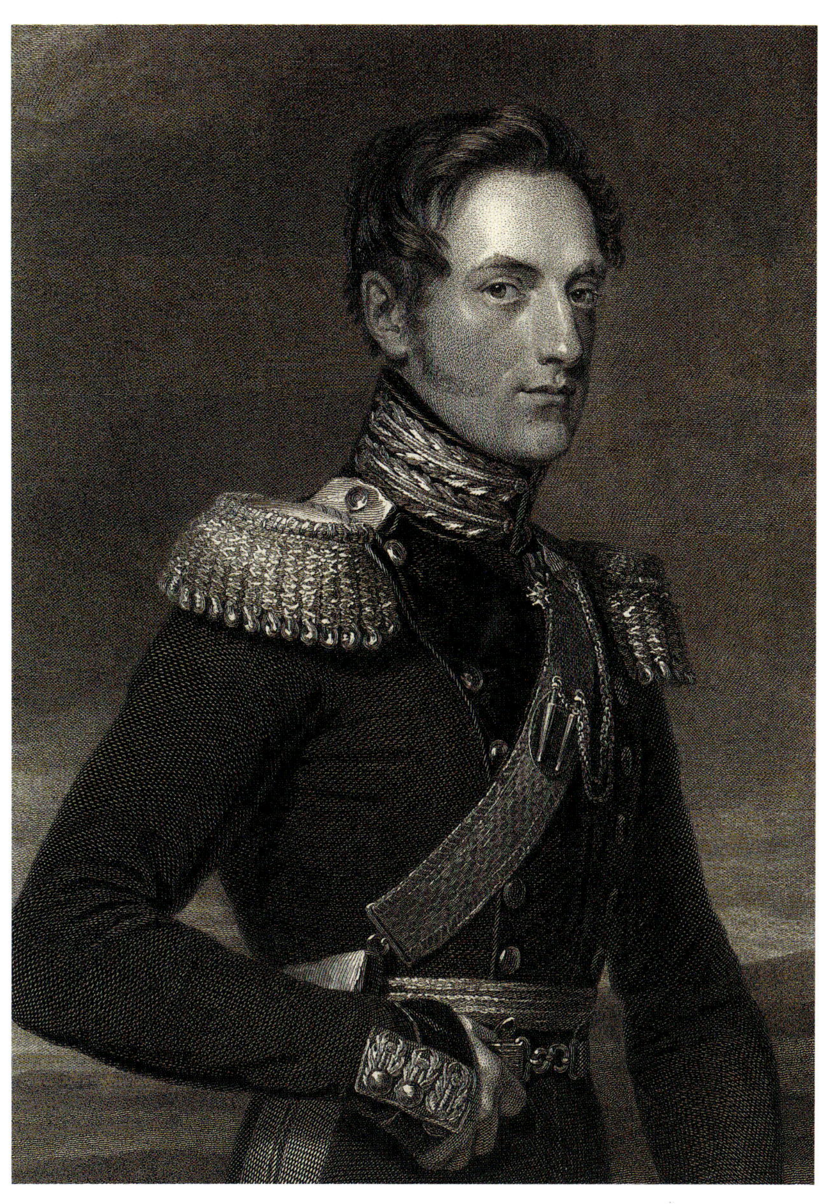

against it, Alexander II (1818–81) famously stated in 1856 that it was better for serfdom to be abolished from above than below. Two years later, the government's programme to free the serfs was announced. The euphoric reaction to this news was encapsulated by Alexander Herzen, one of Russia's most trenchant political writers, who lived in exile in London from 1852 to 1865 (plate 1). In an article of unfettered emotion, Herzen exulted the tsar with the paean, 'Man of Galilee, you have won'.[2]

The limitations of the Emancipation of the Serfs and other reforms of the 1860s nonetheless soon became apparent. The Emancipation of 1861 freed some twenty-two million peasant men, women and children, but failed to attend sufficiently to their livelihood and welfare. They were often allocated the least fertile strips of land to farm and had to pay their previous owners forms of recompense that they could ill afford.[3] Reforms to the judiciary, the

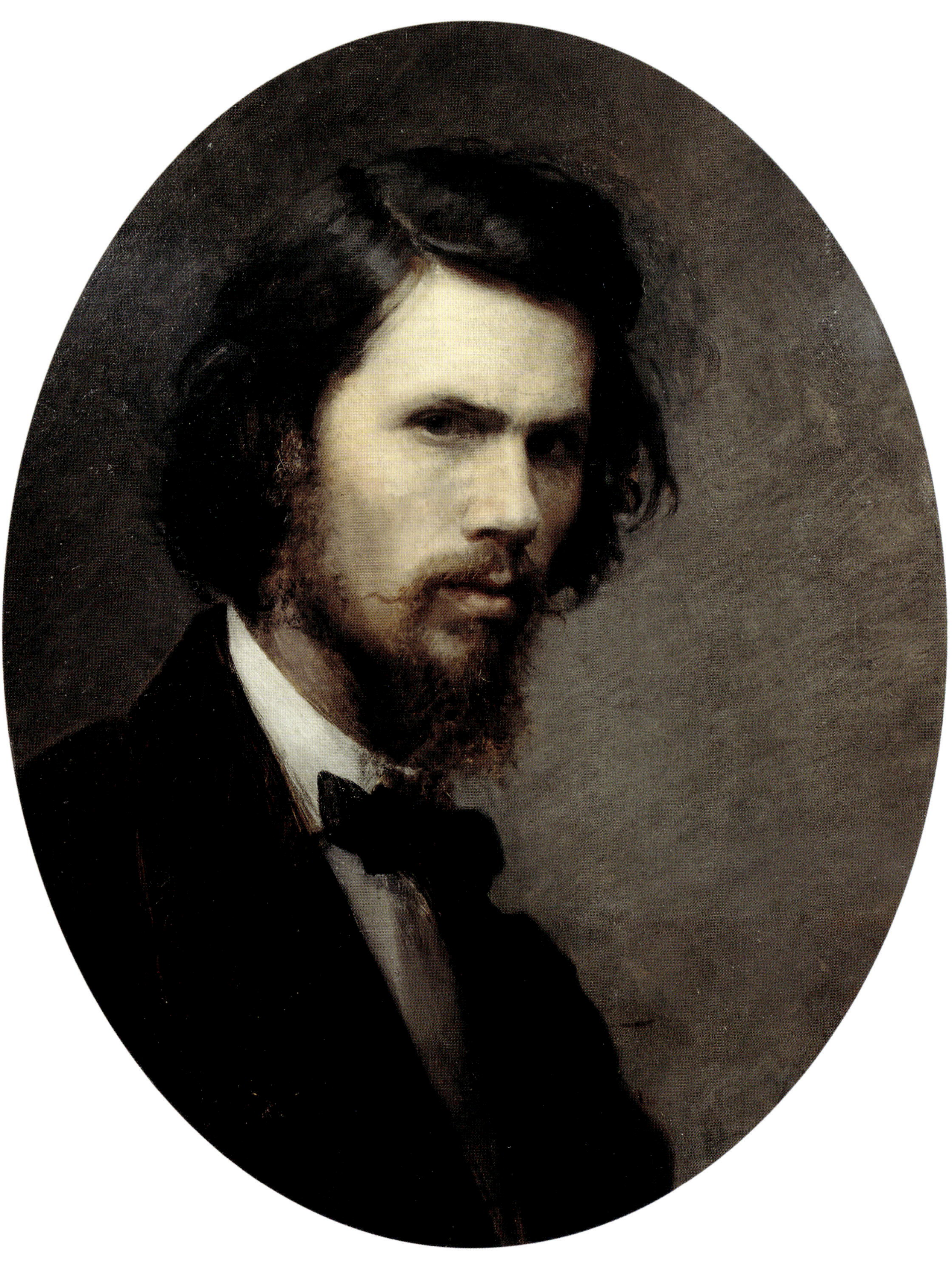

military and local government were similarly flawed, fuelling a period of malaise and uncertainty that resounded in the art world.

In the Academy, long-simmering discontent came to a head in 1863, when fourteen of its more vociferous students objected to the institution's persistence in setting a theme for the annual gold medal in history painting. When the students requested but were denied the right to choose their own subject, they left the Academy in what became known as the Revolt of the Fourteen, filing silently but resolutely out of the ceremonial Council Hall. Led by Ivan Kramskoy, a hot-headed young painter from Voronezh (Fig. 2.5), the secessionists set up an alternative artistic collective in rented premises in the centre of St Petersburg. They were soon advertising their services in the press and plying a brisk trade, stoking the communal samovar as they debated the role and responsibilities of modern artists long into the night.

Plans were afoot for a new artistic society in Moscow too, culminating in the foundation of the Association of Travelling Art Exhibitions in 1870. The Association's stated aim was to organise exhibitions 'in all towns of the empire' in order to foster public understanding of art, to bring this to people in the provinces as well as the capital cities, and to develop new markets for artists' work.[4] Its members accordingly became known as the Peredvizhniki, from the Russian verb meaning to move something from place to place. From modest beginnings, the Association would become the first independent artistic organisation to flourish in imperial Russia and would exhibit the work of almost every significant artist of the next twenty years. The Academy was initially welcoming of the new enterprise and agreed to host its first shows. The inaugural exhibition duly opened there on 29 November 1871, with forty-seven exhibits that were praised in the press for their uniformly high standard. Of these, ten were portraits, portending the importance that portraiture would come to play in the Association's work.

Kramskoy, a man keenly alert to the nuance of social standing, chose to exhibit three paintings of fellow artists, perhaps to emphasise their status as working professionals. These included an intriguing monochromatic portrait of Fedor Vasilev (Fig. 2.6), a brilliant young landscapist then seeking a cure in the Crimea for the tuberculosis that would kill him two years later, at the age of twenty-three. Vasilev's plight moved many and none more so than Kramskoy, who regularly petitioned on the dying artist's behalf. Significantly, though, Kramskoy avoids any stereotype of the ailing genius in his portrait. Vasilev appears instead as a dapper young professional, dignified and thoughtful with his fob watch and tailored three-piece suit. This is no romanticised exaltation of youthful talent, but a celebration of Vasilev's business-like demeanour, which reinforced the Association's initial focus on pragmatic concerns.

All three of the portraits that Kramskoy exhibited at the first Peredvizhnik exhibition were painted in monochrome and must have presented a highly idiosyncratic triptych. His unusual approach perhaps owed a debt to his earlier career as a retoucher for an itinerant photographer, with whom Kramskoy had travelled widely in central Russia and Ukraine, as well as more recently in photographic studios in St Petersburg. More luxuriant portraits were also on display at the first Peredvizhnik exhibition, among them Vasily Perov's iconic image of the playwright Alexander Ostrovsky (plate 2). This was followed by a series of paintings of similarly distinguished sitters that Perov unveiled at the annual Peredvizhnik shows. No fewer than six of his portraits were displayed at the second exhibition in 1872, among them a rather haunting image of the veteran writer and philologist Vladimir Dal (plate 3).

Dal lay at the heart of a movement to draw on and enrich native literary traditions, which had yielded extraordinary results in recent decades. In 1852 Ivan Turgenev had published an acclaimed collection of short stories known as *A Sportsman's Sketches*, which shone a spotlight on the commonplace of rural practices and peasant life. Turgenev followed this with a wealth of novels, short stories and plays that established him as one of the most lyrical chroniclers of Russian life, and led to the bestowal of an Honorary Doctorate of Civil Law from

Fig. 2.5
Self-portrait
Ivan Kramskoy, 1867

the University of Oxford in 1879 – the first novelist of any nationality to be honoured in this way.[5] Fedor Dostoevsky, for his part, had mined the darker seams of urban existence ever since his debut novel *Poor Folk*, which had been published in 1846. Keen to inscribe these giants of Russian literature into his collection, Pavel Tretyakov commissioned Perov to paint portraits of Turgenev and Dostoevsky in 1872. These featured alongside Dal's portrait at the Peredvizhnik exhibition that year, but it was the image of Dostoevsky that caught the public imagination, not least as it had the distinction of being the only portrait of the writer to be painted from life (plate 4).[6] The portrait was clearly identifiable on the right-hand side of an illustration of the exhibition that appeared in a popular periodical the following year (Fig. 2.7), and was repeatedly discussed and admired.

Reactions to Perov's portrait of Turgenev, however, were more reserved. Even Tretyakov was unconvinced. With a steely objectivity that belied his gentle demeanour, the patron had no compunction in saying if he disliked a painting that he had commissioned. He was also increasingly ambitious in his mission to establish a portrait gallery of Russia's social, political and intellectual luminaries, even if they were living abroad. In 1874 Tretyakov therefore commissioned another portrait of Turgenev, on this occasion turning to Ilia Repin, who, like the writer, was living in Paris at the time (plate 5).

Repin came from humble stock as the son of a military settler in Ukraine, but moved to St Petersburg in the early 1860s and a decade later had established a reputation as one of the most promising artists of his generation. While still a student at the Academy, he had painted *Barge Haulers on the Volga* (Fig. 2.8), a masterpiece of Russian Realism that focused on the

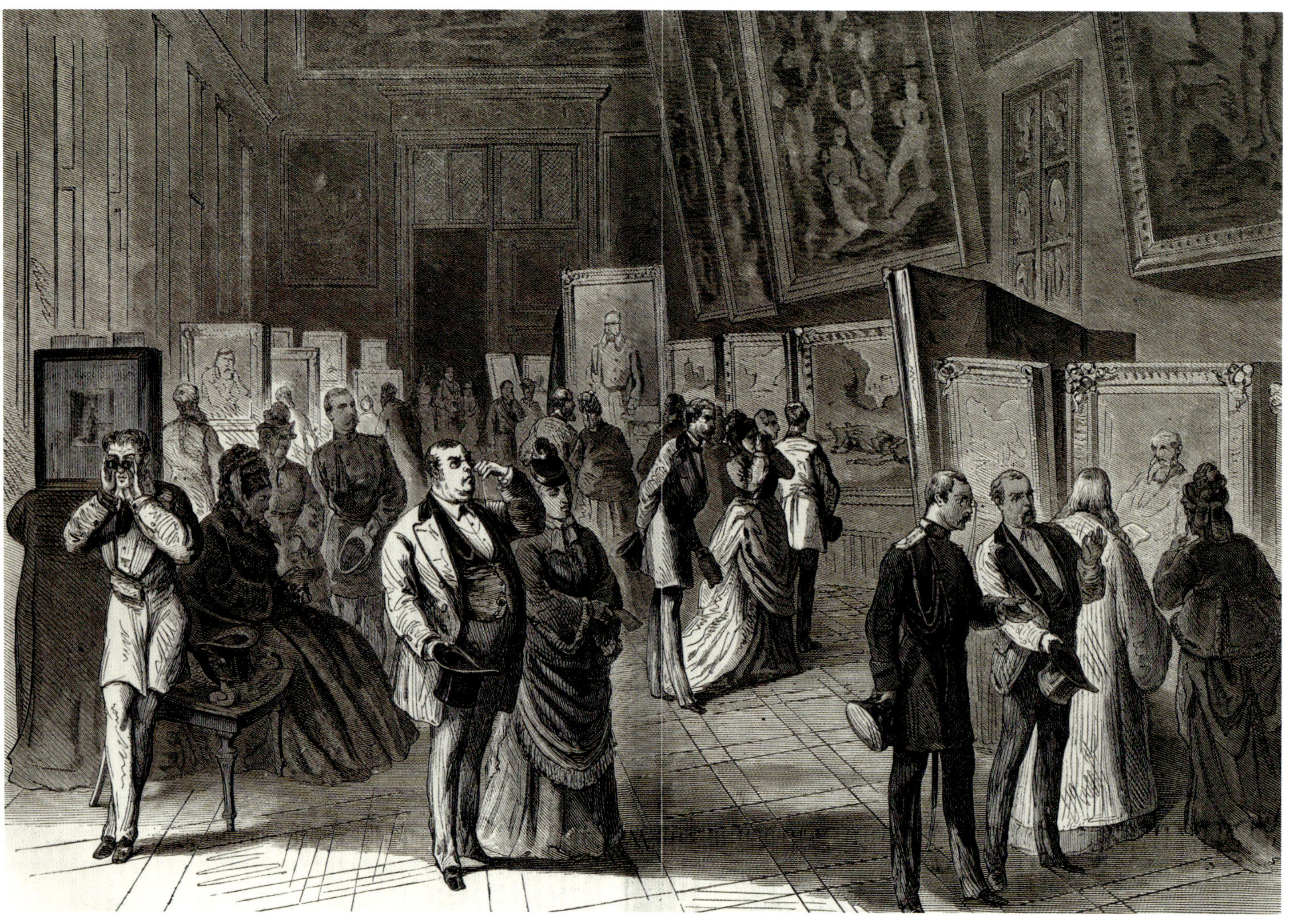

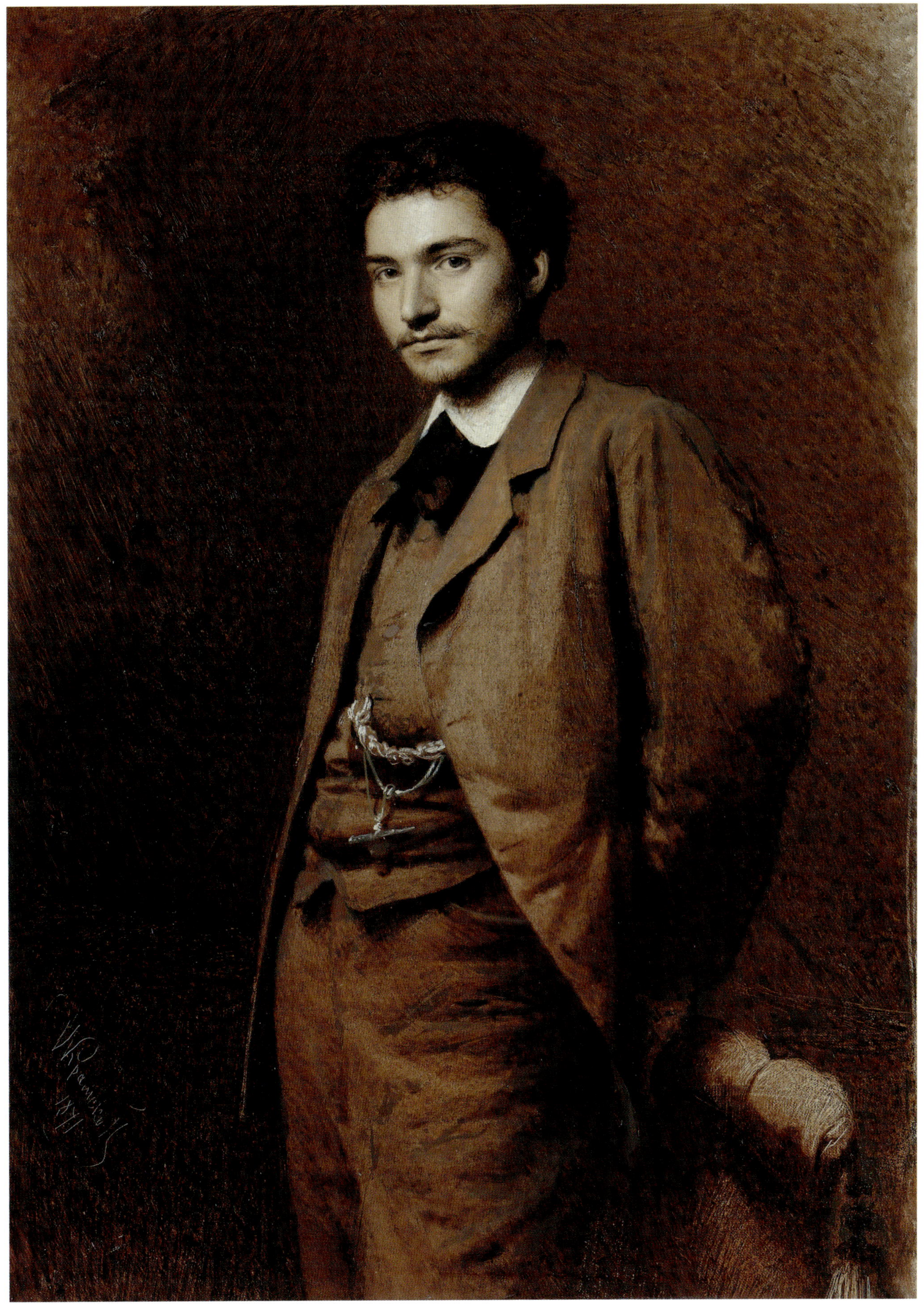

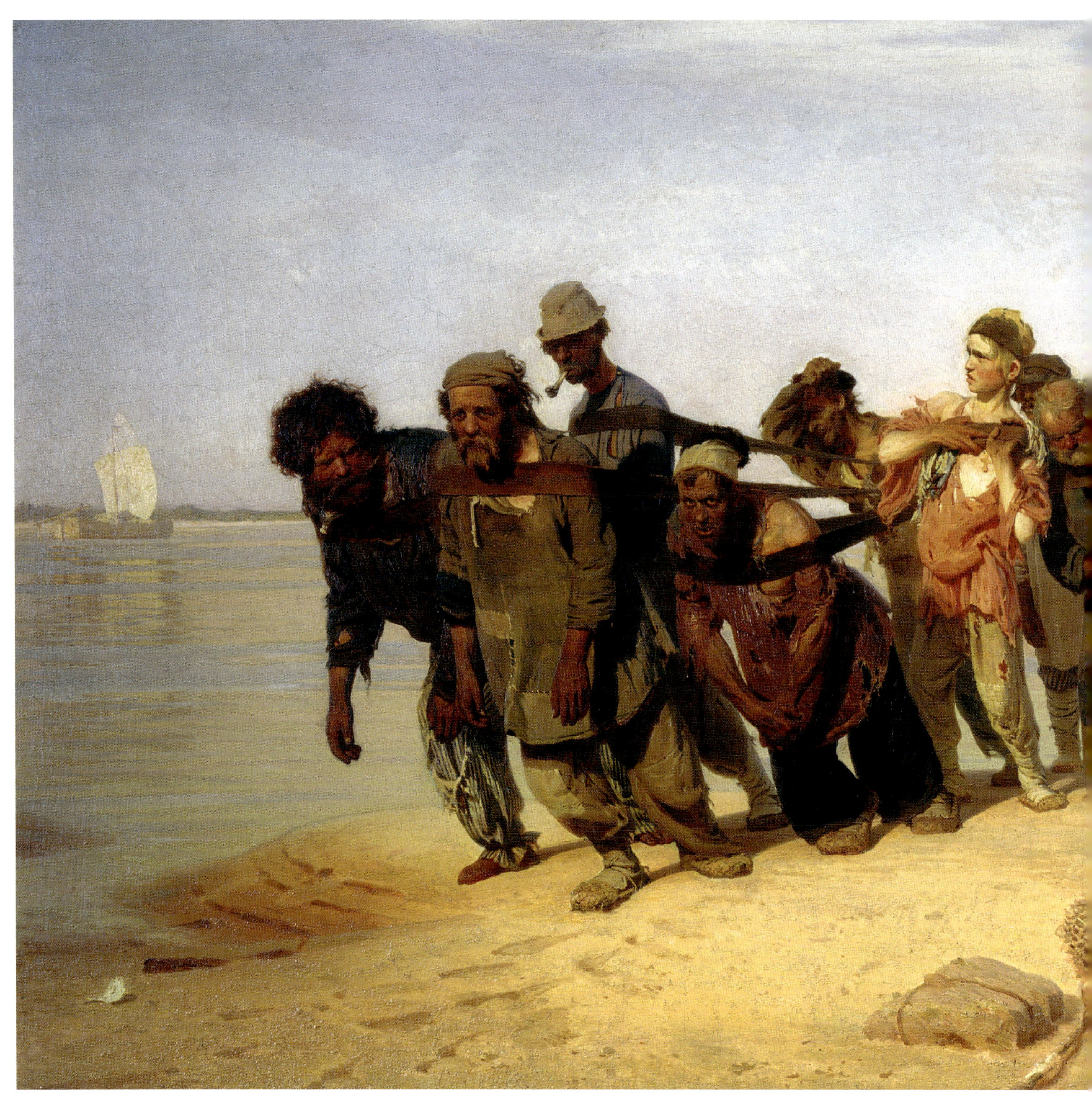

brutish custom of harnessing men to haul riverboats. The practice was in steep decline with the arrival of steam-powered transport – a development that Repin acknowledged by including a distant smokestack on the far right of his canvas. *Barge Haulers* was nonetheless hailed by progressive critics as a semi-political painting that confronted the canker of social injustice and abuse.

For all the contentious nature of its subject, *Barge Haulers* found favour in official circles. It had been commissioned by a member of the imperial family (Grand Duke Vladimir Aleksandrovich, the tsar's second son), and in 1873 it was a showpiece of the Russian section at the International Exhibition in Vienna, where it won a bronze medal. The young artist left

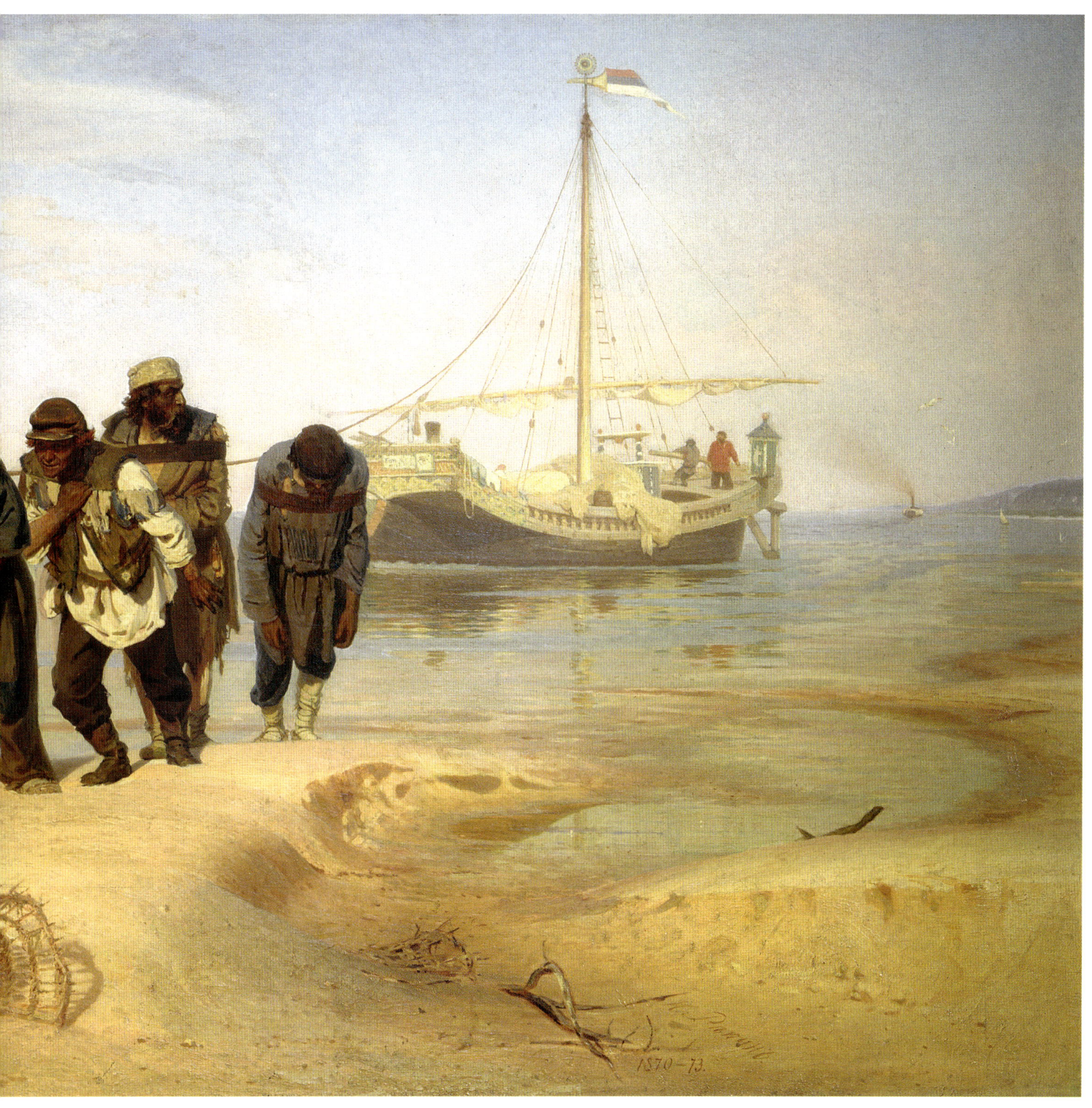

for France on a scholarship from the Academy the same year. He would doubtless have been thrilled at Tretyakov's commission to paint a writer as celebrated as Turgenev, who was the undisputed figurehead of the Russian artistic community in France. Turgenev, for his part, held Repin (Fig. 2.9) in high regard, having written to the critic Vladimir Stasov in 1871, 'I was delighted to learn that the young man is moving ahead so vigorously and rapidly. He has great talent and unquestionably the *temperament* of a painter, which is most important of all.'[7] The partnership augured well.

However, Turgenev was in thrall to Pauline Viardot, a French mezzo-soprano of Spanish descent with whom he lived, together with her husband, in an indeterminate but apparently

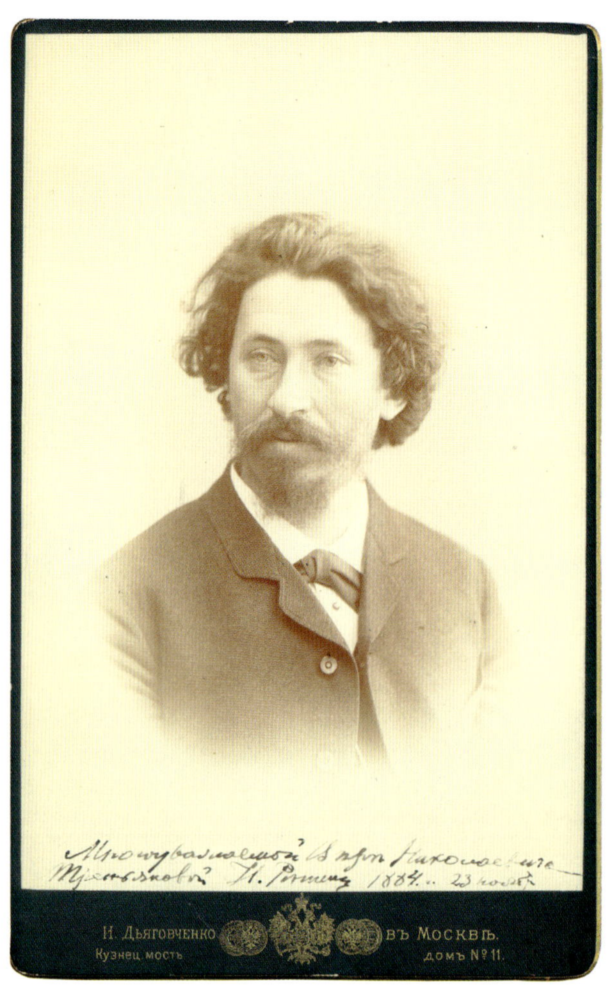

Fig. 2.9
Ilia Repin
Photographed by I. Diagovchenko, 1884

contented *ménage à trois*. 'Turgenev's robust and vigorous heart was then taken up with the fascinating Spanish woman – Mme Viardot. And I was witness to this matchless fascination,' Repin later recalled.[8] A woman of strong views and a fierce defender of Turgenev's reputation, Viardot expressed reservations about Repin's first sketch, and matters deteriorated from that point on. A coolness soon characterised relations between the artist and sitter, both of whom were dissatisfied with the final work.

The troubled history of Repin's portrait of Turgenev (plate 5) reflects not just personal differences of opinion, but much deeper anxieties concerning the future direction of Russian art. At the crux of this lay the question as to whether Russian artists should continue to look to the West for inspiration, or draw on national subject matter and develop their own distinctive style. Turgenev was a staunch enthusiast of modern French painting, which he believed should serve as a model for Russian artists. He particularly admired Alexei Kharlamov, a Russian painter based in Paris, who emulated fashionable French portraitists such as Léon Bonnat so closely as to be known as 'the Russian Bonnat'.[9] Turgenev flattered Repin to follow similar lines, as Repin recognised in April 1874: 'Turgenev said that only when he saw Kharlamov's work and the way in which I did the hands in his portrait did he begin to believe in Russian painting. In this respect he is clearly a man of French attitudes.'[10]

Back in Russia, however, the likes of Stasov and Kramskoy were far more circumspect about the influence of French technique on Russian artists. In a barrage of letters, they were ever impressing their concerns on Repin, whom they believed could become the greatest exponent yet of a native school of art. While Repin in fact maintained a healthy interest in French practice, writing at one point of painting a portrait 'à la Manet', he came to share

Stasov's disdain for Turgenev's views on art. He sneered at the sort of paintings that Turgenev bought, and derided his fixation on the virtuosic brushwork that Kharlamov was seen to represent. 'To think that Turgenev compares him to Velázquez! … Kharlamov establishing a Russian school! Kharlamov is a mere extract of French manners, and is incapable of understanding anything Russian.'[11] Turgenev, for his part, came to see Repin as a parochial artist who should return home 'where his true soil and milieu are to be found'.[12]

In light of these passionate artistic standpoints, it is unsurprising that Repin's portrait of Turgenev prompted such heated debate, caught as it was in the crossfire between those who maintained Russia's indebtedness to Western painting and those who believed Russian artists should plough their own furrow. The respective merits of these two positions would soon exercise painters and critics as never before, and come to polarise opinion as the century progressed.

Notes

1   *The Speeches of the Right Honourable William Pitt in the House of Commons*, 2nd edn, vol. 3 (London, 1808), p.216.

2   A.I. Herzen, 'Cherez tri goda', in *Sobranie sochinenii v tridtsati tomakh*, vol. 13 (Izdatel'stvo Akademii nauk SSSR, Moscow, 1958), pp.195, 197.

3   On the roots and ramifications of the Emancipation, see David Moon, *The Abolition of Serfdom in Russia* (Longman, Abingdon, 2001).

4   'Ustav Tovarishchestva peredvizhnykh khudozhestvennykh vystavok', in *Tovarishchestvo peredvizhnykh khudozhestvennykh vystavok: pis'ma, dokumenty 1869–1899*, vol. 1, ed. Sofia N. Goldshtein (Iskusstvo, Moscow, 1987), p.57.

5   J.S.G. Simmons, 'Turgenev and Oxford', *Oxoniensia*, vol. 31 (1967), pp.146–52.

6   For the limited iconography of Dostoevsky, see Anatoly Ivanov-Natov, *Ikonografiia F.M. Dostoevskogo* (Tovarishchestvo zarubezhnykh pisatelei, Bayville, 1981).

7   Letter from Ivan Turgenev to Vladimir Stasov of 29 November 1871, in Ilia S. Zilbershtein, *Repin i Turgenev* (Izdatel'stvo Akademii nauk SSSR, Moscow and Leningrad, 1945), p.13.

8   Elizabeth Kridl Valkenier, *Ilya Repin and the World of Russian Art* (Columbia University Press, New York, 1990), p.67.

9   Zilbershtein, op. cit., pp.27–30.

10 Letter to Vladimir Stasov, Paris, 13 April 1874, in *I. Repin: Izbrannye pis'ma v dvukh tomakh, 1867–1930*, vol. 1, ed. I.A. Brodsky (Iskusstvo, Moscow, 1969), p.128.

11 Letter to Vladimir Stasov, Paris, 25 May 1874, in Brodsky, op. cit., pp.134–5.

12 Zilbershtein, op. cit., p.45.

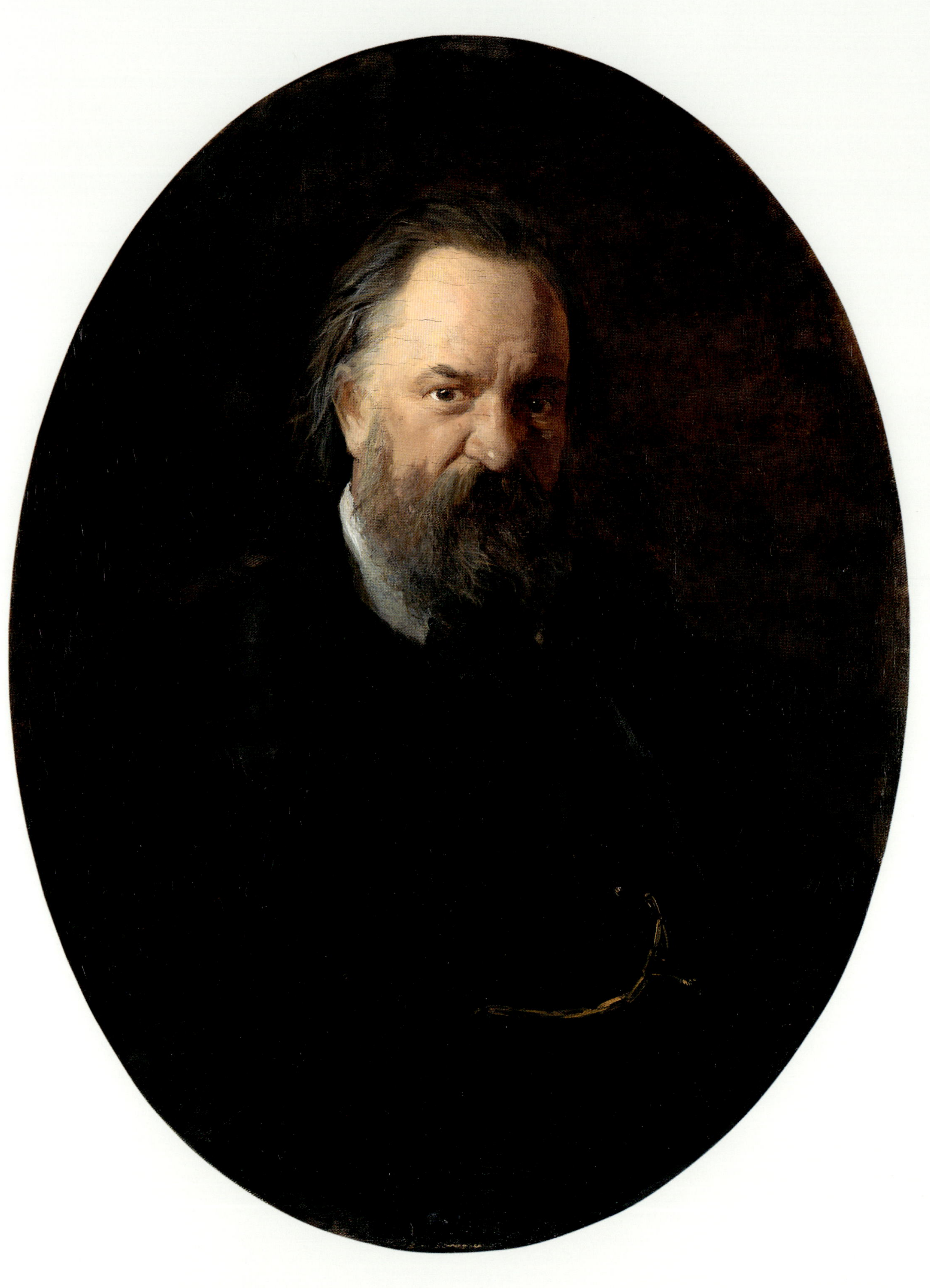

Plate 1

Alexander Herzen
Nikolai Ge, 1867
Oil on canvas, 795 x 630mm

Alexander Herzen (1812–70) was a leading writer, journalist and political thinker, who initially focused on fiction in a moralistic and occasionally socially critical vein. In 1847 he emigrated from Russia to Europe and was profoundly affected by a series of devastating events: the revolutions of 1848, to which he was an eye-witness in Paris; the drowning of his mother and son in a shipwreck in 1851; and the death of his wife the following year. His writing underwent a profound reorientation, as he largely abandoned fiction in favour of émigré journalism, essays and memoir literature in works such as *From the Other Shore* (1847–50) and *My Past and Thoughts* (1868).

In 1852, Herzen moved to London, where he founded the Free Russian Press and launched the seminal literary and socio-political almanacs *Polar Star* (1855–69) and *The Bell* (1857–67). The debates that were aired in these publications exerted enormous influence. However, Herzen became disillusioned in the wake of the ill-formulated reforms of the 1860s in Russia, and was gradually ostracised by liberals and radicals alike. In 1865, he left London for Geneva, and two years later travelled to Florence, where he was painted by Nikolai Ge (1831–94), a progressive young painter who had lived in Italy for some years.

Ge captured with painful insight the simultaneous defiance and despondency of a man who had battled for social and political change in Russia at enormous personal cost, which included foreign exile for twenty-three of his fifty-seven years. Maximising the aesthetic potential of the half-lit face, Ge produced a portrait that transcended the exigencies of the moment, and came instead to symbolise a generation of courageous political commentators who had propelled reformist discourse in Russia, but were now receding into the shadows. Herzen approved of the portrait, which he termed 'rembrandtisch'.[1] Ge, for his part, left a bleak assessment of this scourge of the Russian establishment in what would prove to be the twilight of his life. 'Herzen, that brilliant talent, was a deeply unhappy man. I saw in him a boundless love for his homeland that was forever closed to him, alongside an aversion to everything that surrounded him in the West. … How hard it was to see this talent broken.'[2] The artist smuggled the picture back into Russia by covering Herzen's image with a depiction of the prophet Moses. It is small wonder that Tretyakov took pains to secure it for his collection. Ge withstood Tretyakov's overtures for many years until financial necessity compelled him to part with the portrait. It entered Tretyakov's collection in 1878 and has been a linchpin of its pantheon of exemplary Russians ever since.

1   Letter from Alexander Herzen to Nikolai Ogarev, 13 February 1867, in *Nikolai Nikolaevich Ge: Pis'ma, Stat'i, Kritika – Vospominaniia sovremennikov*, ed. N.Iu. Zograf (Iskusstvo, Moscow, 1978), p.73.

2   *Nikolai Nikolaevich Ge, ego zhizn', proizvedeniia i perepiska*, ed. V.V. Stasov (Posrednika, Moscow, 1904), p.168.

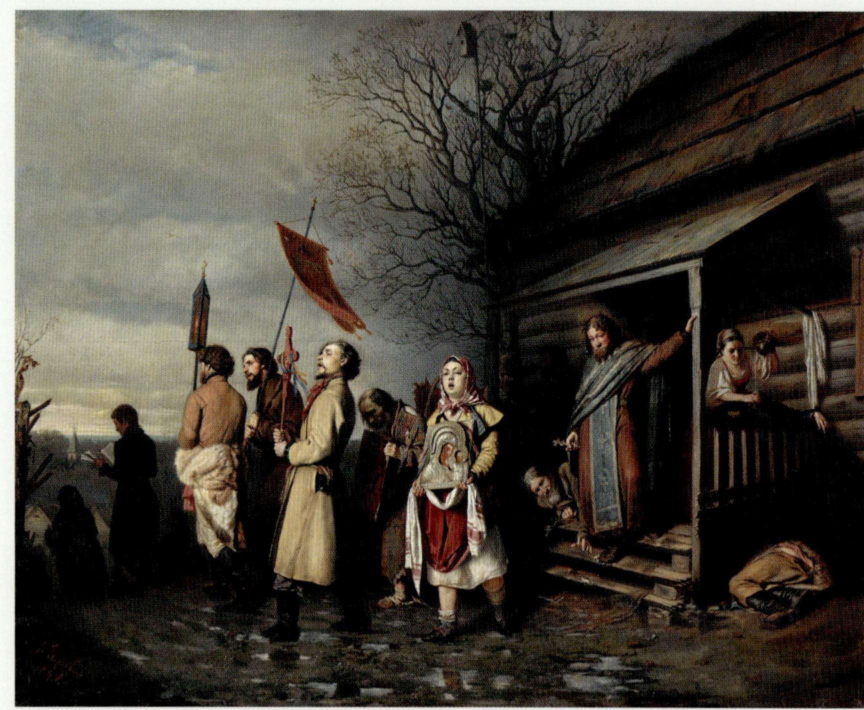

Plate 2

Alexander Ostrovsky
Vasily Perov, 1871
Oil on canvas, 1035 x 807mm

Vasily Perov (1834–82), who painted the playwright Alexander Ostrovsky (1823–86), was one of the most acerbic artists of the 1860s, renowned for his barbed critique of impiety within the Orthodox Church. In *The Village Religious Procession at Easter* (Fig. 2.10), for example, the solemn event of a procession of icons is profaned by the inebriation of church leaders and their acolytes. A priest crushes an Easter egg as he lurches down the steps, while others collapse around him. Money changes hands in the background. An icon is held upside-down.

Ostrovsky in turn targeted the venality and obscurantism of Moscow's merchant and business classes in a series of plays that both scandalised and enraptured the city's theatre-goers. Perov's portrait of the playwright thus marked an encounter of great significance between two of Russia's sharpest social commentators, who in their different media had lampooned institutional corruption and moral turpitude as never before.

Perov elected to portray Ostrovsky square-on, intimating the stature of his sitter in the bulk of his frame. The playwright's broad hands, so agile with a pen, rest quietly on his thighs while he fixes the viewer with an unflinching gaze. The composition relies on a subtle interplay of triangles. That formed by Ostrovsky's face and hands is underpinned by the sheepskin of his collar and, within this, the strangely illegible triangle beneath his chin. At the same time, the artist conjures with great skill the different textures and tonalities of the velvety outer sheepskin against its fleece lining, the full moustache overhanging a moistened lower lip, the thinning hair against the balding pate. The result is a portrait of quiet assurance that avoids the distraction of external paraphernalia in order to focus on the sitter's physicality and intellectual life. Tretyakov snapped it up for his collection, clearly sharing Perov's fascination in a writer who had persistently compelled Russia's middle classes to confront the ignorance and solipsism that at times lay at their core. Many of Ostrovsky's plays maintained their popularity into the twentieth century, with the Czech composer Leoš Janáček basing his opera *Katya Kabanova* (1921) on Ostrovsky's play *The Storm* (1860).

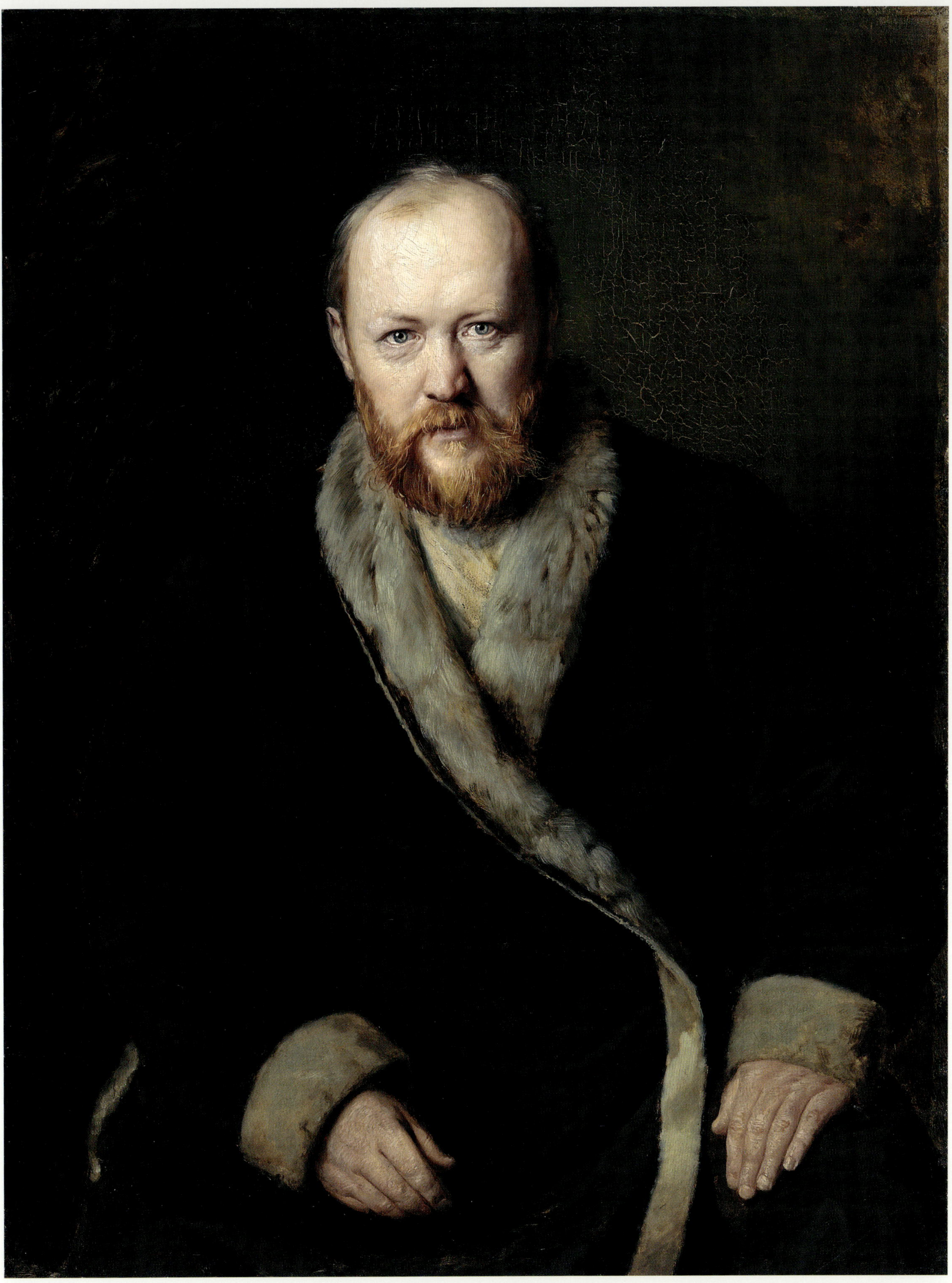

Plate 3

Vladimir Dal
Vasily Perov, 1872
Oil on canvas, 940 x 805mm

Vladimir Dal (1801–72) graduated from the Naval Cadet School in St Petersburg in 1819, and served in the Russian fleet of the Baltic and the Black Sea. He then studied medicine and worked as a military doctor in campaigns against Poland and Turkey. Falling foul of his superiors, he left the military and worked in administration for the Ministry of the Interior, until retiring from service in 1859.

It was during his civilian employment that Dal came to prominence as a writer and philologist. His first literary work, *Russian Fairy Tales – First Group of Five* (1832), was heralded as an innovative contribution to Russian literature at a time when foreign models were still all the rage. A man of prodigious mental energy, Dal then dedicated years to the compilation and preservation of Russian proverbs, folk songs and fairytales. He published these in a number of meticulously researched and richly annotated volumes, including *On the Beliefs, Superstitions and Prejudices of the Russian People* (1845–6) and *Proverbs of the Russian People* (1862). He also laboured over the peculiarities of his native tongue, culminating in the *Reasoned Dictionary of the Living Russian Language*, which appeared in four magisterial volumes from 1863 to 1866. This was a man at the heart of the quest to capture and celebrate the glories of the Russian language in oral and literary form.

Dal was seventy-one in the year that Perov painted him, and the effects of ageing are undisguised. The body, shrunken in its heavy gown, seems encased in the high-backed leather chair. There is a slackness to the skin that clings to sunken cheeks, an incipient cloudiness to the eyes. Yet the overall effect is of intellect undimmed. The acclaimed lexicographer died later the same year. Dal's *Reasoned Dictionary* long remained in print, and remains an unsurpassed fount of regional and dialectical idiosyncrasies.

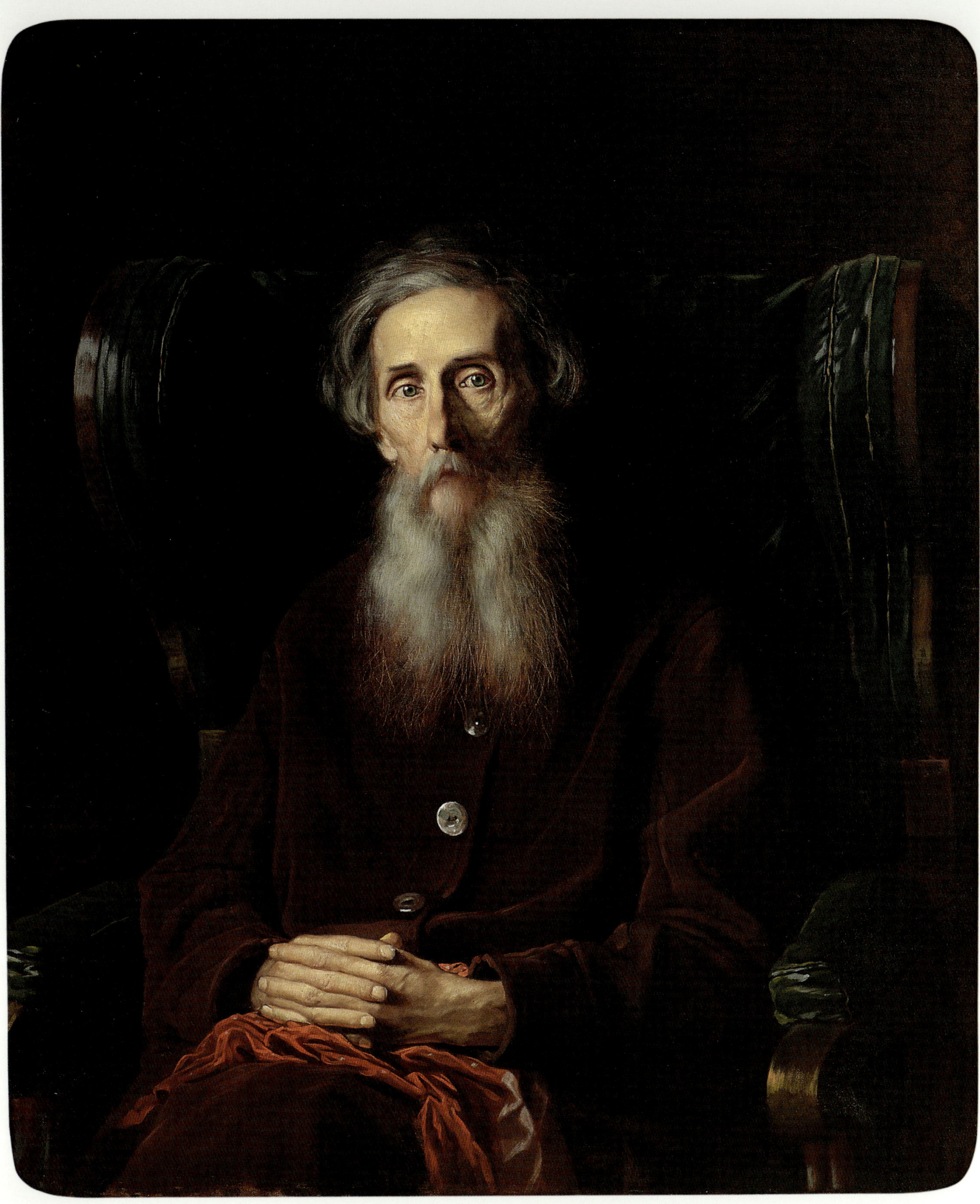

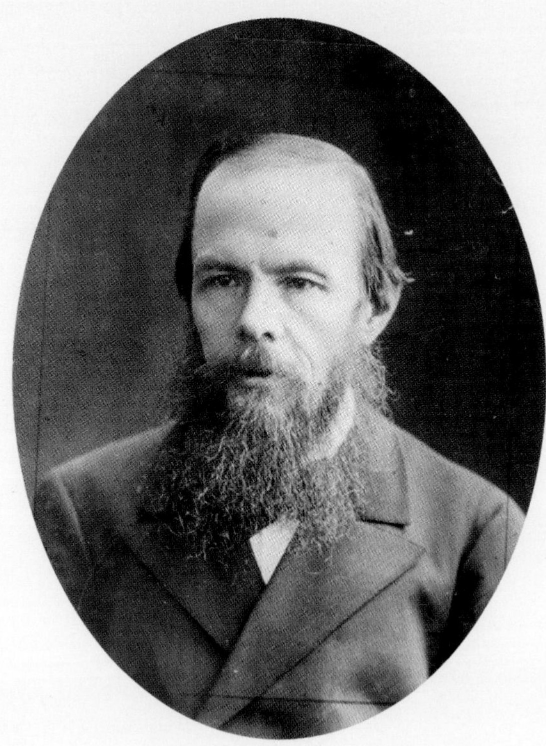

Fig. 2.11
Fedor Dostoevsky
Photographed by
Constantin Chapiro, 1871

Plate 4

Fedor Dostoevsky
Vasily Perov, 1872
Oil on canvas, 996 x 810mm

Fedor Dostoevsky (1821–81) was one of the most prominent figures to suffer from the extraordinary caprice and cruelty of Nicholas I's reign. In 1849 the 28-year-old writer was arrested for his involvement in an underground society of socialist and utopian persuasion known as the Petrashevsky Circle. Condemned to death along with the other conspirators, it was only when he was lined up in front of the firing squad that an order arrived from the tsar to commute the sentence to penal servitude in Siberia. The mock execution was enough to unhinge the most robust of men, and one of Dostoevsky's co-accused went permanently insane.

Serving four years in unspeakable conditions in a prison labour camp in Omsk, with hands and feet shackled and scant protection from the extremes of heat and cold, Dostoevsky then endured half a decade of enforced military service, before returning to St Petersburg in 1859. His mental and physical health forever jeopardised by the trauma of his sentence, he nonetheless proceeded to write some of the greatest novels of the century, among them *Crime and Punishment* (1866) and *The Idiot*, which he finished three years later. By the time he sat for Perov in St Petersburg in 1872, he was a figure of almost unimaginable authority in the public consciousness, a hardened veteran of the country's most extreme punitive measures who had returned to speak of crime and depravity, of illness and

insanity, of the abject depths to which degradation and irrationality could lead.

Perov responded with an image of great economy that quietly suggested but never sensationalised the weight of Dostoevsky's past. Oblivious to his audience, the writer folds in on himself, the antithesis of any ostentatious posturing or hyperbolic display. If first impressions are of stasis and reflection, there is a tension that speaks of a fiercely creative but unquiet mind: the shoulders are slightly raised, the fingers firmly enmeshed in their strangely exaggerated interlace. Meanwhile, the colouring was inspired by the likes of Velázquez and Van Dyck, whose work Perov had copied in the Hermitage. For Dostoevsky's wife, Perov captured the writer's 'moment of creation' as he 'peered into himself', while Kramskoy praised 'the sharpness and energy' of the contours and believed the painting to be one of the greatest Russian portraits of all time.[1] Unceasingly praised in the writer's lifetime and reproduced since on everything from stamps to biscuit tins, the portrait confirmed Dostoevsky's image as a troubled visionary who achieved unprecedented psychological intensity in his work.

1   Ivan N. Kramskoy, 'O portrete F.M. Dostoevskogo', in *Pis'ma, stat'i v dvukh tomakh*, vol. 2, ed. Sofia N. Goldshtein (Iskusstvo, Moscow, 1966), p.356.

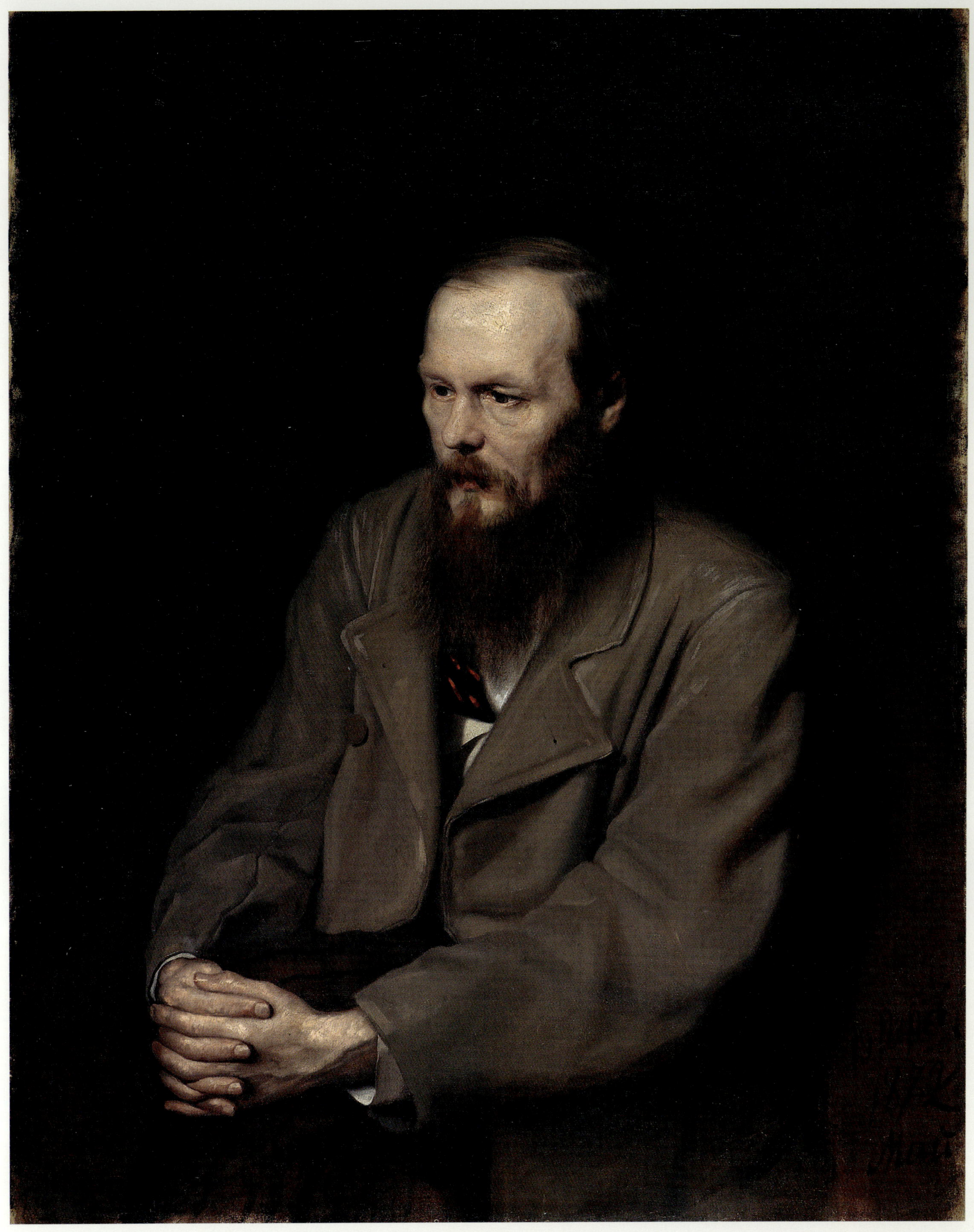

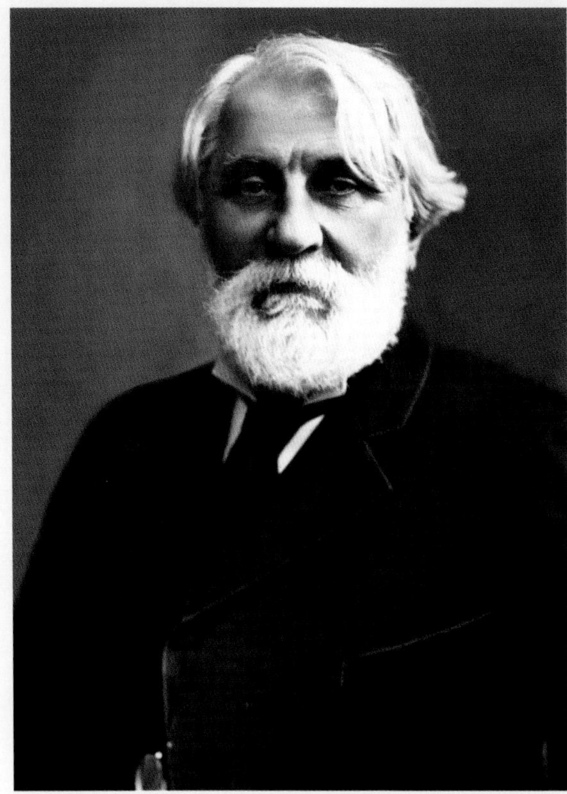

Fig. 2.12
Ivan Turgenev
Photographed by Nadar
(Gaspard-Félix Tournachon), 1877

Plate 5

Ivan Turgenev
Ilia Repin, 1874

Oil on canvas, 1165 x 890mm

Tretyakov commissioned Ilia Repin (1844–1930) to paint Ivan Turgenev (1818–83) when both the artist and the writer were living in Paris. According to Repin, the initial encounter was promising. 'The first sitting went off with blissful good fortune and I was happy. Ivan Sergeevich [Turgenev] congratulated me on my success.'[1] But some of Turgenev's friends voiced concerns about the portrait, whereupon progress faltered. 'I work with Turgenev from 10 to 12 each morning,' Repin wrote to the critic Stasov on 27 March 1874. 'He has rejected one head. It was well painted, but made him look like a shamelessly grinning old roué. … I lost interest in the picture for a while, but now I change it and break it and spoil it as before – I am still searching.'[2]

Repin was more upbeat a couple of weeks later when he wrote to inform Tretyakov that the commission was almost complete. 'Ivan Sergeevich is very pleased with his portrait, and says that it will bring me much honour. … Mme Viardot said to me bravo, Monsieur! The likeness is impeccable.'[3] By late May, however, the writer was openly critical of the finished work. Repin wrote bitterly to Stasov that '[Turgenev] himself admitted to me that he is a bad critic, and this is true'.[4]

Portraits that stem from fraught relations between sitter and artist can nonetheless have their own particular appeal. In this case Turgenev's coolness towards the artist is unconcealed, and perhaps reflects the caginess of a long-term émigré in the face of a talented young compatriot whose star was on the ascendant back at home. The mouth is downturned, the expression one of mild disdain. Tretyakov was far from satisfied, claiming that the portrait failed to capture Turgenev's intelligence and good humour – a verdict with which one could hardly disagree. Resuming his quest for a worthy image of the writer for his collection, Tretyakov would eventually approach no fewer than seven artists, two of whom refused. Even Repin was persuaded to produce further portraits of the writer in 1879 and, after Turgenev's death, in 1883, both of which have been lost. His painting of 1874 is now seen as the most successful of all portraits of Turgenev, the clear friction between artist and sitter giving it undeniable presence as the writer quietly glowers in his richly patterned chair.

1   Elizabeth Kridl Valkenier, *Ilya Repin and the World of Russian Art* (Columbia University Press, New York, 1990), p.66.

2   Letter to Vladimir Stasov, Paris, 27 March 1874, in *I. Repin: Izbrannye pis'ma v dvukh tomakh, 1867–1930*, vol. 1, ed. I.A. Brodsky (Iskusstvo, Moscow, 1969), p.120.

3   Letter to Pavel Tretyakov, Paris, 13 April 1874, ibid., p.128.

4   Letter to Vladimir Stasov, Paris, 25 May 1874, ibid., p.134.

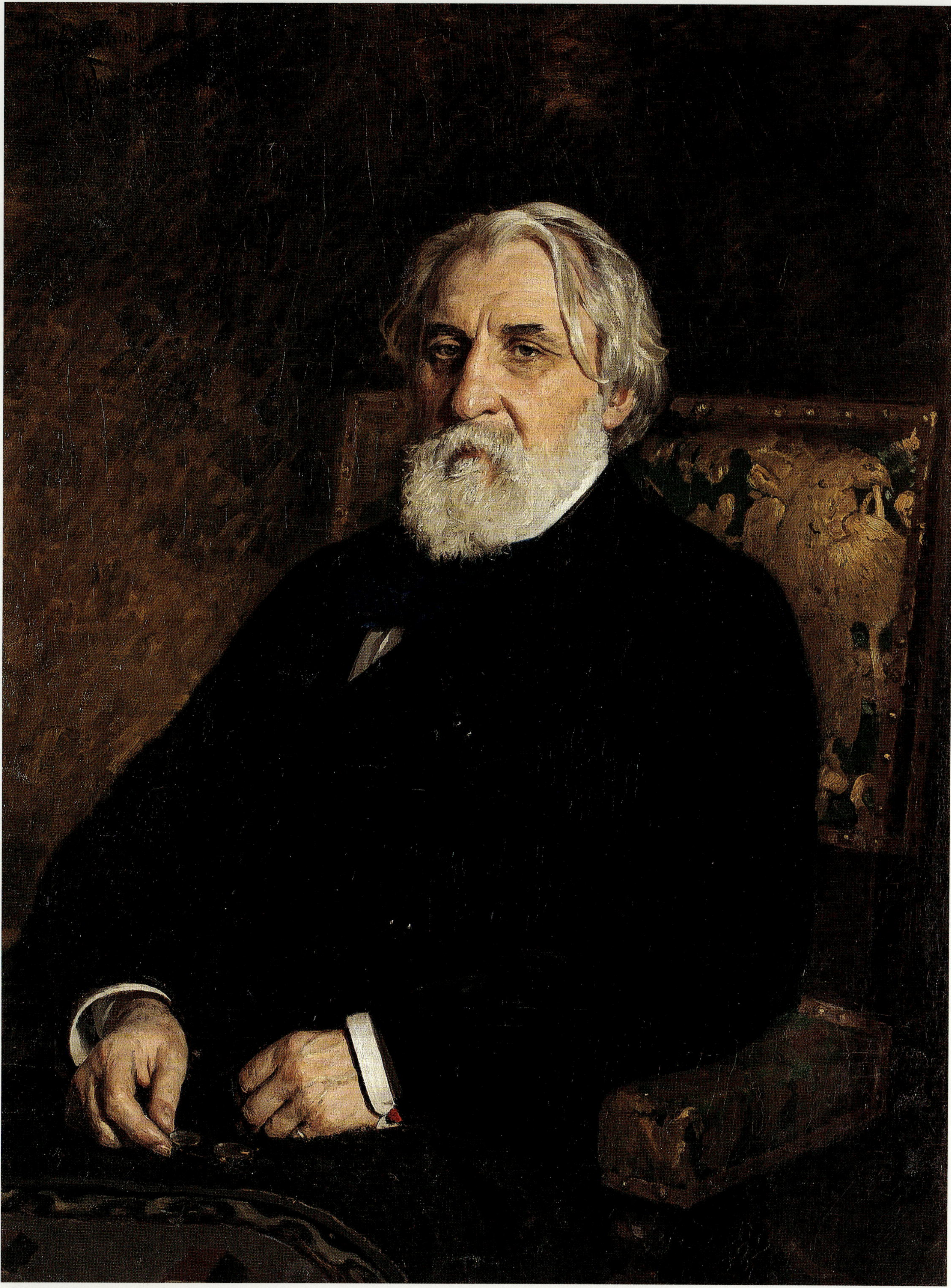

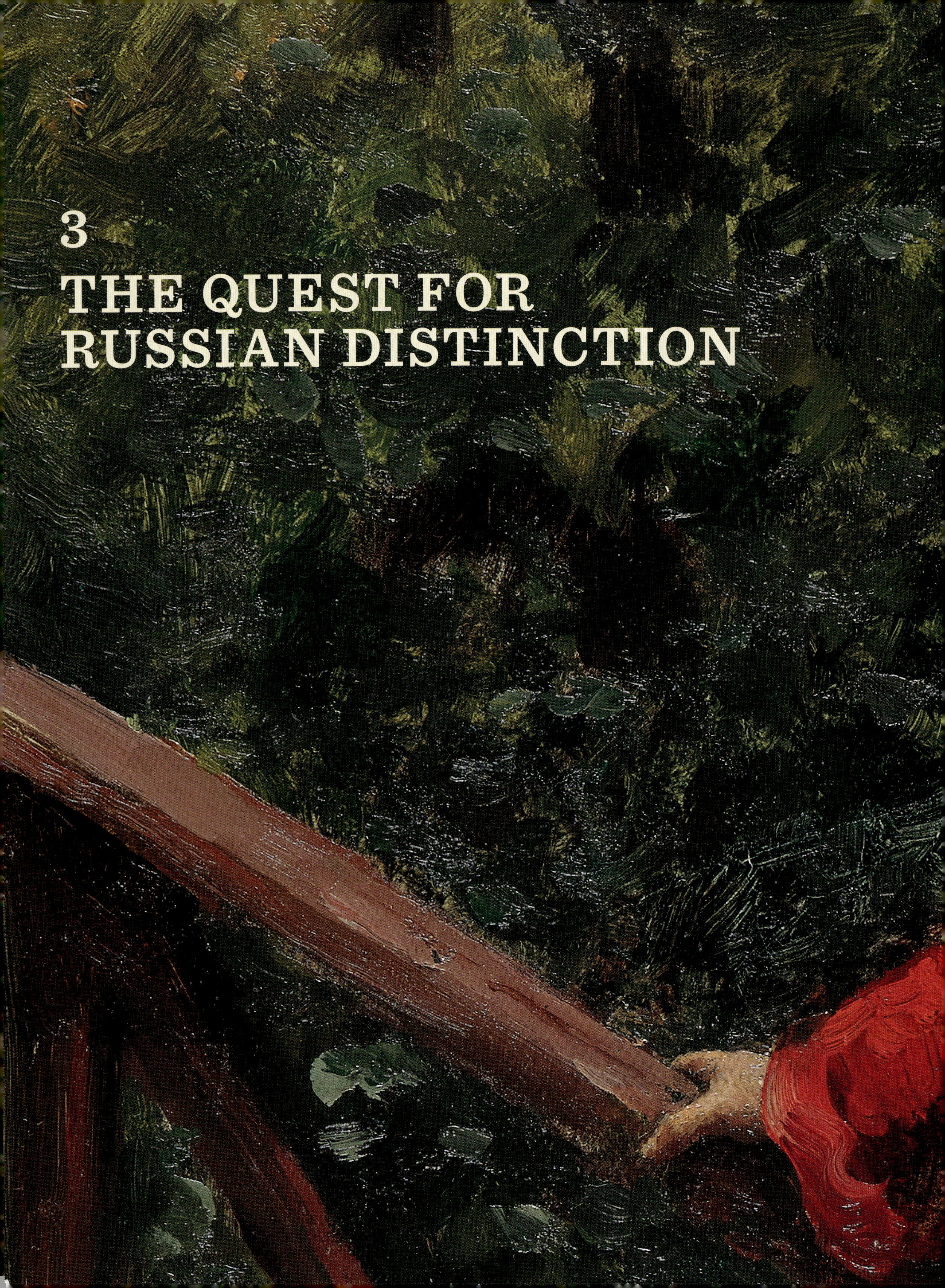
3
THE QUEST FOR
RUSSIAN DISTINCTION

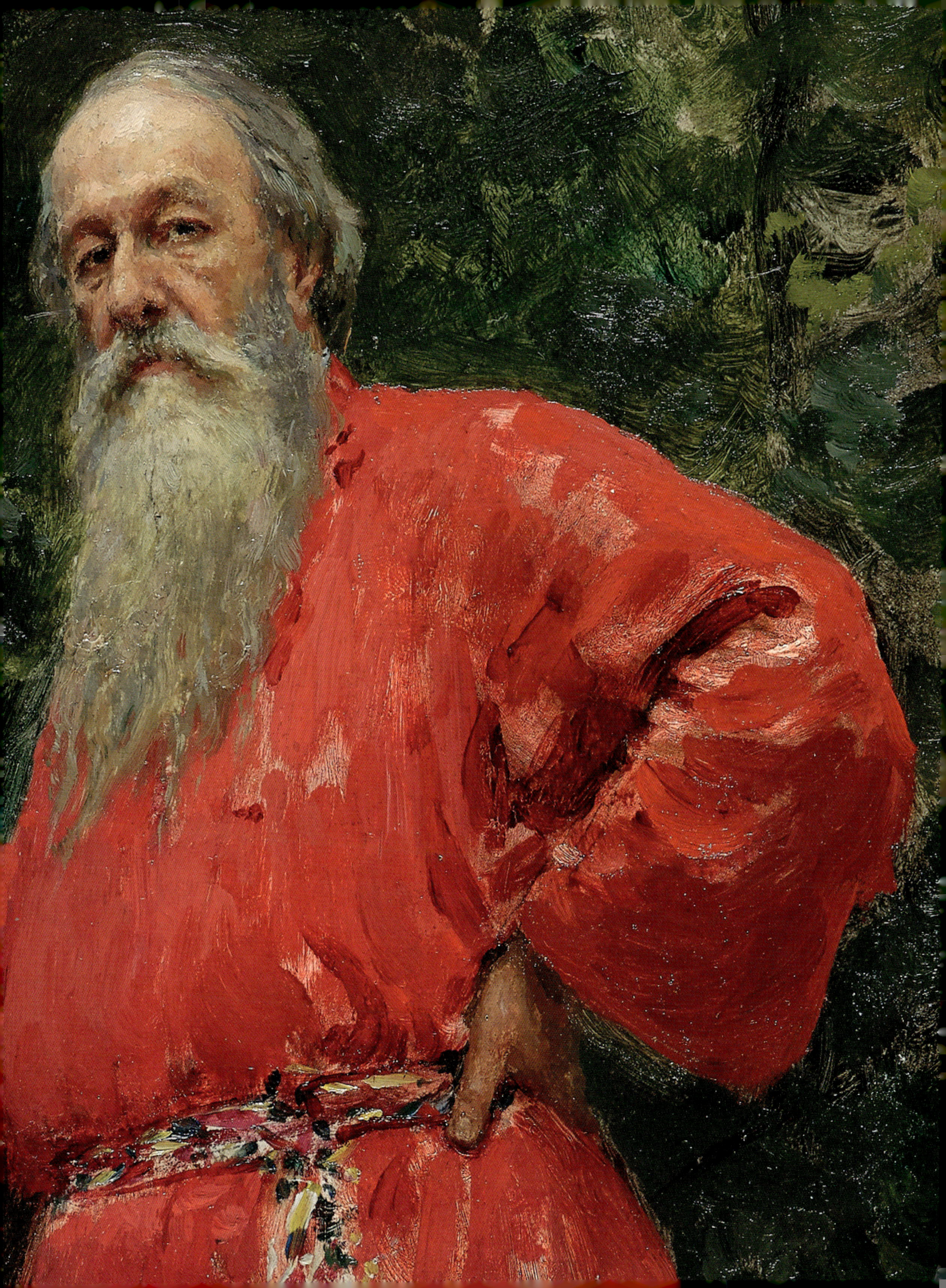

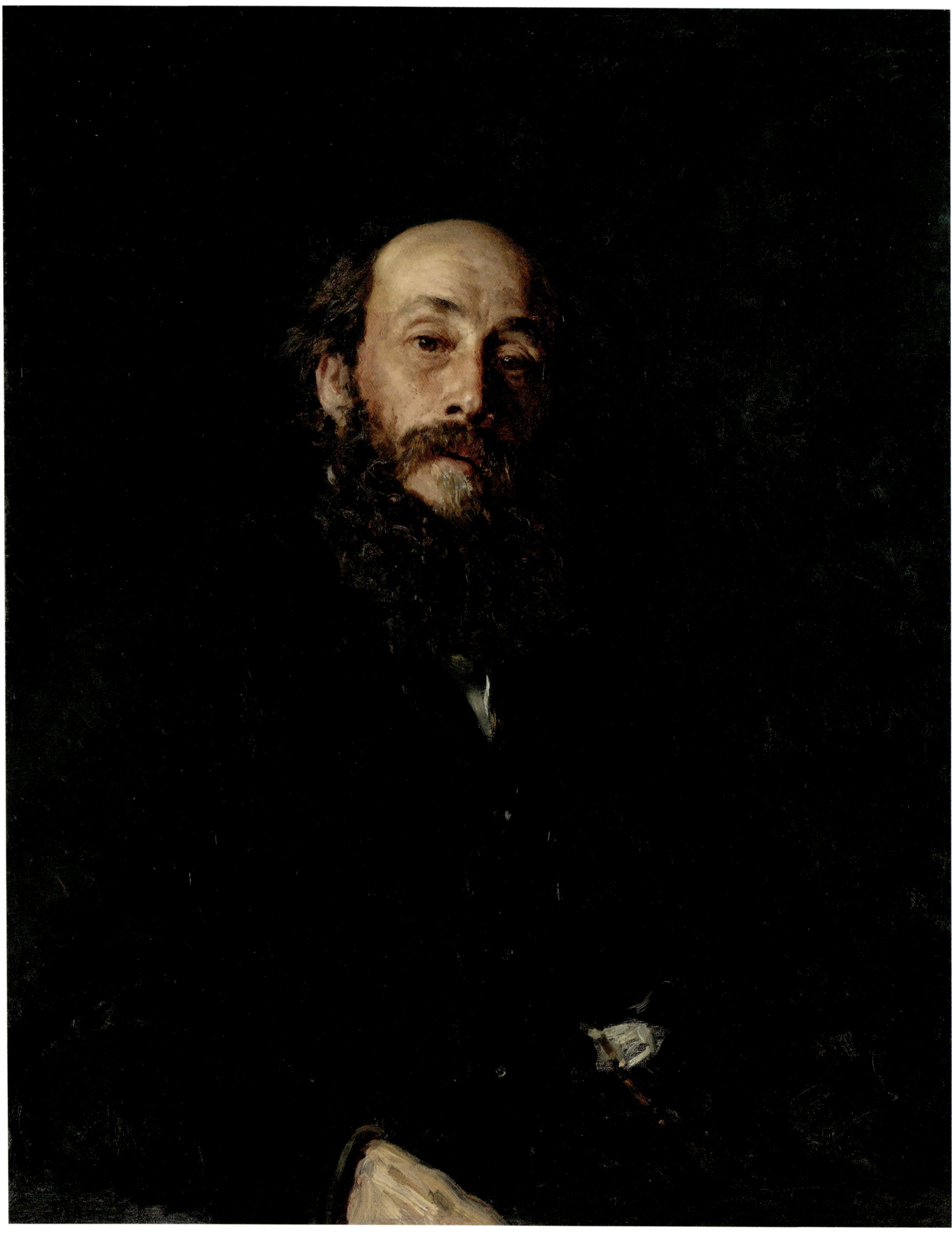

BY THE EARLY 1880s, the arts were enjoying unprecedented popularity in Russia. The annual Peredvizhnik exhibitions were routinely attracting over 15,000 visitors in St Petersburg, as well as thousands more in Moscow and the provincial cities that they toured.[1] The thirteenth exhibition, in 1885, was viewed by nearly 45,000 people in St Petersburg alone, which was just under one-twentieth of the city's population at the time.[2] There was also a surge of new books and periodicals in the final quarter of the century, and writers commanded an unparalleled level of authority. Tretyakov duly stepped up the pace of his campaign to document the country's greatest literary voices in visual form, and increasing numbers of novelists, playwrights and critics graced the walls of his gallery as the decade progressed.

Tretyakov was now sufficiently provident in his patronage to commission portraits not only of writers in their prime, but of those whose heyday was past. Typical in this respect is Repin's portrait of Alexei Pisemsky (plate 6), which was exhibited at the ninth Peredvizhnik exhibition (1881) alongside those of other cultural luminaries. Nikolai Ge, whose portrait of Herzen had captivated Tretyakov a decade previously, peered down from another canvas by Repin, in which bold brushwork captured Ge's aloof expression to great effect (Fig. 3.1). The portraits were accompanied by stunning examples of genre and landscape painting, among them Nikolai Kuznetsov's pellucid *Holiday* (Fig. 3.2) and *Thickets* by Ivan Shishkin (Fig. 3.3), an artist so dedicated to the accurate transcription of Russia's fields and forests that he became known as 'the accountant of leaves'. There was also a showpiece historical painting in the shape of Vasily Surikov's *The Morning of the Execution of the Streltsy*, which took as its subject the rebel soldiers who had defied Peter the Great some two centuries earlier (Fig. 3.4). Clad in white shirts, they prepare to be hanged from gallows specially erected between St Basil's Cathedral and the Kremlin walls, while the merciless tsar, mounted on horseback on the right, coolly surveys the agony of their final moments and family farewells.

These were striking paintings, and in normal circumstances would have prompted avid speculation and debate. Yet the opening of the ninth Peredvizhnik exhibition, on 1 March 1881,

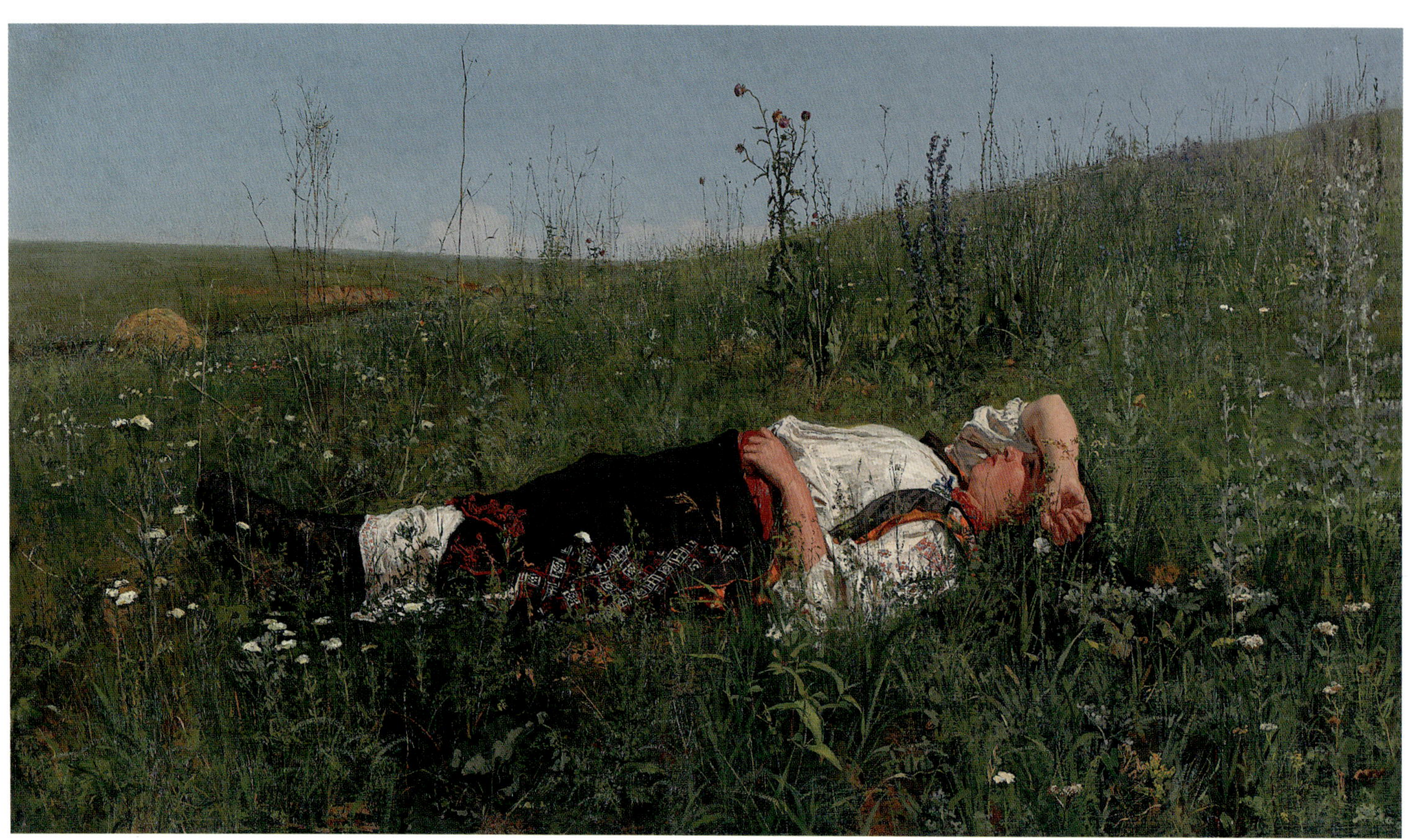

was quickly overlooked, for that very day Alexander II was assassinated as his carriage passed along one of St Petersburg's elegant canals less than a mile away. The first bomb thrown by a member of a radical revolutionary cell failed to harm the tsar, but when he alighted to survey the damage a second bomb found its target to devastating effect. With severed limbs and ruptured arteries, Alexander was taken to the Winter Palace, where he bled to death hours later. The popular society artist Konstantin Makovsky was rushed to the tsar's bedside to paint him during 'a ghastly session' of two hours that same day (Fig. 3.5).[3] A Rubicon had been crossed, but repressive measures were effected across the board to recover authority and control. The tsaricides were hanged a month later in a grim parallel to Surikov's painting, and the imperial family re-established their hold and continued to rule for another thirty-odd years.

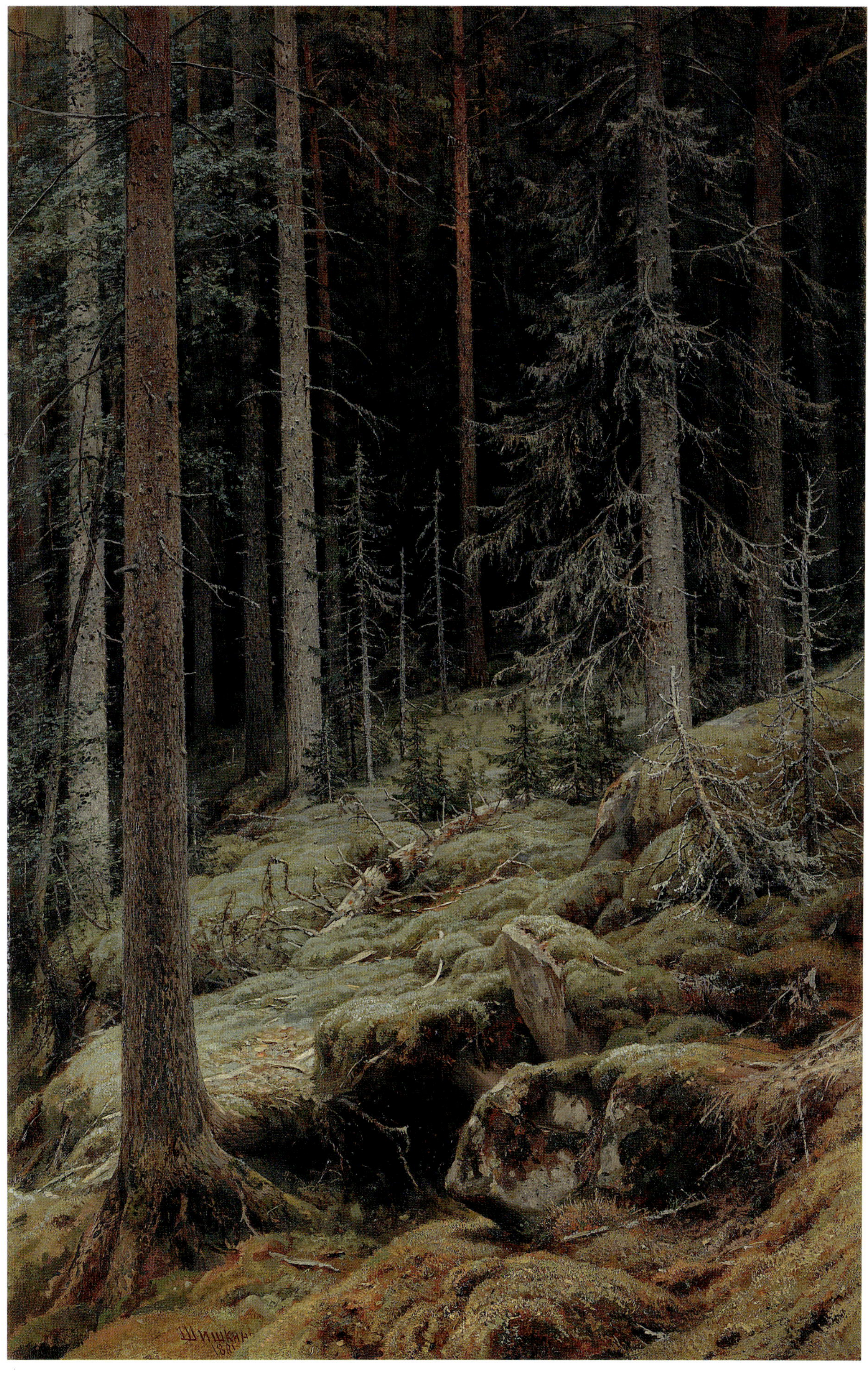

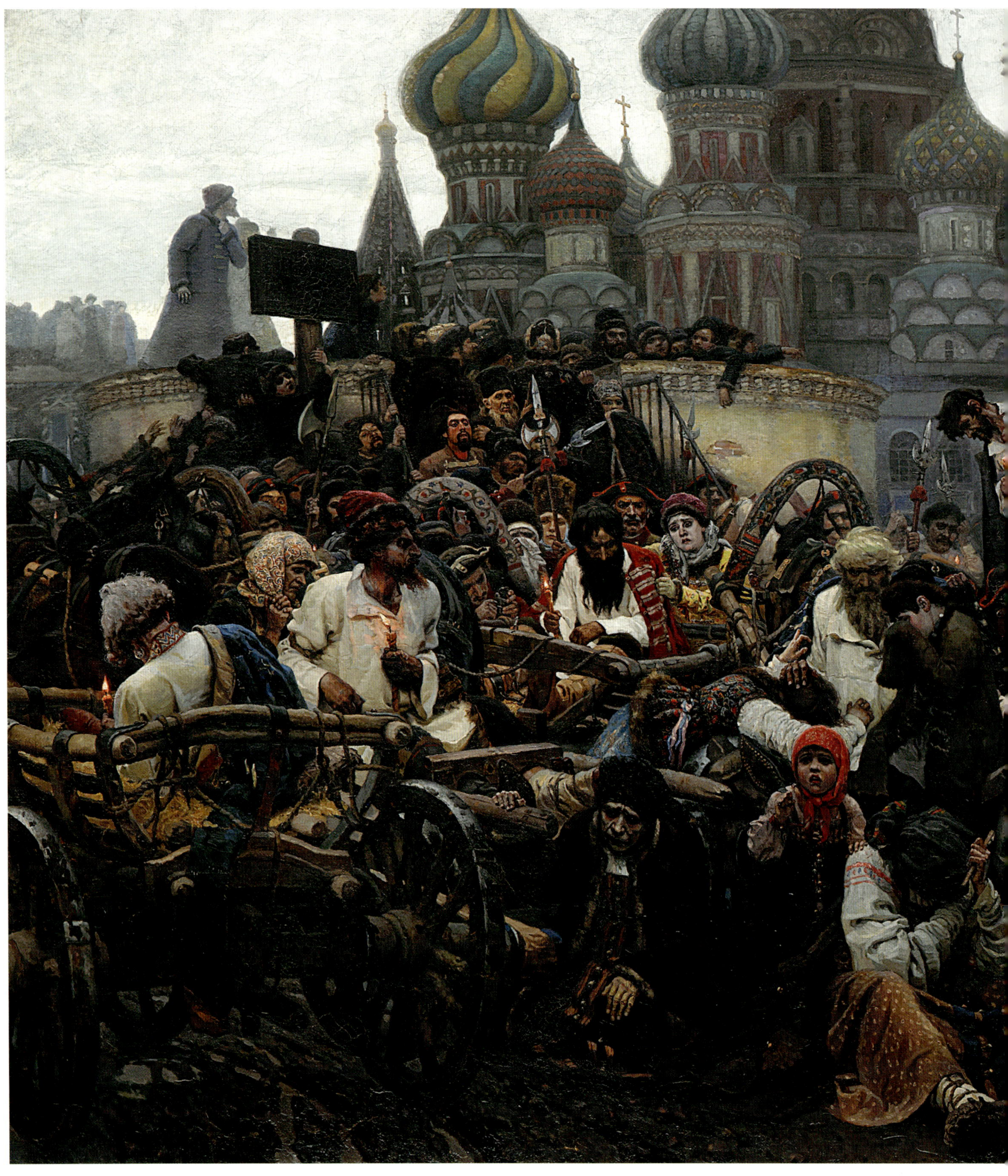

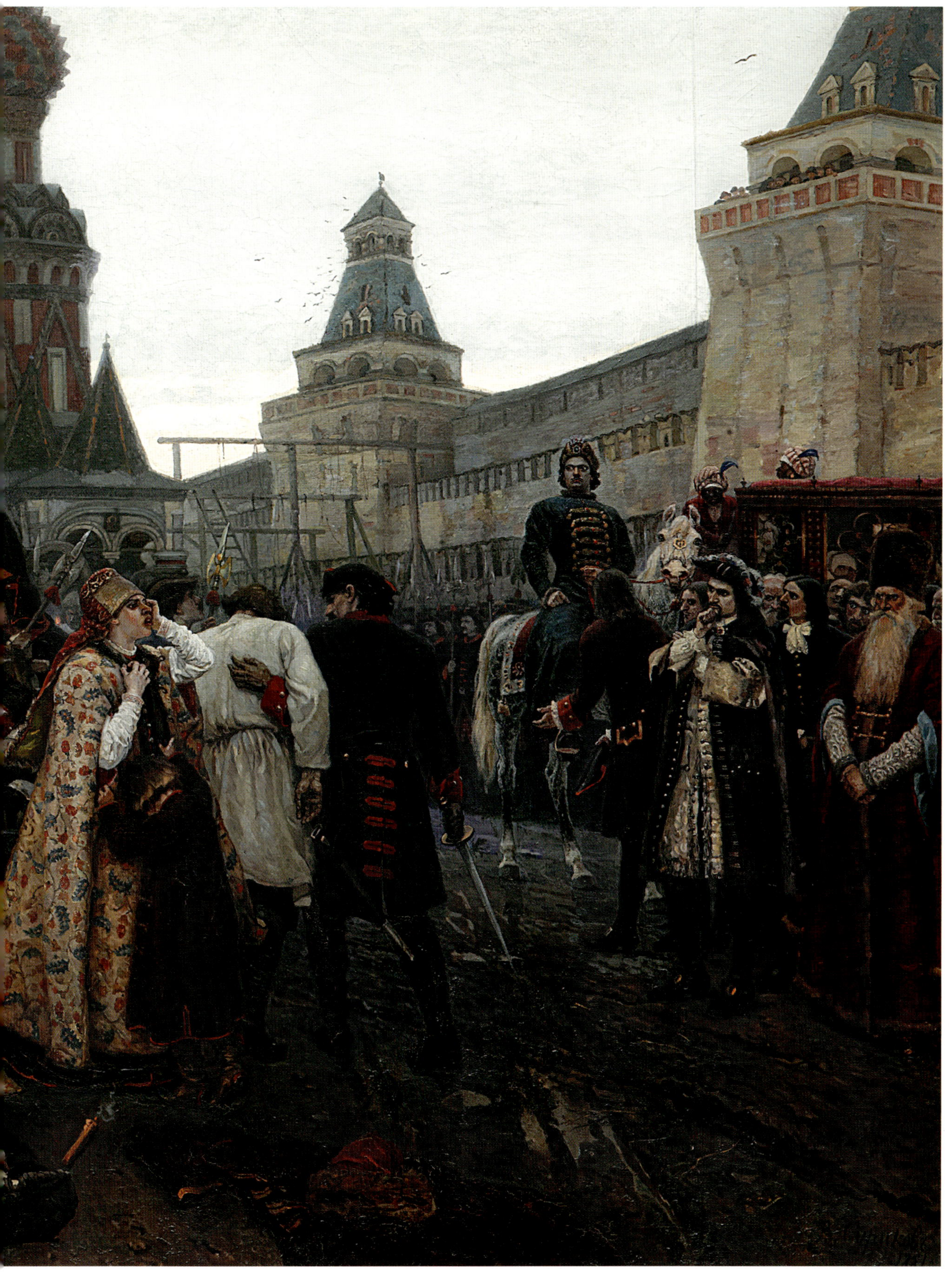

Fig. 3.5
Alexander II on His Deathbed
Konstantin Makovsky, 1881

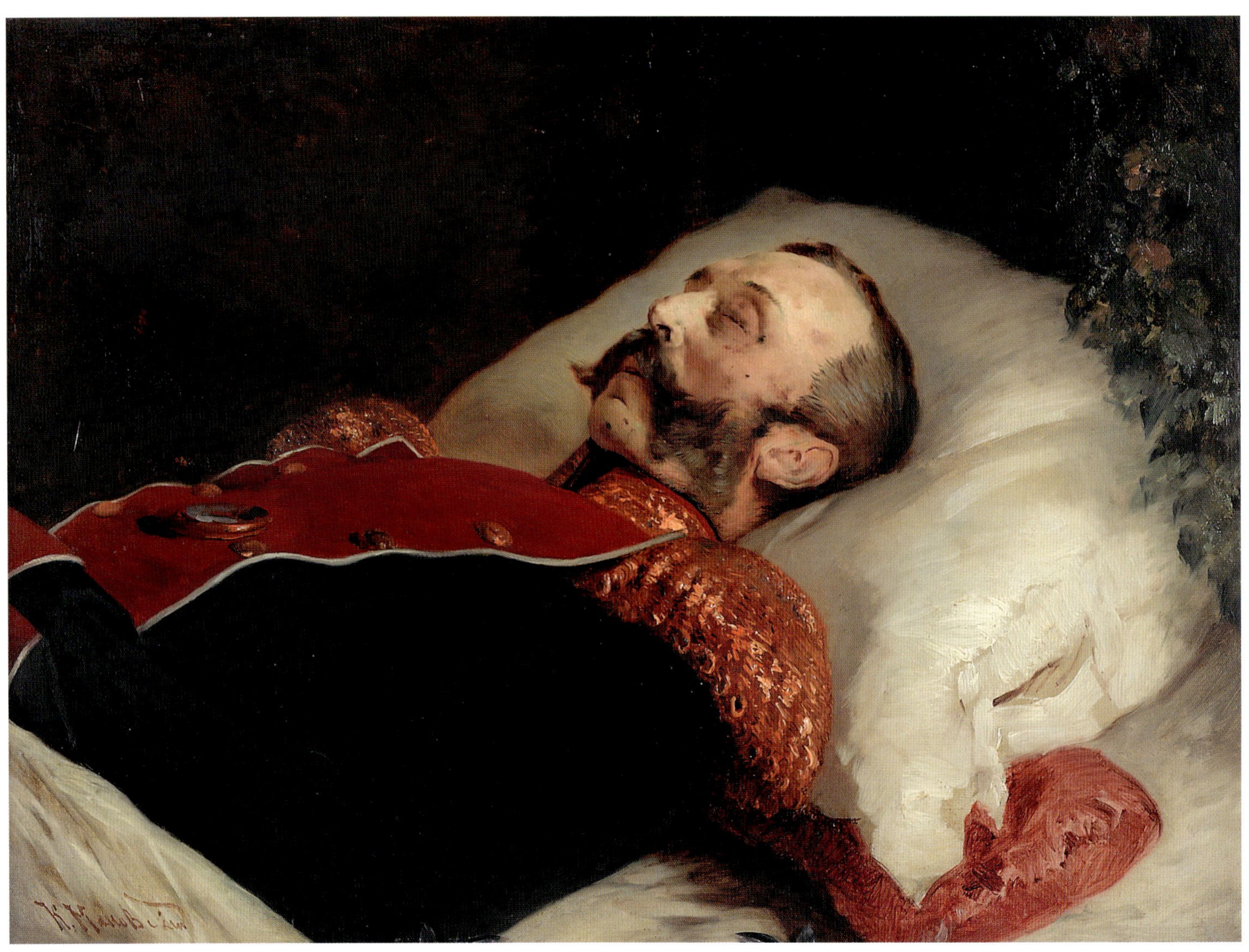

As the news of the tsar's assassination spread, the people of St Petersburg sank at their kitchen tables or stopped in their tracks at work, struggling to come to terms with the enormity of the event. Among them were the composer Modest Mussorgsky, whose rapidly failing health had confined him to hospital, and Repin, who had been commissioned by Tretyakov to paint Mussorgsky as a matter of urgency. The result of their encounter (plate 7) is one of the most affecting of Repin's portraits, and marks the beginning of a lengthy period in which paintings of musicians would feature prominently in Tretyakov's collection and excite public opinion as never before.

Mussorgsky came from a privileged background, the son of a noble land-owning family who lived in a beautiful region of forests and lakes some 250 miles south of St Petersburg. Intended for the family tradition of military service, he entered cadet school in St Petersburg at the age of thirteen, and four years later was commissioned into the Preobrazhensky Regiment, a long-standing elite within the Russian Imperial Guard. Another event that year had a more profound effect, however, for in October 1856 the 17-year-old Mussorgsky met Alexander Borodin, a trainee doctor who would forge a distinguished career as a chemist and surgeon and was an ardent champion of women's rights. Borodin's first impressions of Mussorgsky were of a slightly foppish young man, immaculate in his well-cut uniform and carefully slicked hair, and 'with hands well groomed, like a lord's'. Ladies swooned at his manners and politesse. Mussorgsky was also already an accomplished and flamboyant pianist, whom Borodin recalled performing extracts from *Il Trovatore* and *La Traviata* to admiring cries of 'charmant' and 'délicieux'.[4] Together the two men developed their passion for music, and soon graduated from providing musical entertainment for friends and acquaintances to serious compositions of their own. For Borodin, composing always came second to his medical and scientific work. But for Mussorgsky it was a driving ambition, a seductive and exacting taskmaster that dictated the course of his brilliant but truncated career.

Mussorgsky's early compositions adhered to Western models in a manner that had been typical of Russian music since the eighteenth century. Gradually, however, he gravitated towards other composers in St Petersburg who were experimenting with forms of music that were identifiably Russian rather than pale derivations of European styles. They soon attracted the attention of Vladimir Stasov, who was as keen to promote native traditions in music as he was in art. Famously, in 1867 Stasov concluded a review of a concert that had featured compositions by Alexander Dargomyzhsky, Mikhail Glinka, Mily Balakirev and Nikolai Rimsky-Korsakov with the words: 'God grant that our Slav guests will never forget today's concert; God grant that they will always remember how much poetry, feeling, talent and intelligence there is in this small but already mighty handful of Russian musicians.'[5] Stasov would later attract derision for his blinkered nationalism, but his closing description became a powerful rallying cry. A new group formed around Balakirev, comprising Rimsky-Korsakov, Borodin, Mussorgsky and César Cui, who collectively became known as the Mighty Handful, or simply the Five.

Stasov was soon zealously promoting the Five as exemplars of a national musical tradition, just as he would champion the Peredvizhniki as Russia's first wholly national school of painting. His categorisations were highly problematic. Many of Stasov's preferred painters were more outward-looking and heterogeneous in approach than he would have his audiences believe. Similarly, the Five sang from very different songsheets at times. Mussorgsky, for one, gradually distanced himself from the charismatic and controlling Balakirev to explore other avenues of musical expression. The nationalistic credentials that Stasov identified nonetheless exerted a powerful allure and helped to establish Mussorgsky's reputation as a talent to watch. His professional ascent was not without its obstacles: his startlingly original orchestral piece *Night on Bald Mountain* (1867), for example, was dismissed with a sneer by

Balakirev, and never performed during Mussorgsky's lifetime. By the early 1870s, however, the composer was sharing rooms with Rimsky-Korsakov in the centre of St Petersburg, and writing works of precocious creativity for the city's main opera houses and concert halls. The year 1874 alone saw the premier of the opera *Boris Godunov* at the Mariinsky Theatre, and the completion of *Pictures at an Exhibition*. The latter, a piano suite of exquisite range and balance, had been prompted by a retrospective exhibition of the work of Viktor Hartmann, an architect friend of Mussorgsky's who had died from an aneurysm at the age of thirty-nine the previous year.

Sadly, Mussorgsky's professional success went hand in hand with chronic alcoholism, which was romanticised by the talented but tormented creative types who frequented St Petersburg's taverns and bars. He would drink for days on end, despite the entreaties of well-meaning friends and the devastating loss of others to alcohol-related illnesses. By early 1881, his condition was serious enough for him to be hospitalised. At Tretyakov's bidding, Repin arrived post-haste from Moscow and painted the composer between 2 and 5 March. He had hoped for a final sitting, but Mussorgsky, who had been sober for a while, fell off the wagon and died on 16 March.

Repin's portrait of Mussorgsky was not the only image of a musician that he painted that year. On 17 October 1881, almost seven months to the day after Mussorgsky's death, Tretyakov commissioned him to portray the conductor, composer and pianist Anton Rubinstein (plate 8). A musical prodigy who had met the likes of Frédéric Chopin and Franz Liszt when he toured Europe as a child, Rubinstein had played for Nicholas I and his family in the Winter Palace in 1843, at the age of just fourteen. The subsequent years had not been easy, with the death of his father in 1846 leading to considerable family poverty. By the 1850s, however, Rubinstein had an international following as one of Russia's leading conductors and soloists. As a fellow pianist later recalled, he 'captivated you with the elegance and grace of his playing, his tempestuous, fiery temperament, and his warmth and charm. His *crescendo* had no limits to the rising power of its sonority, while his *diminuendo* reached an unbelievable *pianissimo*, resounding in the farthest corners of the enormous hall.'[6]

As Rubinstein's career soared, so he became determined to advance Russia's musical frontiers. In 1859, together with his loyal patron and mentor Grand Duchess Elena Pavlovna (the tsar's aunt by marriage), he founded the Russian Musical Society to improve standards in musical education and performance. This was soon complemented by the Free Music School and, more ambitiously, the St Petersburg Conservatoire, which Rubinstein established in 1862. His younger brother, Nikolai, another fine pianist, conductor and composer, followed suit and launched the Moscow Conservatoire four years later.

For many observers these were patriotic acts, providing Russia with its first professional music schools where young musicians could train and perform. Others, however, criticised the conservatoires for employing foreign professors to teach an alien educational system and perpetuating the musical repertoire of the West. For Mussorgsky, the professors 'first pollute their students' minds, then seal them with various abominations'.[7] Stasov was equally scathing, seeing the conservatoires as the antithesis of the nationalistic orientation of the Five, with Anton Rubinstein and Mussorgsky occupying two opposing poles. Whatever the truth to these claims, the debates cast interesting light on Tretyakov's decision to commission portraits of both composers in the same year. Swayed by neither the vagaries of fashion nor any specific ideological faction, the patron remained emphatically inclusive and catholic in his approach.

Repin's paintings of Mussorgsky and Rubinstein mark a small but significant shift in Russian portraiture. The compositions have been carefully considered, but the poses are looser and less formal than in earlier works. While Perov's portraits of Dal and Dostoevsky (plates 3 and 4) speak of lengthy sittings and enforced immobility, Repin's portraits have a more spontaneous quality, as if the two musicians, preoccupied with other matters, were

Fig. 3.6
Leo Tolstoy
Ivan Kramskoy, 1873

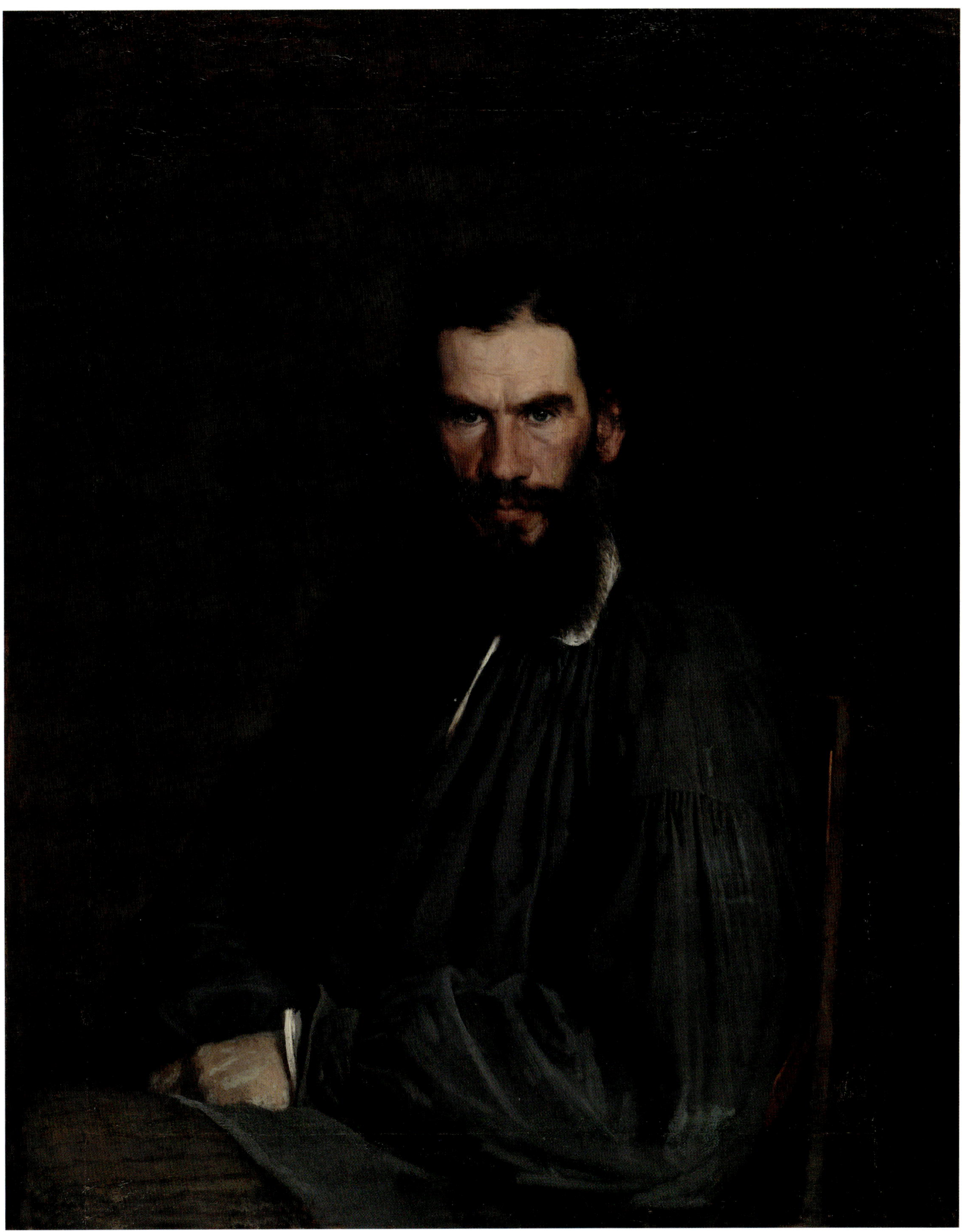

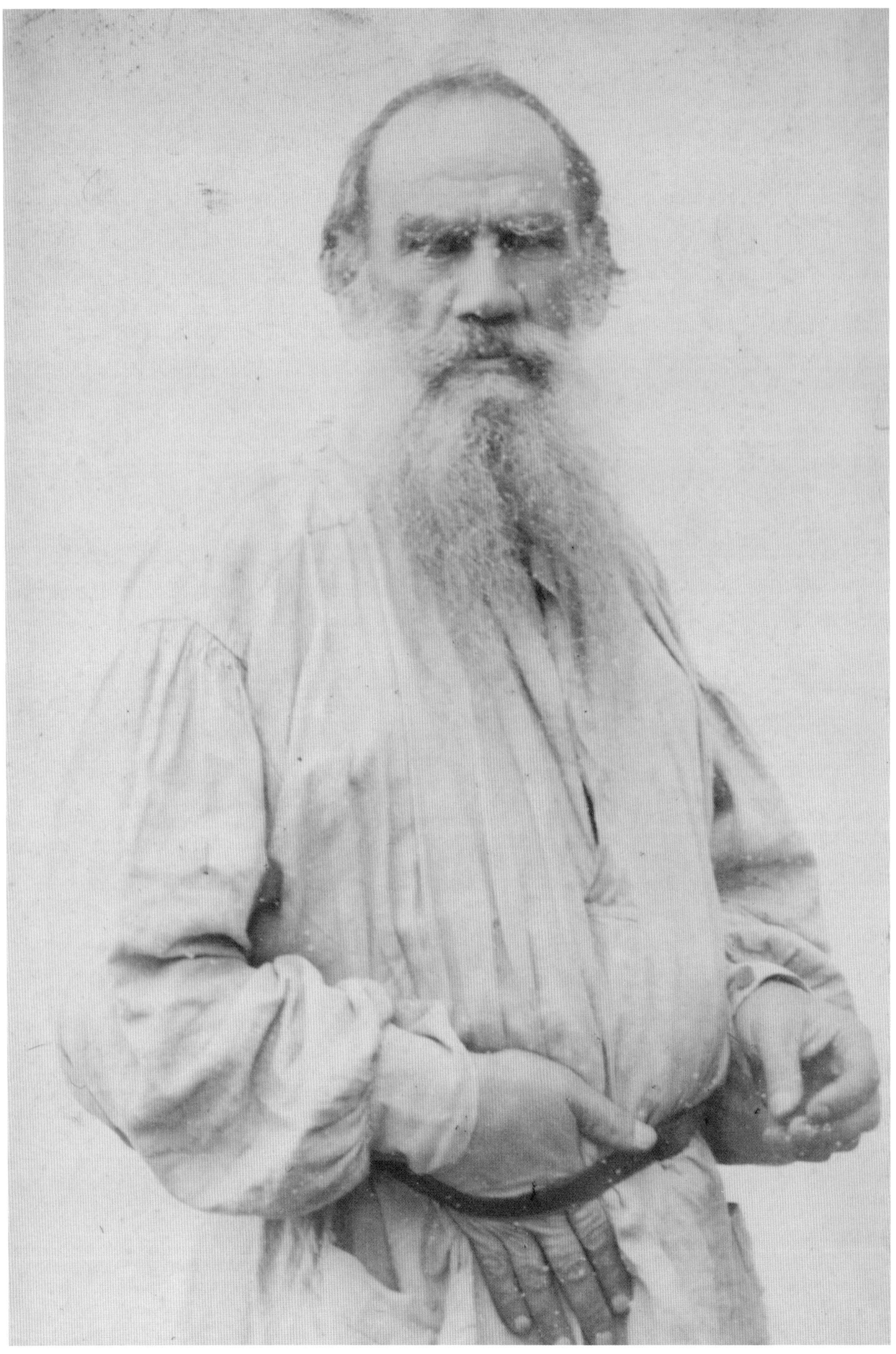

impatient to move on. This sense of animation and immediacy would become increasingly pronounced in the 1880s, as the subjects of Russian portraits began to engage in some activity, rather than sitting motionless in the half-length portrait that had proved so popular the decade before. This was often true of portraits of stage professionals (plates 9 and 10), and was certainly the case with Ge's celebrated image of Leo Tolstoy of 1884 (plate 11).

Tolstoy had first courted attention in his mid twenties with a trilogy of semi-autobiographical novels entitled *Childhood, Boyhood* and *Youth* (1852–6). *Sevastopol Sketches* (1855), whose harrowing detail drew on Tolstoy's experience in an artillery regiment during the Crimean War, then catapulted him into the public eye. Over the following two decades, Tolstoy cemented his position as one of the greatest writers of the century with *War and Peace* (1869), his audaciously ambitious historical novel that follows the lives of scores of characters from the battlefields of the Napoleonic wars to the court of Alexander I. Less expansive but no less virtuosic is *Anna Karenina* (1877), with its mesmeric tapestry of sexual abandon intertwined with maternal devotion, of social intrigue versus noble self-sacrifice, of deathly railway tracks set against the wholesomeness of agricultural work. Kramskoy painted Tolstoy in the period between these two iconic novels in a sombre but compelling portrait for which Tretyakov paid 500 roubles in 1874 (Fig. 3.6).

By the 1880s, however, Tolstoy had renounced his earlier fiction in order to devote himself to religious and philosophical enquiry. In doing so, he sacrificed the happiness of his marriage, distanced himself from his privileged gentry background and disclaimed the copyright to his earlier works. Adopting an increasingly ascetic lifestyle, the writer expounded a set of idiosyncratic Christian beliefs predicated on pacifism and self-denial in tracts such as *A Confession* (1882) and *What I Believe* (1884). These and other diatribes brought him into growing conflict with the Russian Orthodox Church, which eventually excommunicated him in 1901. Tolstoy's ideas nonetheless cut through class divides and reverberated across continents, making him one of the most influential thinkers of his age.

Tolstoy's renunciation of earthly pleasures led him to advocate chastity (this after the birth of thirteen children, the twelfth of whom was born in the year of Ge's portrait), and wear peasant dress (Fig. 3.7) to till the fields of Yasnaya Polyana, his inherited family estate. Repin visited him there for eight days in August 1887, and painted the writer in a series of candid and charismatic works. These included a small canvas of him guiding a plough in bright sunlight (Fig. 3.8) and a much larger portrait in which Tolstoy marks not one but two places in his book, as if to emphasise his assiduous reading habits (Fig. 3.9). These paintings embrace the spectrum of Tolstoy's Olympian reputation by this time, as an endlessly probing thinker and writer, and a man who believed Russia's effete and superficial *beau monde* to be of no value compared to the common people who worked the land.

The trajectory of Tolstoy's iconography, from the sobriety of Kramskoy's portrait of 1873 to Repin's effulgent image of him steering a plough, was reflected in other portraiture of the period. In 1873, Repin depicted Stasov as a seated dignitary, the soft curve of his beard echoed in the gleaming arc of his watch chain (Fig. 3.10). In 1889, however, he painted the critic in a strikingly different mode, small scale but full length, and clad in the peasant attire that was popular among those who, like Tolstoy, were keen to revive native traditions and promote Russian concerns (plate 12).

The critic was now indefatigable in his advocacy of Russian idioms and motifs in music and painting, and coruscating in his criticism of lily-livered artists and composers who fawned unthinkingly on the example of the West. To Stasov's delight, the tide of influence was now turning, with Russian culture attracting admiration abroad. The harmonic and compositional innovations of Russian composers had a growing band of foreign devotees, among them the German pianist Sophie Menter (plate 13). After a faltering start at international exhibitions, with no representation at all at the Great Exhibition of 1851 and what Stasov felt to be a highly

Fig. 3.7
Count Leo Tolstoy
Unknown photographer, *c.*1894

Fig. 3.8 (overleaf)
The Ploughman. Leo Tolstoy ploughing
Ilia Repin, 1887

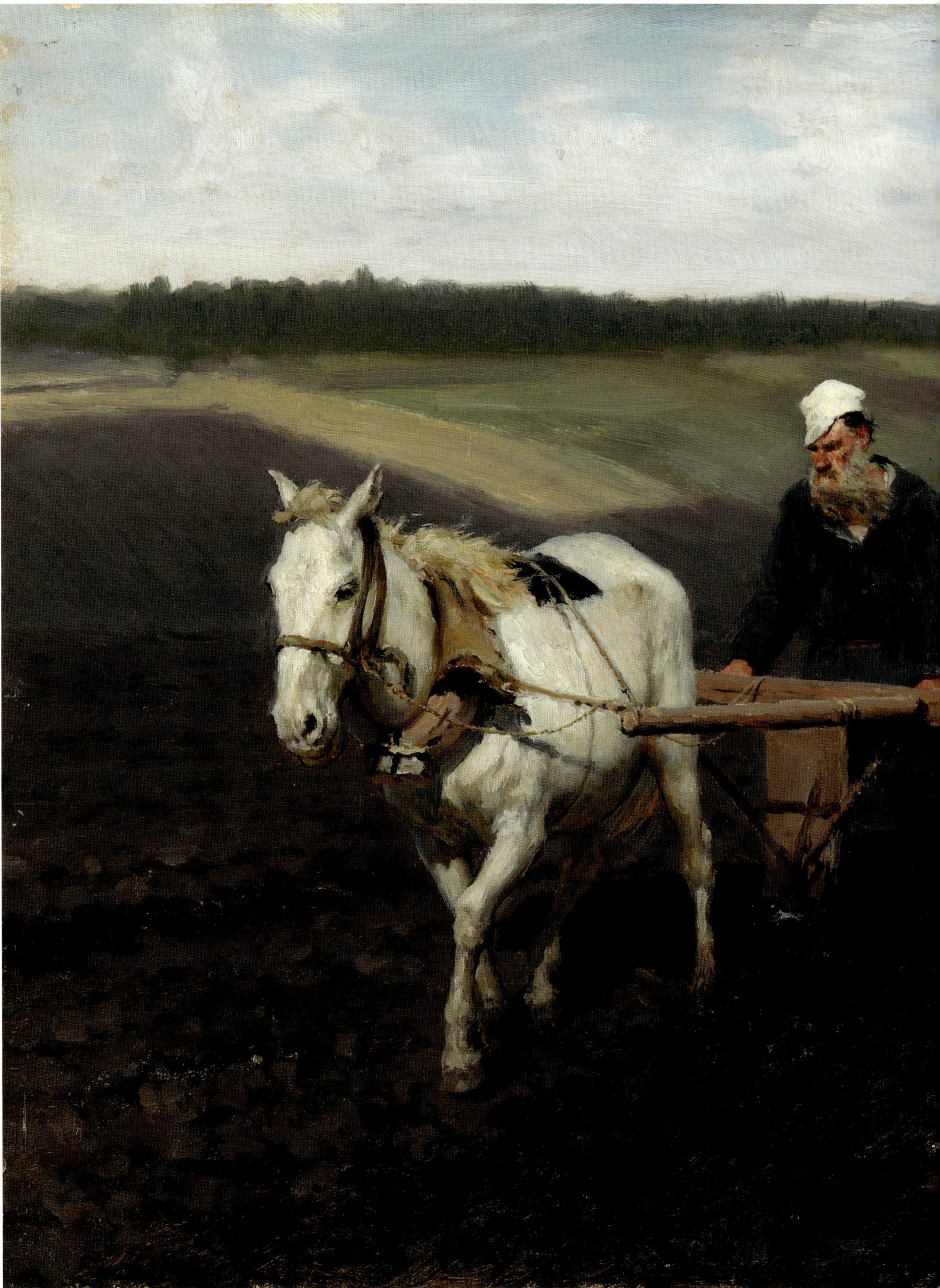

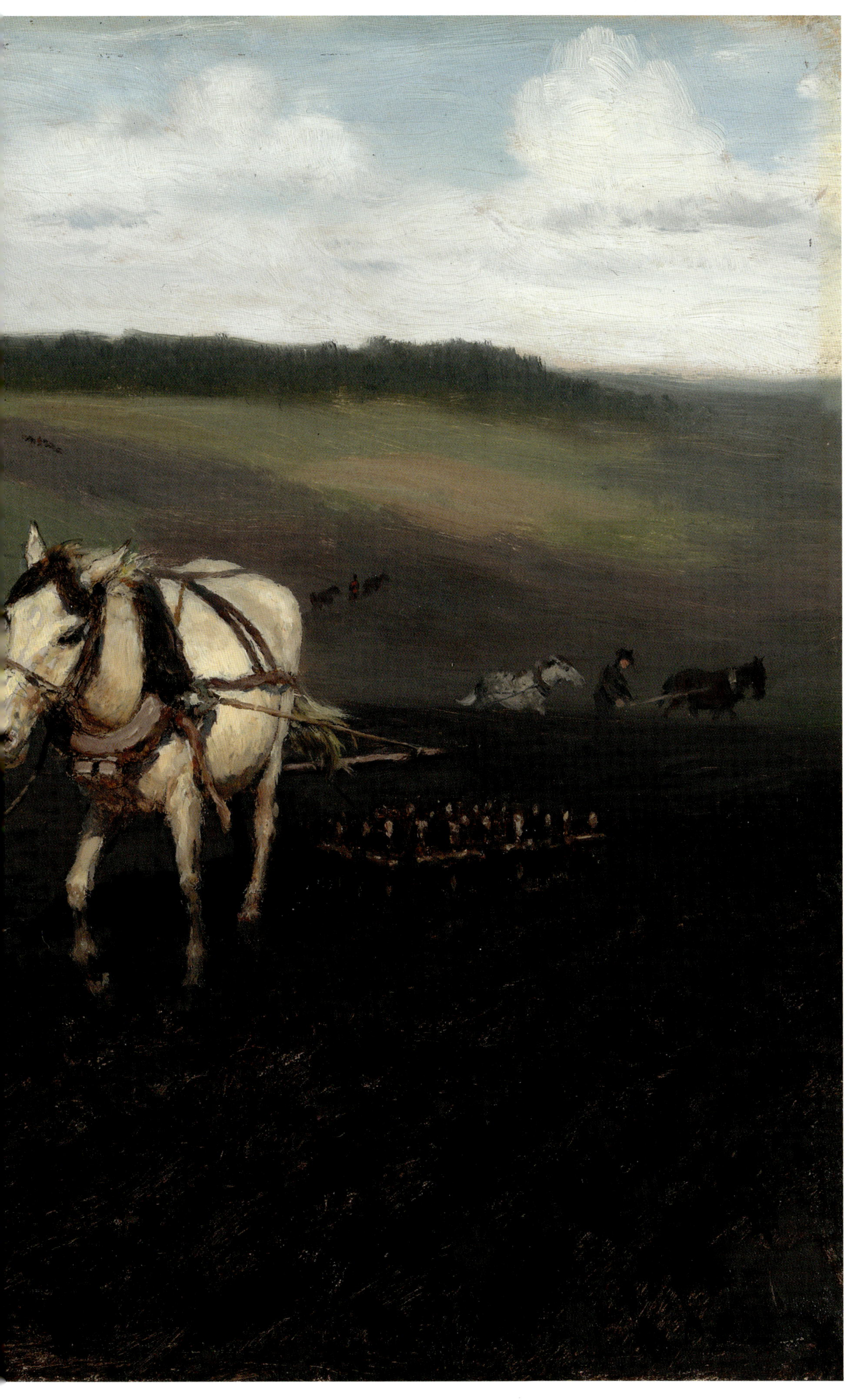

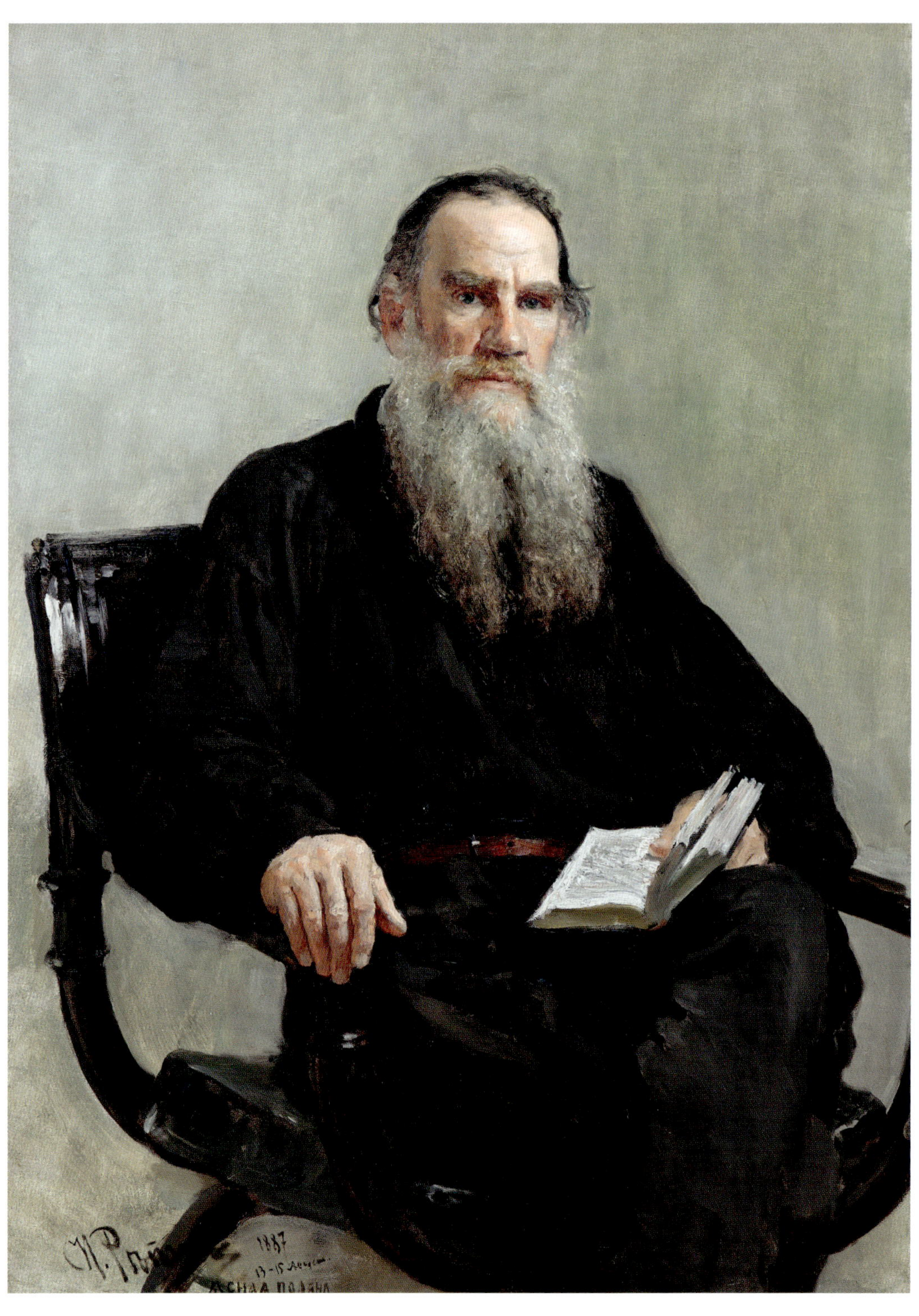

Fig. 3.9
Leo Tolstoy
Ilia Repin, 1887

partial submission at the International Exhibition in London in 1862, Russian painting was also being recognised abroad.

The extent to which Russian artists should look inward or outward for their inspiration was, however, becoming an increasingly contentious debate. If Stasov was adamant that they should develop and celebrate their difference, other critics and artists were equally convinced that the full realisation of Russia's artistic potential depended on fertile engagement with the West. These arguments would come to a head in the 1890s, leading to an explosion of stylistic innovation and a profound cultural reorientation as the century came to an end.

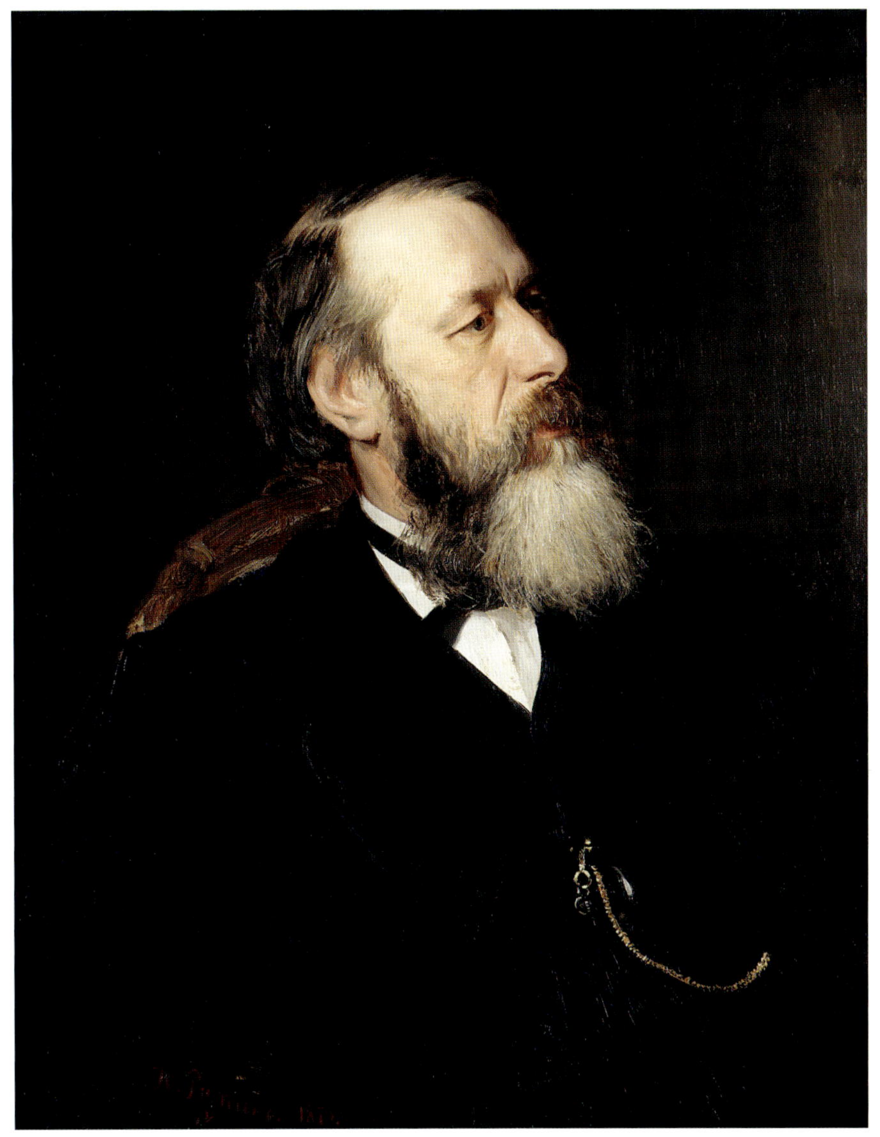

Fig. 3.10
Vladimir Stasov
Ilia Repin, 1873

Notes

1 For summary figures of audiences at many of the exhibitions in the 1870s and 1880s, see 'Otchet, zachitannyi G.G. Miasoedovym obshchemy sobraniiu chlenov Tovarishchestva peredvizhnykh khudozhestvennykh vystavok' in *Tovarishchestvo peredvizhnykh khudozhestvennykh vystavok: pis'ma, dokumenty 1869–1899*, vol. 1, ed. Sofia N. Goldshtein (Iskusstvo, Moscow, 1987), p.334.

2 There were approximately 884,000 residents in St Petersburg in 1885. *Entsiklopedicheskii slovar'*, eds K.K. Arsenev and F.F. Petrushevsky (St Petersburg, 1900), vol. 18, p.313.

3 *Gosudarstvennaia Tretiakovskaia galereia: katalog sobraniia*, vol. 4, book 1, *Zhivopis' vtoroi poloviny XIX veka*, ed. Ia.V. Bruk and L.I. Iovleva (Krasnaia ploshchad', Moscow, 2001), p.411.

4 A.P. Borodin, 'Vospominaniia o M.P. Musorgskom', in *M.P. Musorgsky [sic] v vospominaniiakh sovremennikov*, ed. E.M. Gordeeva (Muzyka, Moscow, 1989), pp.86–7.

5 Vladimir V. Stasov, 'Slavianskii kontsert G. Balakireva', first published in *Sankt-Peterburgskie vedomosti*, in *Izbrannye sochineniia v trekh tomakh* (Iskusstvo, Moscow, 1952), vol. 1, p.173.

6 *Vospominaniia o Rakhmaninove*, ed. Z.A. Apetian (Muzyka, Moscow, 1988), vol. 1, p.194.

7 Quoted in Francis Maes, *A History of Russian Music: From Kamarinskaya to Babi Yar*, trans. Arnold J. Pomerans and Erica Pomerans (University of California Press, Berkeley, Los Angeles and London, 2002), p.39.

Plate 6

Alexei Pisemsky
Ilia Repin, 1880
Oil on canvas, 895 x 715mm

A sharp and often sardonic observer, Alexei Pisemsky (1821–81) moved from his native Kostroma to St Petersburg in 1854, and made his name with a series of novels and plays that picked away at some of Russia's festering sores. His finest novel, *One Thousand Serfs* (1858), charted the rise and fall of a power-hungry young man from the provinces, its title alluding to the number of serfs that a landowner needed to own to be considered wealthy. More sensational still was the staging of infanticide in Pisemsky's play *A Bitter Fate* (1859), in which a peasant returning home after a lengthy absence discovers that his wife has had a child with their serf-owner during a loving and consensual affair. Driven to the point of insanity by this betrayal, the cuckolded husband promptly kills the child. While not for the faint-hearted, *A Bitter Fate* was widely admired and won the prestigious Uvarov prize for outstanding writers and historians. Pisemsky became something of a social curiosity, intriguing Russia's literary sophisticates with his provincial accent and uncouth ways.

More recently, however, Pisemsky's writing was seen to have run its course as a younger generation of more radical writers came to the fore. He dismissed them as nothing but 'witty windbags', loathing their claim to the moral high ground when the young Turks were just as self-interested as earlier writers had been.[1] Not yet ready to hang up his spurs, Pisemsky continued to write into the 1870s, now targeting the evils of Russia's emergent capitalism. But these later works had lost the bite of his earlier writing and were largely ignored. That Tretyakov chose to commission a portrait of him in 1880 was, therefore, compelling evidence of the patron's intent to document the broad sweep of Russia's literary achievement, rather than her most fashionable writers alone. Pisemsky was by now something of a curmudgeon at times, contemptuous of much modern writing and despairing of his own waning star. Repin's portrait is nonetheless a sympathetic one. The signs of ageing are present in the walking stick and pouchy eyes, while the rumpled coat and drooping bow-tie suggest a man no longer in the spotlight. Yet there is a sense still of a sparkling and irreverent raconteur behind the alert pose and watchful gaze.

1   See Charles A. Moser, 'Pisemsky', in *Handbook of Russian Literature*, ed. Victor Terras (Yale University Press, New Haven and London, 1985), p.340.

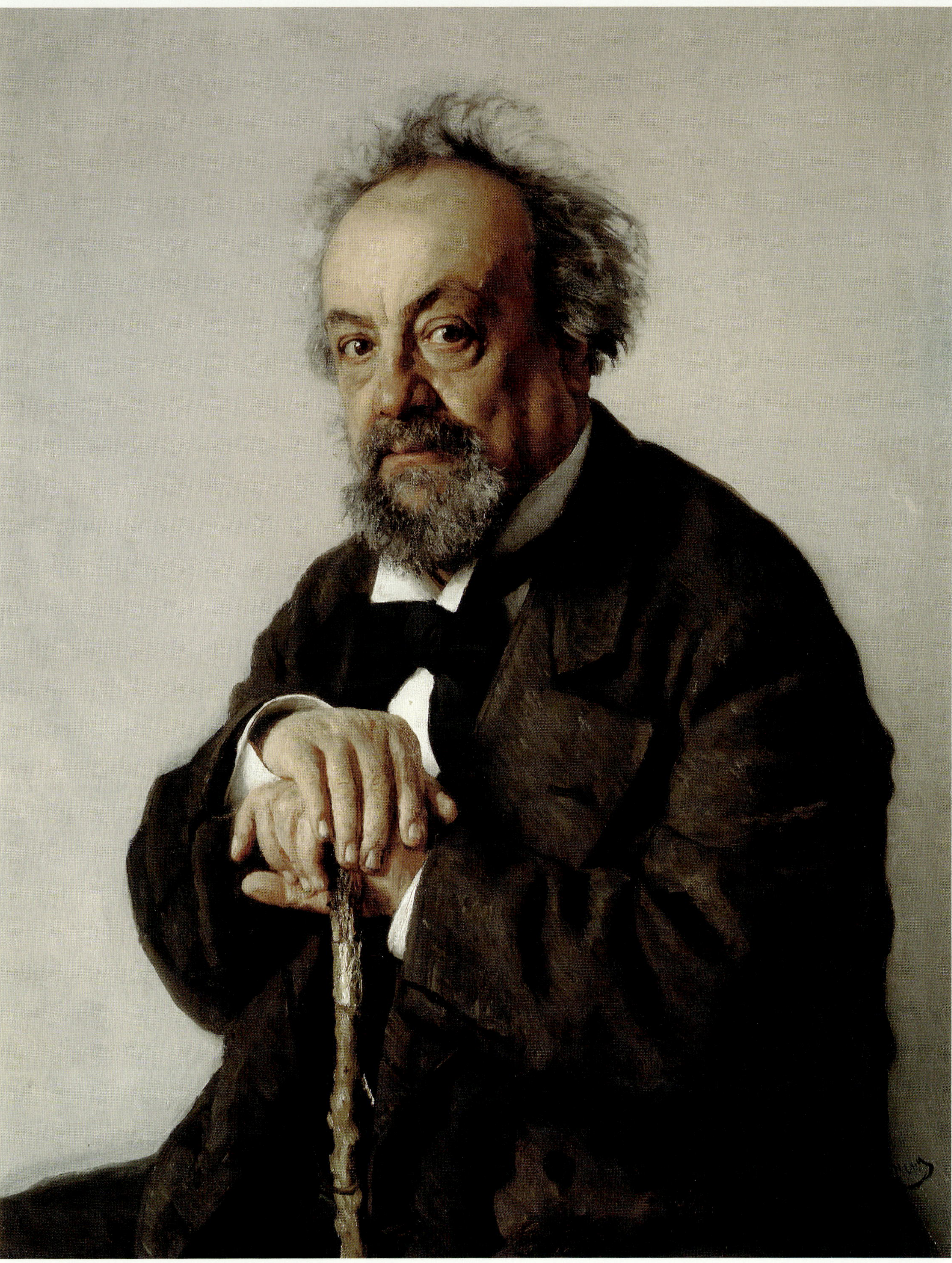

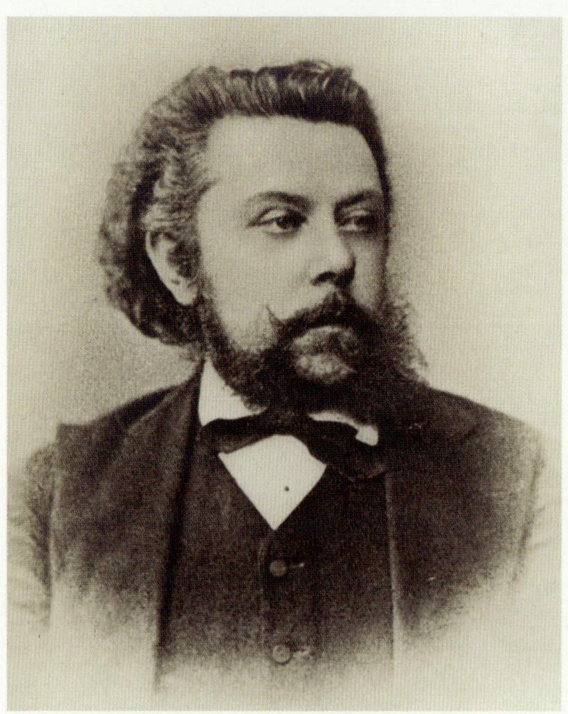

Plate 7

Modest Mussorgsky
Ilia Repin, 1881

Oil on canvas, 718 x 585mm

Repin began his portrait of Modest Mussorgsky (1839–81) on 2 March 1881, the day after the assassination of Alexander II, and left a vivid record of his encounter with the composer in the Nikolaevsky Military Hospital ward:

> When I painted M.P.'s [Mussorgsky's] portrait in the Nikolaevsky Hospital, a terrible event had just occurred: the death of Alexander II; and during the breaks between sittings we read a mass of newspapers, all on one and the same terrible topic. … [Mussorgsky] lived under a strict regime of sobriety and was in a particularly fine sober mood. … But as always, alcoholics are gnawed by the worm of Bacchus; and M.P. was already dreaming of rewarding himself for his long patience. Despite strict orders forbidding cognac … an attendant obtained a full bottle of cognac for M.P.'s name day (he was loved by all). … My last session was planned for the next day. But when I arrived at the appointed hour, I did not find M.P. among the living.[1]

For all the trauma that surrounded its production, both inside and outside the hospital ward, Repin's portrait is a *tour de force*, with the striking burgundy lappet of the dressing gown expertly framing the florid features of the incurable dipsomaniac. The expression is one of both stubborn defiance and dread inevitability, with eyes averted as Mussorgsky confronted the fact of his addled body giving up on him at the age of just forty-two. One can imagine the intensity with which Repin applied his paint in rapid, untempered strokes, capturing the disarming flash of pattern on Mussorgsky's shirt, his unkempt beard and curls, the rosacea on his nose. It is an uncompromising and poignant work.

The artist and the composer had in fact met a decade previously and had much in common. In a letter of 1873, Mussorgsky had written to Repin: 'It is the people I want to depict: when I sleep I see them, when I eat I think of them, when I drink they appear to me, complete, large, unvarnished.' Such a statement could equally be applied to much of Repin's work. Repin himself remembered Mussorgsky as 'a natural talent, a medieval warrior, with the appearance of a Black Sea sailor; he was not averse to playing the fool.'[2] The artist's admiration for his sitter seems to underscore the portrait, even as the effects of Mussorgsky's destructive drinking are painfully exposed. Reluctant to profit from the commission, Repin refused to keep the fee that Tretyakov paid him for the portrait, and donated it to a memorial for the composer. Tretyakov was thrilled with the painting, perhaps recognising it to be one of the most emotionally charged deathbed portraits of all time.

1   *M.P. Musorgsky* [*sic*]: *Pis'ma i dokumenty*, ed. A.N. Rimsky-Korsakov (Gosudarstvennoe muzykal'noe izdatel'stvo, Moscow and Leningrad, 1932), p.252.

2   Ibid., letter to Repin, 13 June 1873, pp.251–2.

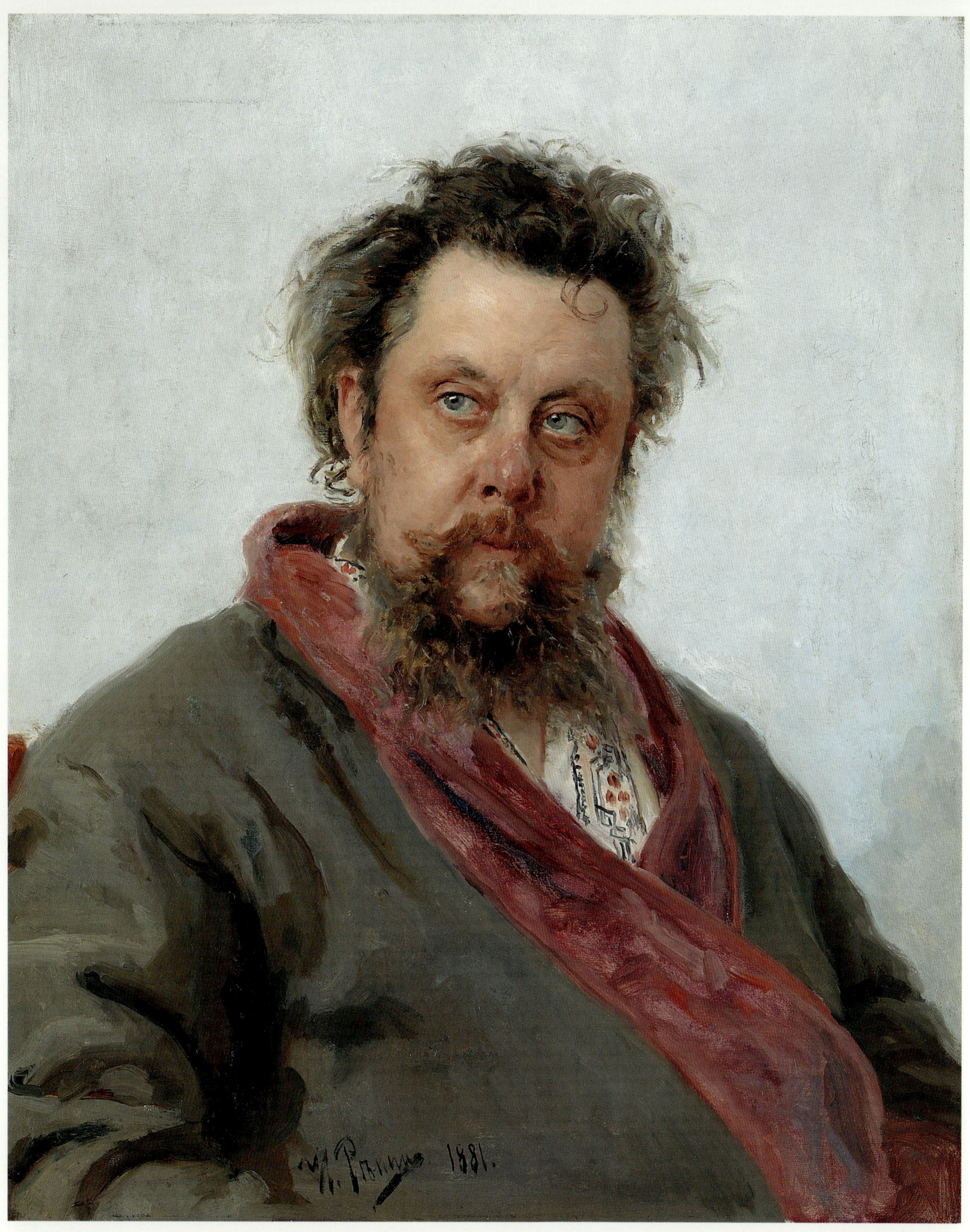

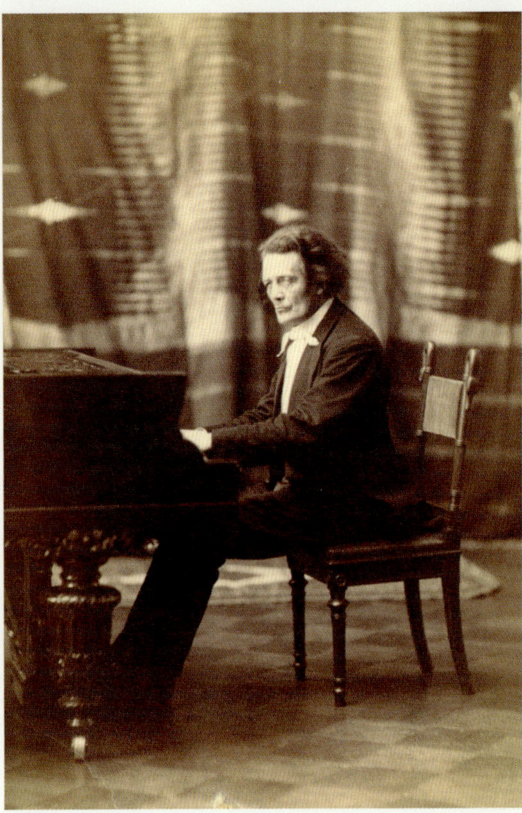

Plate 8

Anton Rubinstein
Ilia Repin, 1881

Oil on canvas, 800 x 623mm

The Rubinstein brothers were taught to play the piano from a young age by their mother, who hit them with a ruler if they struck a wrong note. 'Strictness was still much in fashion then, with sticks and slaps on the face, not at all as it is today,' Anton recalled.[1] He became a renowned child performer and, later, one of the great pianist-composers of his generation, rivalled at the keyboard only by Liszt. Tretyakov and his family were loyal supporters and attended two memorable performances in 1880, as Tretyakov's daughter Vera recalled. 'When Anton Grigorevich [Rubinstein] walked on to the stage to a long round of applause his powerful frame with a head like Beethoven astonished us, and we, all the youngsters there, felt at once that we were in the presence of a giant, a genius. … Mama, who knew Anton Grigorevich, took us to his dressing room. It was the first time that I felt I stood before a great artist: there was something titanic and divine about him, and also something human, deep and tender that was irresistibly appealing.'[2] The power of these performances perhaps prompted Tretyakov to commission Rubinstein's portrait from Repin the following year. The patron had no doubt that Repin was the man for the job, writing that the portrait 'may prove to be even better than Pisemsky's – such a colourful personality for an artist to tackle, so you should take up this work'.[3]

Within two weeks of receiving his commission, Repin was painting Rubinstein, attesting to the expediency with which portraits for Tretyakov's collection were often produced. Repin was clearly drawn to his sitter, writing to Stasov, 'he has an interesting head, and resembles a lion'. But the artist felt rushed, complaining that Rubinstein had little time to spare him and 'poses badly'.[4] The resulting portrait is nonetheless a success, capturing both Rubinstein's restlessness and his leonine aspect. With folded arms and a glorious mane of hair, he sits brooding in his evening suit, as if gracing us briefly with his attention before striding on to the stage. Repin would paint two other portraits of Rubinstein, in which he is shown conducting – in action, turning the pages of his score, with baton raised. But it was the portrait for Tretyakov that captured most effectively Rubinstein's legendary sense of purpose and drive.

1   Anton G. Rubinstein, 'Avtobiograficheskie rasskazy (1829–1867)', in Lev Barenboim, *Anton Grigorevich Rubinstein* (Gosudarstvennoe muzykal'noe izdatel'stvo, Leningrad, 1957), vol. 1, p.401.

2   Vera P. Ziloti, *V dome Tretiakova* (Vysshaia shkola, Moscow, 1998), pp.134–5.

3   Yelena Terkel, 'Pavel Tretyakov and Anton Rubinstein – Fellow Devotees to the Arts', *The Tretyakov Gallery Magazine*, 3 (2012), p.41.

4   Letter to Vladimir Stasov, 31 October 1881, in *I.E. Repin i V.V. Stasov: Perepiska*, ed. A.K. Lebedev and G.K. Burova (Iskusstvo, Moscow and Leningrad, 1949), vol. 2, p.70.

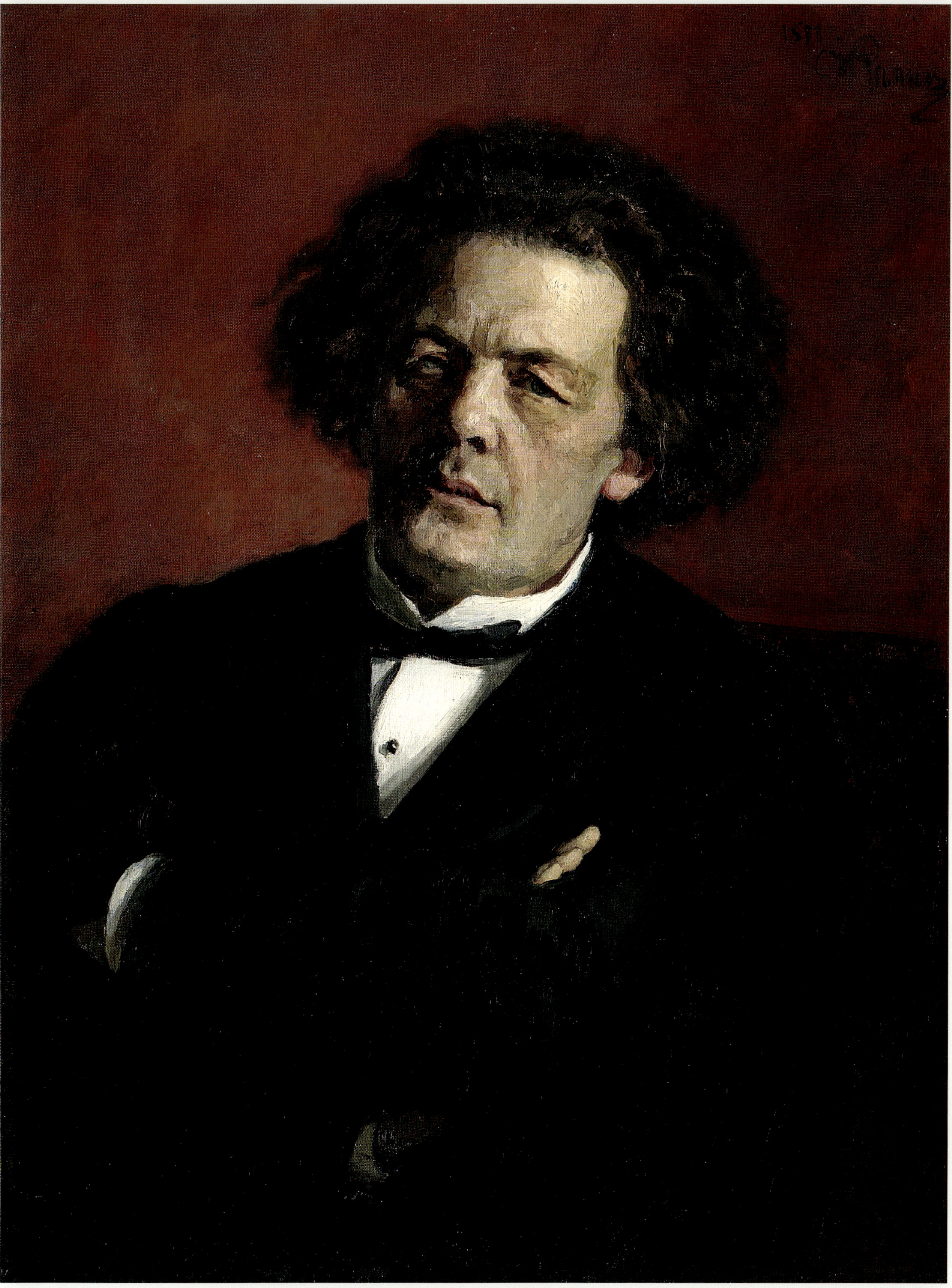

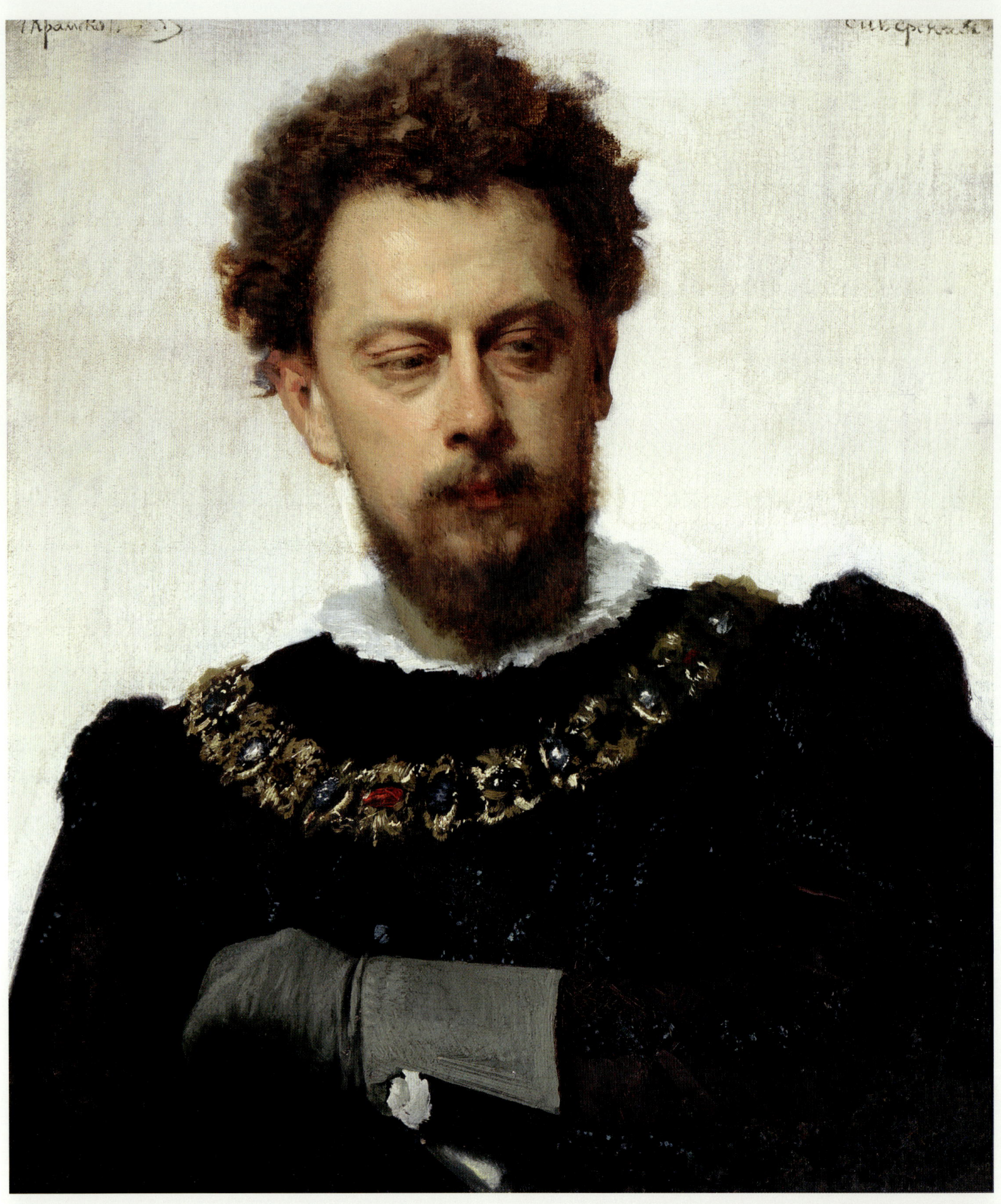

Plate 9

*The Actor Alexander
Lensky as Petruchio
in Shakespeare's*
The Taming of the Shrew
Ivan Kramskoy, 1883

Oil on canvas, 620 x 535mm

The works of William Shakespeare were long admired in Russia. The first Russian translation of one of his plays, *Julius Caesar*, appeared in 1787, and translations of many other plays and sonnets followed. Enthusiasm then intensified with the publication of the first Russian edition of Shakespeare's *Complete Works* in the 1860s.[1] Alexander Lensky (1847–1908), a stalwart of the Maly Theatre in Moscow, rode this wave of popularity to great effect and developed a reputation for his powerful interpretation of Shakespearean roles. A passionate theatrical educator, he also worked as a director at the Maly Theatre, which often chose not to employ professional directors and allowed actors to direct their own shows. His loyalty to the theatre was rewarded when he was appointed its artistic director in his fiftieth year.

The actor became close to Ivan Kramskoy (1837–87) in 1883, taking painting lessons with the artist when he lived and performed in St Petersburg that year. This gave Kramskoy ample opportunity to study his subject at close quarters, leading to a portrait of great insight. The composition is a skilful one, with the leather gauntlet, heavy jewelled chain and white ruff of Lensky's outfit creating tiers of contrasting textures. These are offset by the actor's tousled curls and lowered eyes, which are painted in slightly less focus than his costume, intimating perhaps his temporary divestment of his own identity in order to immerse himself in his theatrical role. Lensky was pleased with the result and acquired the painting, which stayed in his family collection until 1961.

1   Oscar M. Kartoschinsky, 'Shakespeare in Russia', *The Russian Review*, vol. 1 (April 1916), pp.141–6.

Plate 10

Pelageia Strepetova
Nikolai Iaroshenko, 1884
Oil on canvas, 1213 x 790mm

Nikolai Iaroshenko (1846–98), the son of a soldier, served in the artillery and reached the rank of major-general by the time he resigned his commission in 1892. He studied painting while still in the military, for a time with Ivan Kramskoy, and became known for the occasional socio-political image, some routine landscapes and a sensitive characterisation of Russian types. He also acquired a reputation as a staunch ideologue of the Association of Travelling Art Exhibitions when it moved on from its relatively catholic early stage to acquire a reputation for social realism in the 1880s and 1890s.

By the time Iaroshenko painted Pelageia (Polina) Strepetova (1850–1903), she had been a professional actress for some two decades, having made her debut in Riabinsk in 1865. She spent many years playing parts in comedies and vaudeville on the provincial stage, before acquiring fame for her passionate performances in plays by Ostrovsky and Pisemsky (plates 2 and 6). She performed in various theatres in Moscow and became a member of the Alexandrinsky Theatre troupe in St Petersburg. Ilia Repin was one of many artist-admirers of her work, and painted her both in and out of role (Fig. 6.4).

Iaroshenko avoids any hyperbole in his portrait, choosing instead to highlight the poise and focus that Strepetova brought to her roles. The composition is one of great economy and the palette is equally restrained, yet the finely judged counterbalance of face and hands, with their bright white accents of lace collar and cuffs, give the canvas an internal energy that intimates the actress's own. Kramskoy, who was no stranger to florid prose, wrote in a letter to Alexei Suvorin, an influential publisher and journalist: 'I have decided to prophesy that, when we have all left the scene, the portrait of Strepetova will stop everyone in their tracks. … Everyone will see the depth of tragedy expressed in the eyes, the endless suffering that marked this person's life.'[1] Suvorin could not have disagreed more, leading to a heated exchange between the two men on the qualities or otherwise of Iaroshenko's work.

1   Letter to Alexei Suvorin, 4 March 1884, in Ivan N. Kramskoy, *Pis'ma v dvykh tomakh*, vol. 2 (Gosudarstvennoe izdatel'stvo izobrazitel'nykh iskusstvo, Leningrad, 1937), p.276.

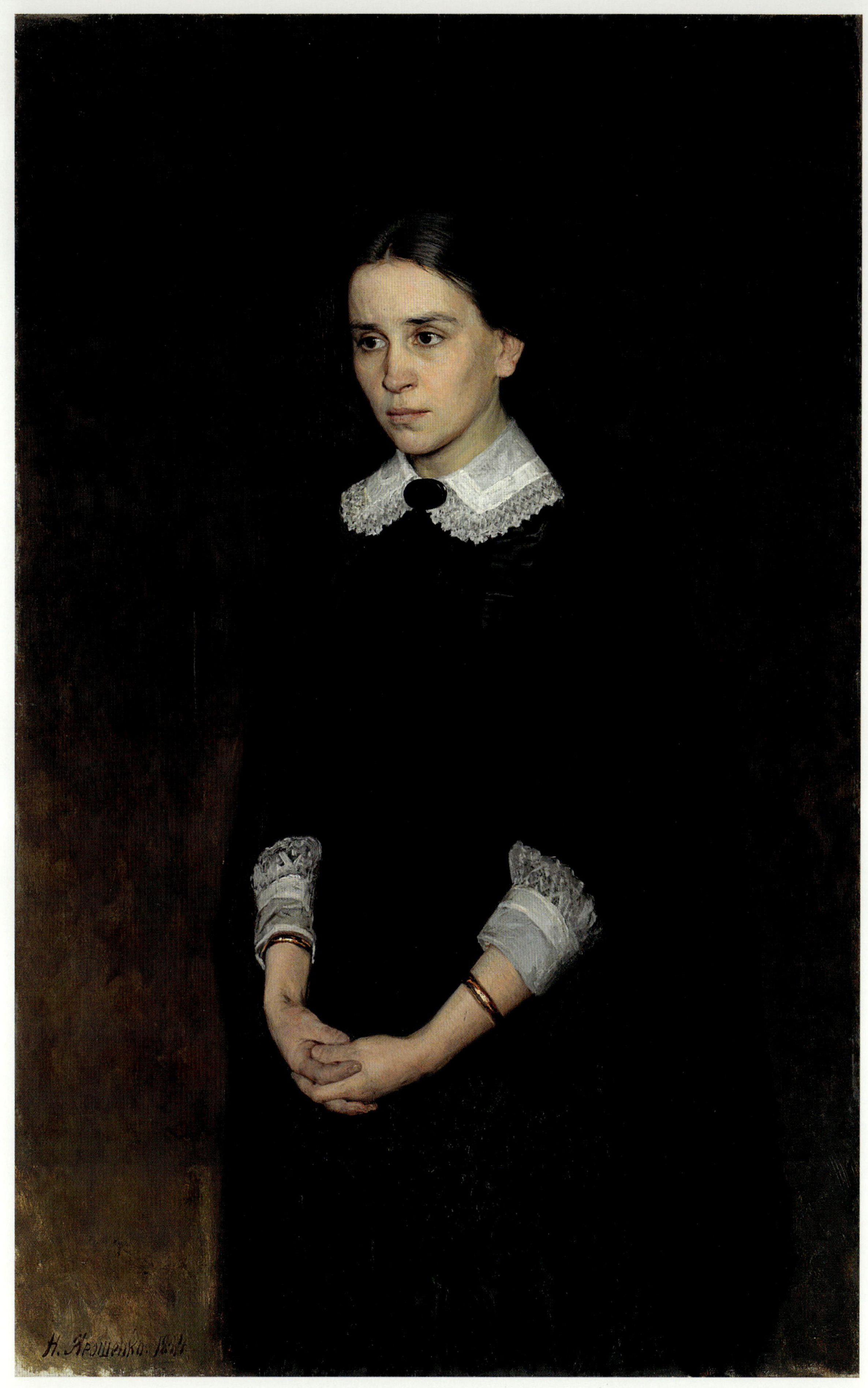

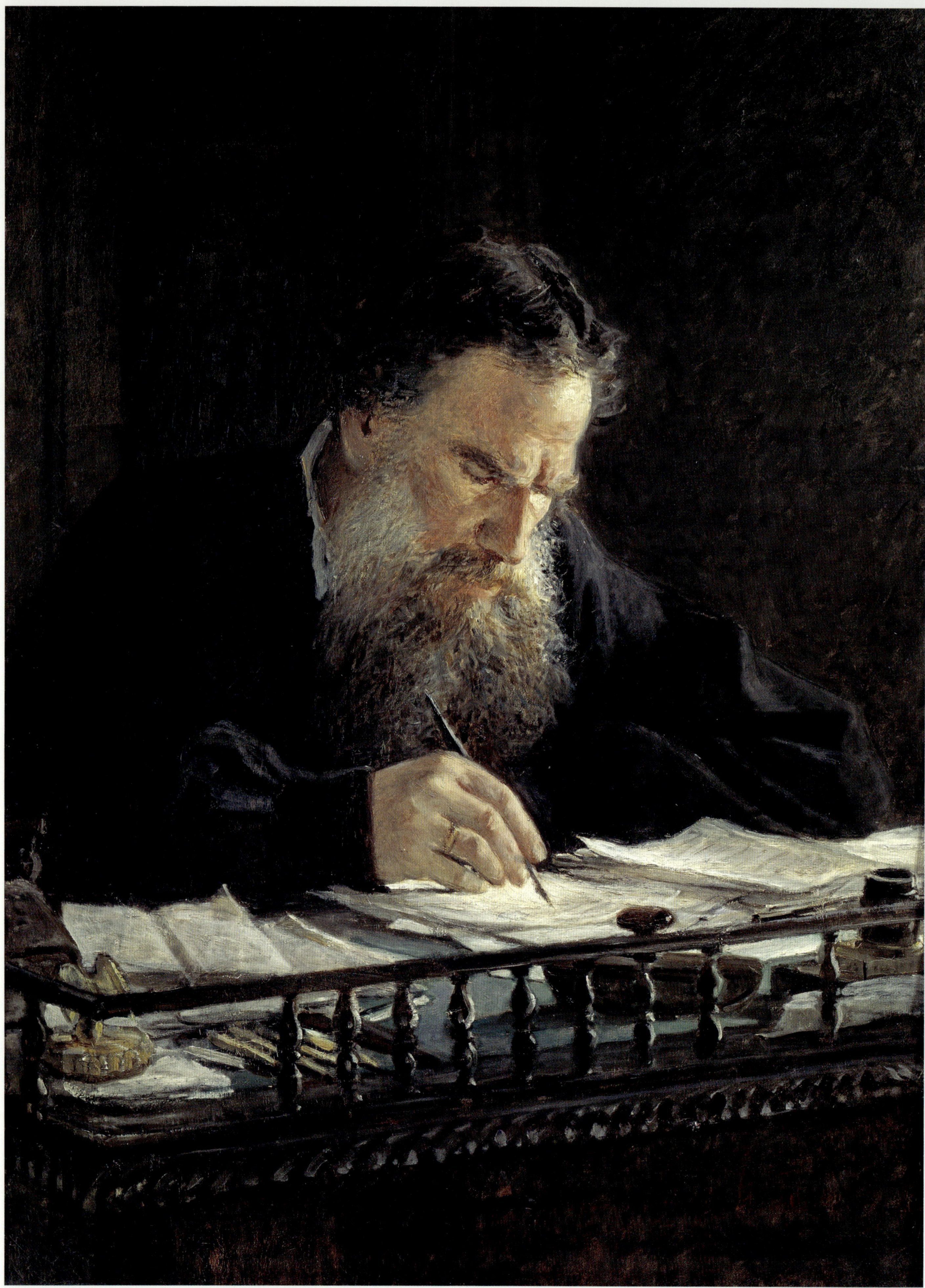

Plate 11

Leo Tolstoy
Nikolai Ge, 1884
Oil on canvas, 962 x 717mm

By the 1880s, Leo Tolstoy was a writer of international repute. Nikolai Ge, a highly introspective and spiritual artist, had been drawn like a moth to Tolstoy's flame, and was already a close friend of the writer by the time he painted him in the study of Tolstoy's Moscow home in 1884. Tolstoy is shown with lowered gaze and furrowed brow, deep at work on the manuscript for his philosophical disquisition *What I Believe*, which would soon be banned. Tolstoy's puritanical leanings are intimated in the plain background and simple black shirt, but there are hints at the luxury of his material world in the handsome desk with its blotter and golden paperweight. Ge's visual conceit is to leave the revered sage undisturbed at his work, with a clear pictorial focus on his famous writing hand. Yet there is a beguiling intimacy to the way in which the artist picks out the gleam of Tolstoy's wedding ring, and the splendour of his now greying chestnut beard. 'In this portrait I have conveyed all that is most precious in this wonderful man,' the artist declared.[1]

Ilia Repin, who portrayed Tolstoy on numerous occasions, commented on the forcefulness of his personality. 'When near him I could only submit to his will, as if hypnotised. In his presence, every statement he uttered seemed incontrovertible to me.'[2] The writer's influence would eventually extend as far as Mahatma Gandhi, with whom he corresponded in the last year of his life, and led to almost cultish status by the time of his death. Fleeing his estate of Yasnaya Polyana after a bitter estrangement from his wife, he caught pneumonia miles from home and was given shelter in a provincial stationmaster's house. Such was the circus of attention that surrounded his demise that a French film crew arrived to cover the event. Tolstoy's long-suffering wife and amanuensis, who had transcribed the manuscript of *War and Peace* no fewer than seven times, arrived with their children, but was prevented from seeing him until he had lost consciousness. He died on 20 November 1910, without receiving the last rites.

1   Letter to V.P. Gaevsky, 6 February 1884, in *Nikolai Nikolaevich Ge*, op. cit., p.118.

2   Ilia E. Repin, *Dalekoe blizkoe*, 9th edn (Khudozhnik RSFSR, Leningrad, 1986), p.365.

Plate 12

*Vladimir Stasov at
His Dacha in the Village
of Starozhilovka near
Pargolovo*
Ilia Repin, 1889–90
Oil on canvas, 400 x 376mm

Vladimir Stasov (1824–1906), an employee and later librarian of the art section at the Imperial Public Library in St Petersburg from 1857 to 1906, was the leading Russian critic of music and the visual arts in the nineteenth century. He was also a tireless campaigner for a distinct Russian school in both disciplines, and believed this to have been realised most fully in Russian Realist painting and in the music of the Five.

The steps that Stasov took to promote this cause knew no bounds, and occasioned not only one-sided interpretation, but even wilful misrepresentation of an artist's work. In 1875, for example, Stasov excised any positive mention of modern Western painting from the letters that he had received from Repin in Paris, and published these without the painter's permission. Repin, who appeared parochial as a result, remonstrated with the critic, but perceptions of him as a patriotic artist uninterested in the West remained. His and Stasov's friendship nonetheless survived, and they later travelled to Europe together. Stasov also championed other Realist artists in a constant stream of articles and reviews, and was of inestimable influence in the success of the Russian Realist school. He was elected a Fellow of the Russian Academy of Sciences in 1900, along with Tolstoy.

Repin started this portrait on Stasov's birthday at the critic's dacha outside St Petersburg in the summer of 1889, working on a small scale that seemed to be a direct inverse of the critic's expansive and often overbearing personality. Rain prevented Repin from finishing the painting, so he revisited it in August 1890 and made many changes, as letters from Stasov attest. The critic's pose was altered, as were the colours of his clothing: the shirt changed from white to red, and the trousers from red calico to black velvet.[1] Stasov's preoccupation with Russian identity is signalled by his choice of traditional peasant attire. The nationalistic notes to the painting ring louder still thanks to Repin's majestic use of red, which has special significance in Russia as a dominant colour of long-standing visual traditions. It appears in highly regulated form in icon painting and heraldic imagery, and the specific corner of any dwelling where icons are displayed and venerated is known as the 'red corner'. For many viewers, Repin's 1889 portrait of Stasov was, therefore, an assertion of the critic's allegiance to an unalloyed national style.

1   *Repin i Stasov*, op. cit., vol. 2, pp.144, 371–2.

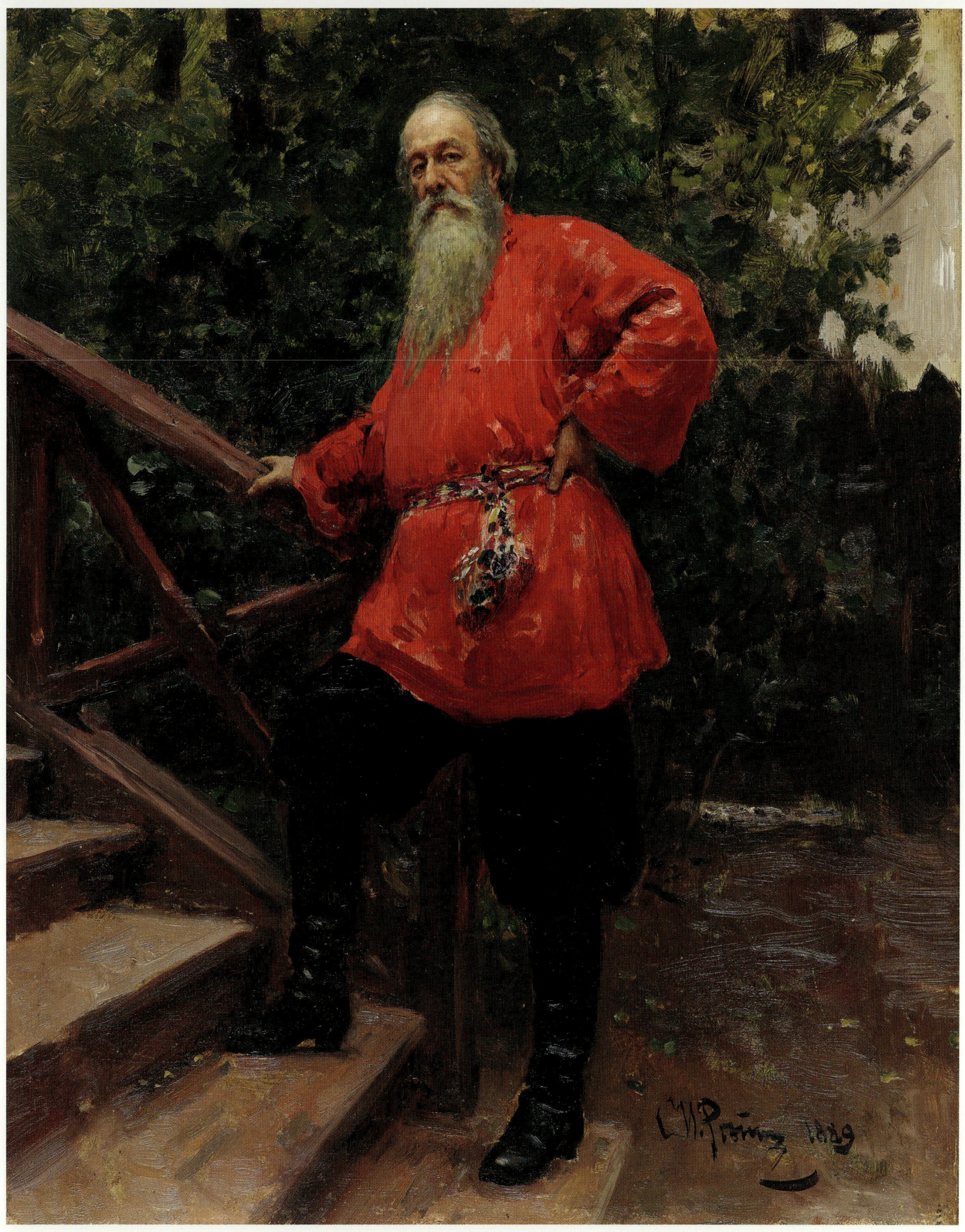

И.Репинъ 1889

Plate 13

Sophie Menter
Ilia Repin, 1887
Oil on canvas, 1215 x 1245mm

Sophie Menter (1846–1918), the German pianist and composer, was a protégée of Franz Liszt from the age of twenty-three. The Hungarian composer and virtuoso pianist claimed that 'no woman can touch her', and particularly admired her 'singing hand'.[1] Menter was also the wife of the cellist David Popper from 1872 to 1886. In 1883 she was awarded honorary membership of the Royal Philharmonic Society in England and appointed professor of piano at the St Petersburg Conservatoire. The following year she acquired Itter Castle, a spectacular medieval castle in North Tyrol, where she hosted many musical and cultural luminaries.

In St Petersburg, Menter taught not only the rising talent, but also such established musicians as Balakirev, before resigning in 1886 to focus on her concert career. As well as performing in elite venues, she took part in the concerts of the Free Music School, demonstrating the strength of her commitment to Russian music. It was perhaps in recognition of this that when Anton Rubinstein dedicated each of the nine pieces of his *Soirées musicales, Op. 109* to a contemporary pianist, Menter was among the dedicatees. George Bernard Shaw, who heard her play in 1890, was reduced to rhapsodies. 'Mme Menter seems to play with splendid swiftness, yet she never plays faster than the ear can follow, as many players can and do; and it is the distinctness of attack and intention given to each note that makes her execution so irresistibly impetuous.'[2] Tchaikovsky was another admirer, dedicating the score of his *Concert Fantasia* to her, and scoring her *Concerto in the Hungarian Style* for piano and orchestra while staying with Menter at Itter Castle in 1892.

In Repin's portrait, Menter is a powerful, enigmatic presence, coiling over her keyboard in an extravagant evening gown with the tender flesh of her underarms provocatively exposed. There are echoes of Manet's *Olympia* (1863, Musée d'Orsay, Paris) in the contrast between the bouquet of flowers and the whiteness of Menter's skin, the seductive allure of the hand (in this case the agent of the pianist's talent and success) and the self-assurance of her gaze. The portrait is one of two that Repin painted of Menter when he visited her at Itter Castle during his European tour of 1887. The artist brought it back to St Petersburg and sold it in 1917, whereupon it passed through various hands before entering the Tretyakov Gallery in 1951. The other portrait stayed with Menter in Itter Castle, and ended up in a private collection in Tel Aviv.

1   Harold C. Schonberg, *The Great Pianists* (Simon & Schuster, New York, 1987), p.262.

2   Ibid.

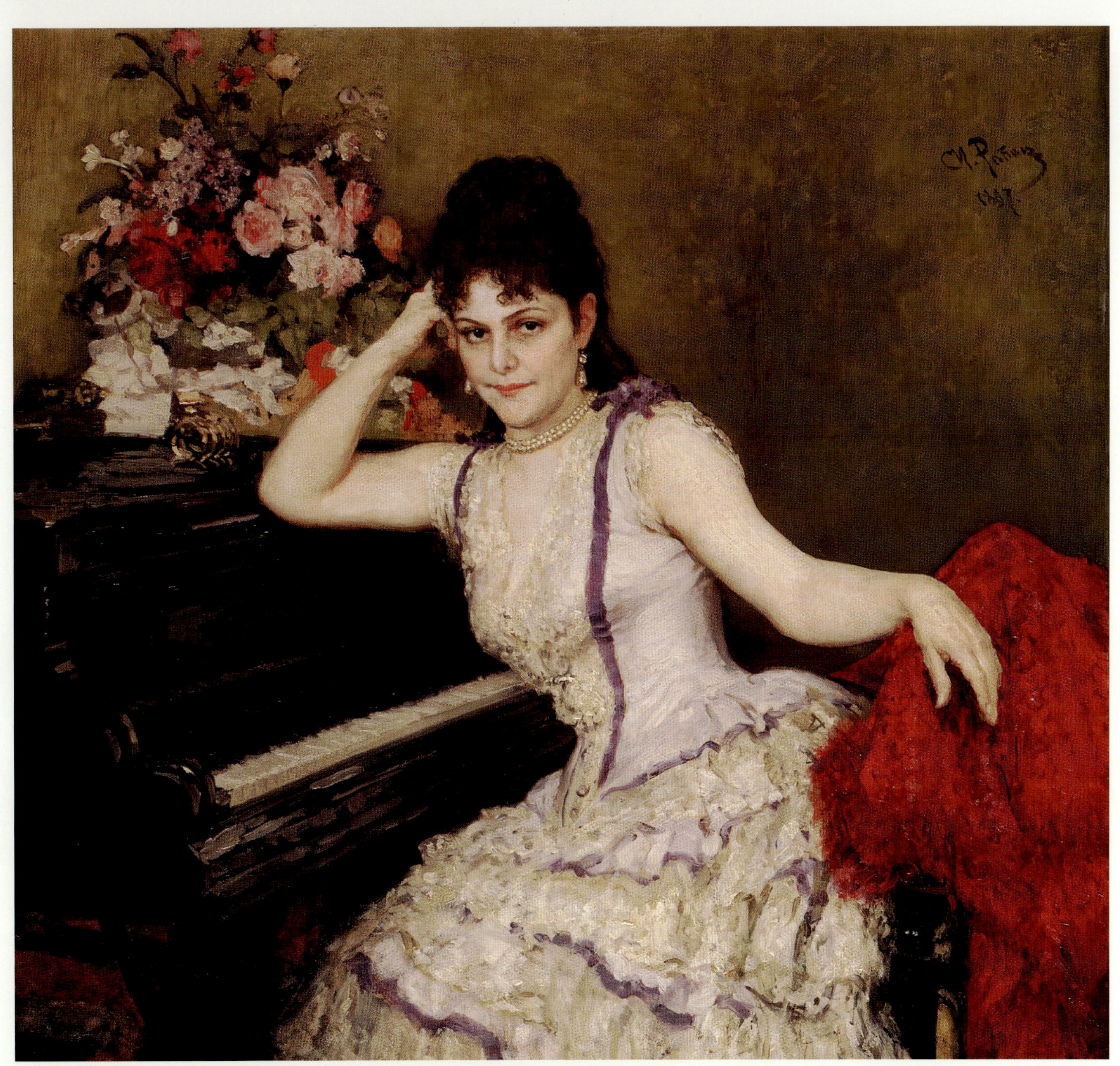

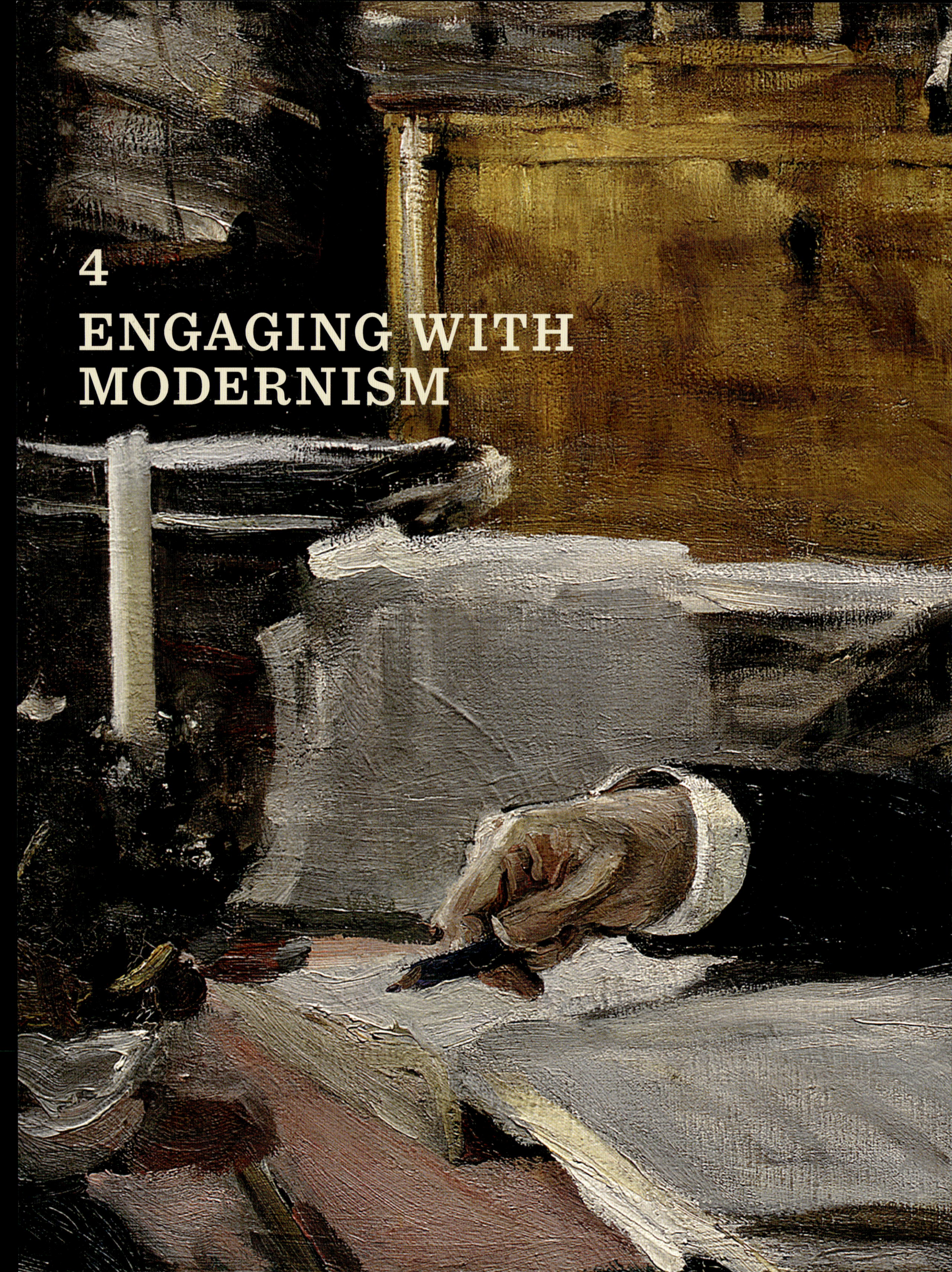
4
ENGAGING WITH
MODERNISM

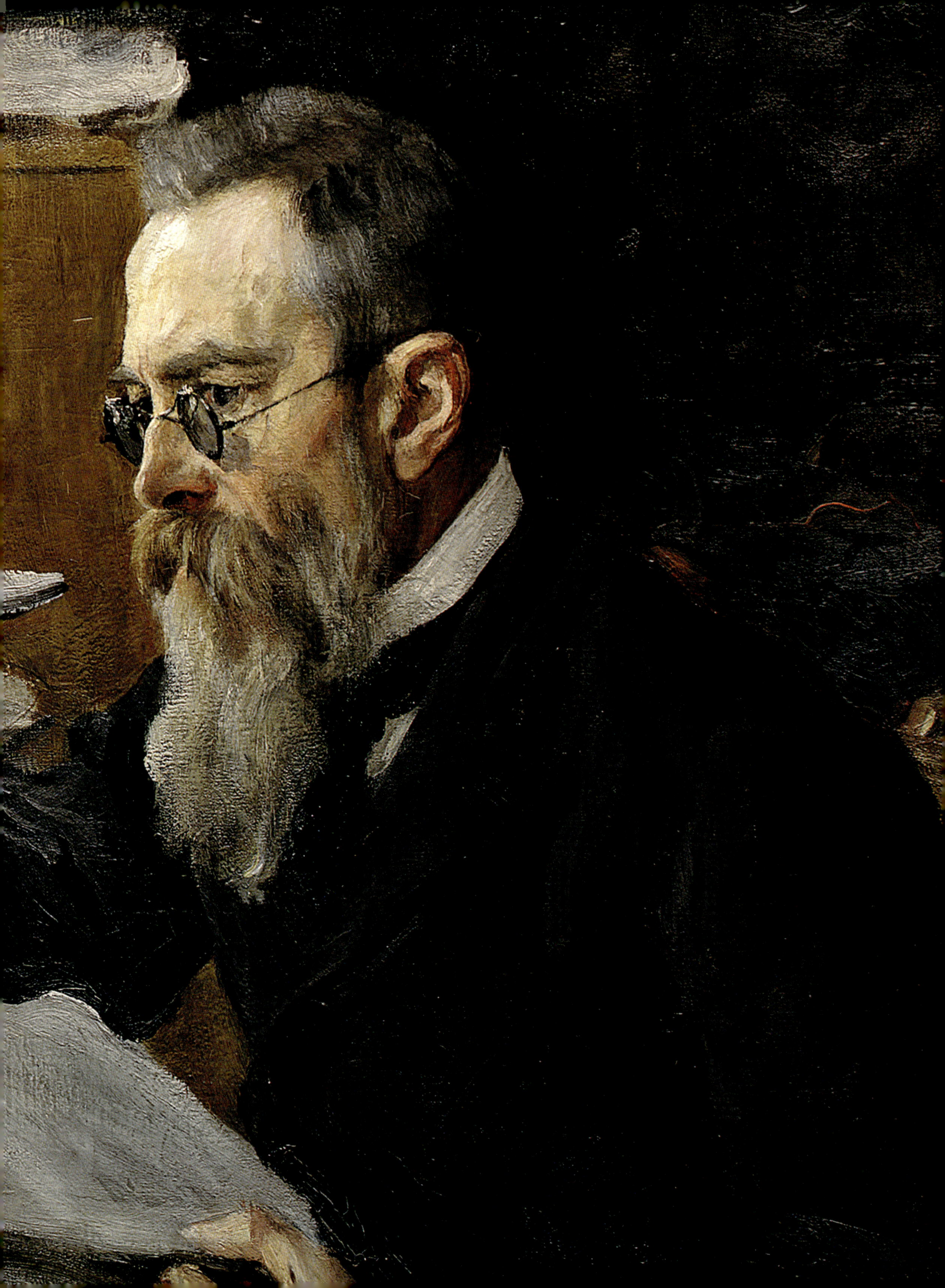

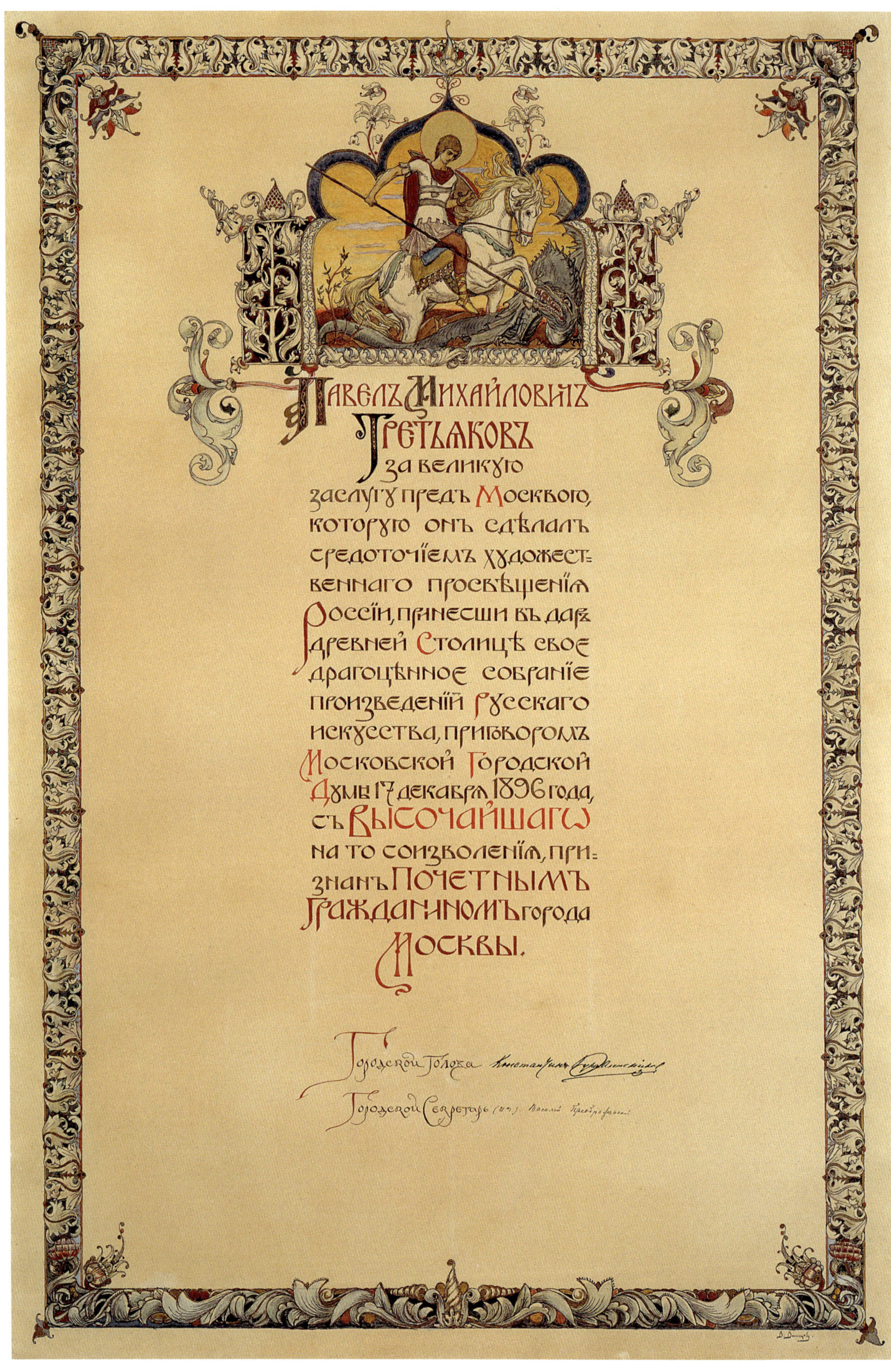

ПАВЕЛЪ МИХАЙЛОВИЧЪ
ТРЕТЬЯКОВЪ
за великую
заслугу предъ Москвою,
которую онъ сдѣлалъ
средоточіемъ художест-
веннаго просвѣщенія
Россіи, принесши въ даръ
древней Столицѣ свое
драгоцѣнное собраніе
произведеній русскаго
искусства, приговоромъ
Московской Городской
Думы 17 декабря 1896 года,
съ ВЫСОЧАЙШАГѠ
на то соизволеніи, при-
знанъ ПОЧЕТНЫМЪ
ГРАЖДАНИНОМЪ города
МОСКВЫ.

Городской Голова Константинъ Рукавишниковъ
Городской Секретарь (и.д.) Василій Красноглазовъ

T HE *FIN DE SIÈCLE* WAS A PERIOD of tremendous cultural and aesthetic vitality in Russia. The Academy of Arts underwent a significant overhaul in 1893, introducing new methods into its pedagogy and enticing leading painters into its employ. Russians were also able to study artworks as never before, with private patrons willing to open the doors of their galleries and major advances in the development of a public museum culture. In July 1892, Tretyakov's younger brother Sergei died and left him a rich collection of modern European painting, prompting Pavel to donate his entire gallery to the city of Moscow the following month. It opened as the Pavel and Sergei Tretyakov Moscow City Art Gallery in 1893. Tretyakov was proclaimed an Honourable Citizen of Moscow three years later, with a spectacular certificate embellished in the national revival style that was much in vogue at the time (Fig. 4.1).

Shamed by Tretyakov's generosity, officials in St Petersburg also focused their minds on a public gallery of Russian art, culminating in the opening of the Russian Museum of His Imperial Majesty Alexander III (now the State Russian Museum) in 1898. The museum was housed in the magnificent Mikhailovsky Palace, which had been built in the centre of St Petersburg for Grand Duke Mikhail Pavlovich, Paul I's youngest son. It was there that Mikhail's widow, Grand Duchess Elena Pavlovna, had nurtured the career of Anton Rubinstein and held her famous literary and musical soirées, making the palace's new designation as a museum of the arts particularly apt. Her example was followed by other dynamic salonnières later in the century, among them Baroness Varvara Ikskul von Hildenbandt, whom Repin painted in spectacular style in 1889 (plate 14).

Repin's juxtaposition of bold blocks of colour in his portrait of Hildenbandt speaks of modernist concerns. There is a hint of Impressionist influence in the crisp outlines and slightly lowered viewpoint, with perhaps a nod to Manet's *Olympia* (1863, Musée d'Orsay, Paris) in the steadfastness of Hildenbandt's gaze. Repin had first encountered Impressionism during his stay in Paris from 1873 to 1876, and Russian awareness of modernist practices had risen steadily in

Fig. 4.1
Certificate naming Pavel Tretyakov an
Honourable Citizen of Moscow, 1896

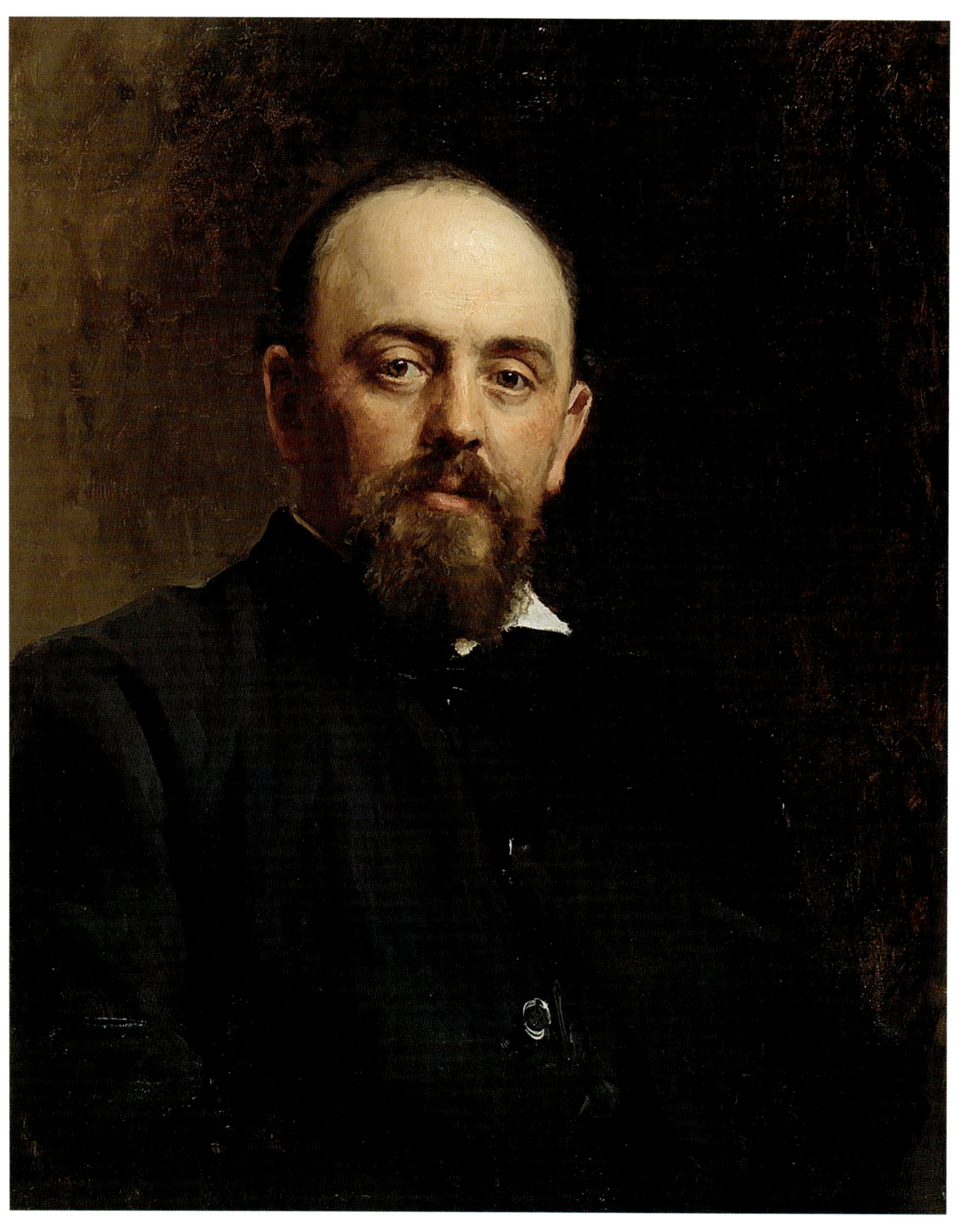

Fig. 4.2
Savva Mamontov
Ilia Repin, 1878

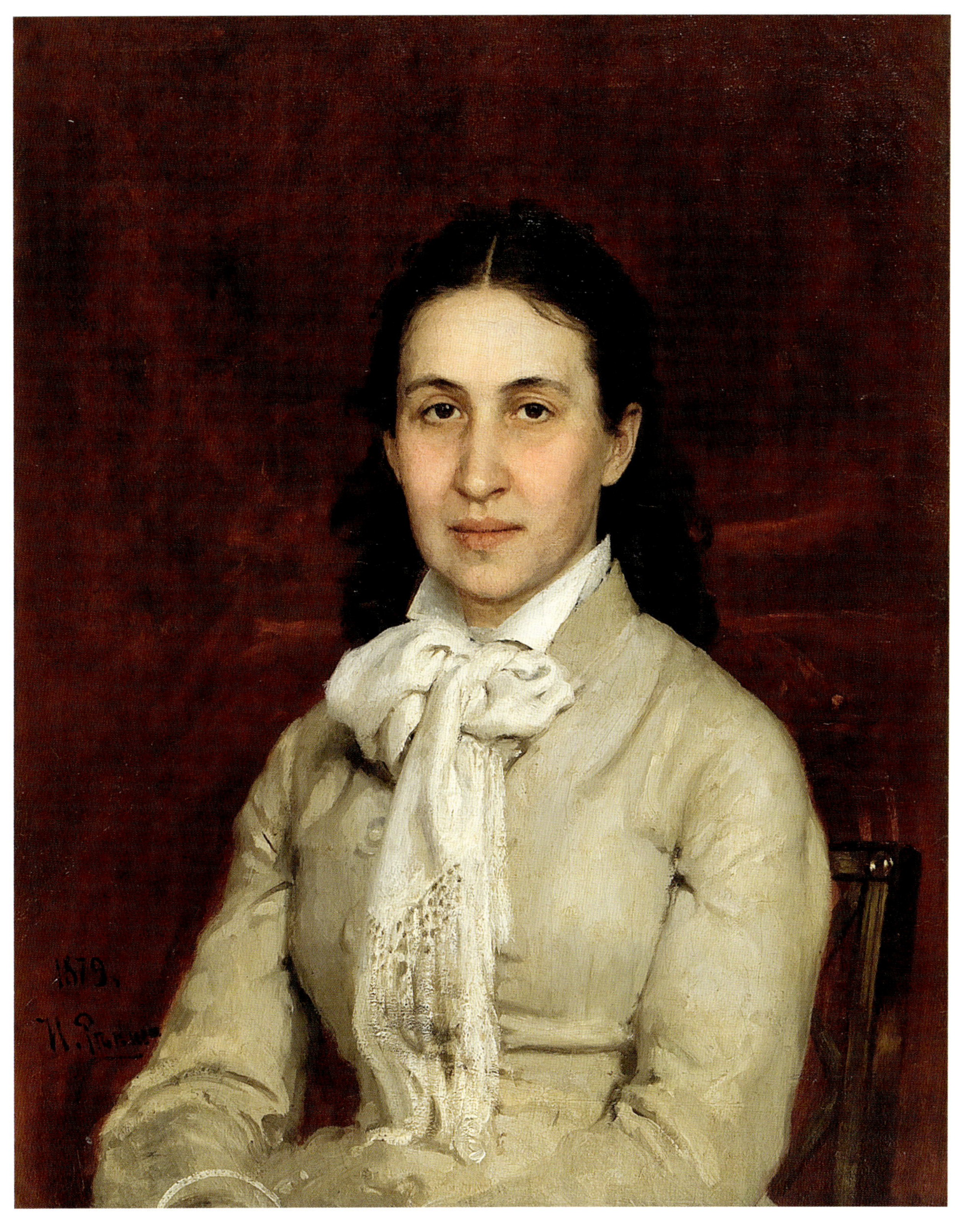

Fig. 4.3
Elizaveta Mamontova
Ilia Repin, 1874–9

recent years. Those Russian artists who travelled abroad now gravitated towards Paris, and returned home eager to regale their friends with stories of the outré practices they had observed. A healthy contingent exhibited at the Exposition Universelle in Paris in 1889, where those lucky enough to visit in person marvelled at the novelty of its subjects and styles. French painting was also well represented in private collections in Moscow and St Petersburg. The French artists whom Russian patrons tended to favour in the late 1880s and early 1890s were far from cutting edge, with a proclivity for the likes of Jules Bastien-Lepage and the Barbizon school. The growing interest in French painting among Russia's private collectors, coupled with the Parisian adventures of her travelling artists, nonetheless fuelled interest in the innovations of the West and propelled Russia's portraitists down increasingly experimental paths.

Among those to exhibit at the Exposition Universelle was Nikolai Kuznetsov, who won a silver medal there. Kuznetsov hailed from the Crimean peninsula where, after a local school education, he had carried out agricultural work on his father's estate until the age of twenty-four. He then studied at the Academy of Arts in the 1870s before returning to the Black Sea, but made regular forays to Moscow and St Petersburg to exhibit his paintings, as when he submitted his limpid *Holiday* to the ninth Peredvizhnik exhibition in 1881 (Fig. 3.2). From the 1880s, Kuznetsov began to travel to western Europe, which led to a marked change in his work. He largely relinquished the anecdotal genre scenes of his early career in favour of portraiture; and the lustrous finish and botanical exactitude of works such as *Holiday* gradually yielded to a more carefree and painterly style as can be seen in his portrait of Tchaikovsky, painted in 1893 (plate 15).

Experimental brushwork was taken further still by Valentin Serov, a brilliant young painter some fifteen years Kuznetsov's junior, whose career epitomises the sense of possibility and purposefulness that gripped many Russian artists in the twilight of imperial rule. The son of two composers, Alexander and Valentina Serov, Valentin was born into the interlocking circles of artists and musicians that were characteristic of Russian cultural life at the time. His father died when he was just six, whereupon Serov's mother sent him to live with a friend in a commune in Smolensk province, and then took him travelling in Europe as she sought to further her musical career. This peripatetic lifestyle had its costs but its benefits too, for in the autumn of 1874 Serov and his mother moved to Paris and met Repin, who took the boy under his wing and gave him daily drawing lessons. Repin would prove a thoughtful and attentive mentor for many years, not least when he smoothed Serov's passage into the Academy in 1880, a year before he reached the official admission age at the time of sixteen. Arguably the most important advantage that Repin's friendship brought came much earlier, though, for it was through Repin and his connections that Serov first met the great patron and impresario Savva Mamontov and his wife Elizaveta in Paris in 1874.

Mamontov, like Tretyakov, epitomised the merchant and industrialist patrons who came to prominence in Russia in the second half of the nineteenth century. While Tretyakov owed his fortune to the textile industry, Mamontov's stemmed from his family's investment in railways, which had been spreading their web across the empire since the 1860s. Mamontov entered the family business and became director of the Moscow-Yaroslavl railway in 1869, overseeing the expansion of the rail network to Russia's inhospitable northern territories. From an early age, however, his heart lay in the arts. He had studied singing in Italy in his twenties but, realising that his would remain an amateur talent, determined to foster artistic development more generally, and was soon extending hospitality to artists at both his Moscow mansion and his country estate of Abramtsevo, where an entire colony of painters and sculptors gathered from the 1870s. An atmosphere of ardent conviviality and creativity emerged in which the resident artists often portrayed Mamontov, Elizaveta and views of their halcyon estate. Repin, a lynchpin of the Mamontov circle, painted memorable portraits of the charismatic couple (Figs 4.2 and 4.3), together with a shimmering image of the terrace in front of the Abramtsevo house

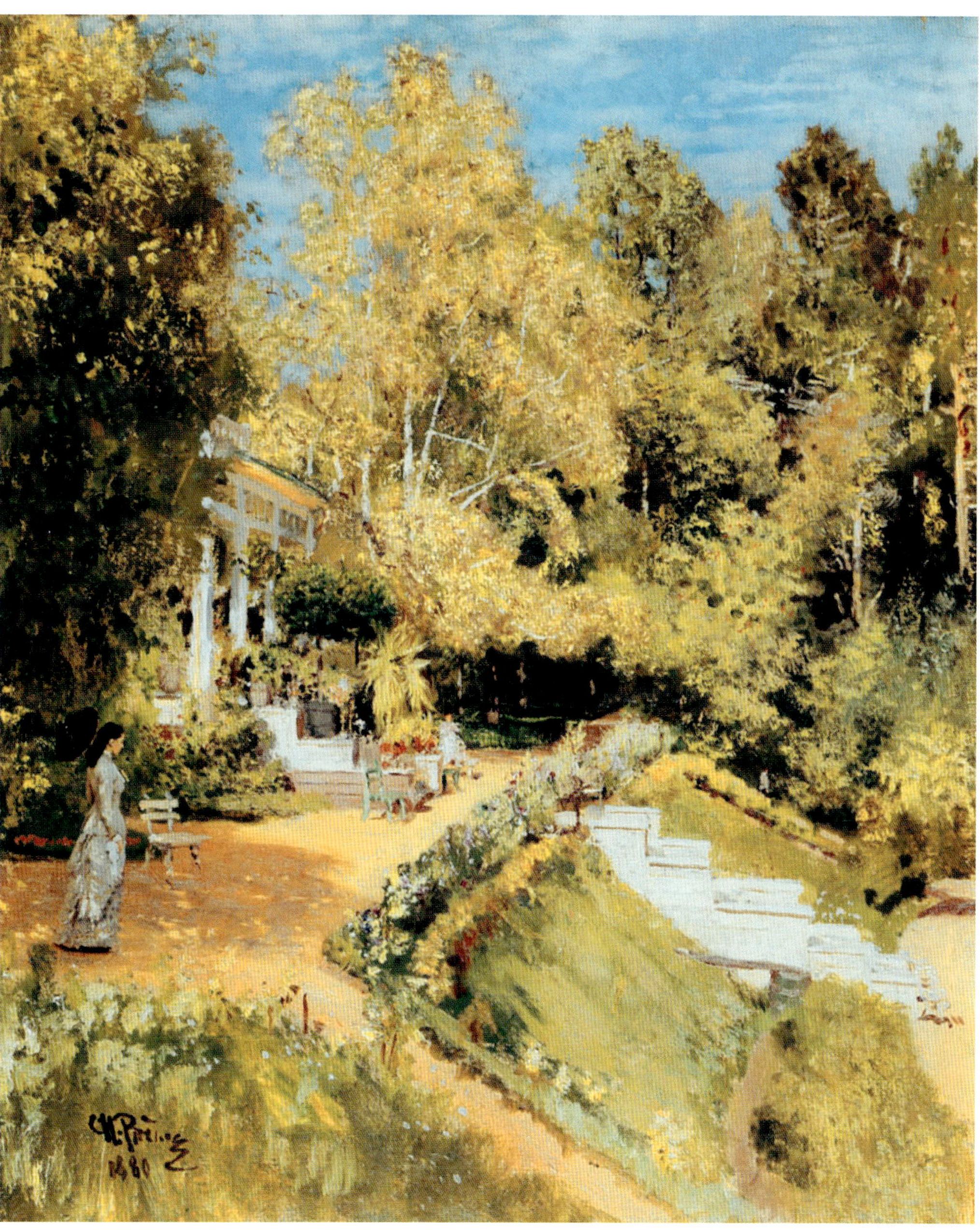

Fig. 4.4
Abramtsevo
Ilia Repin, 1880

the following year (Fig. 4.4). The gregarious Mamontov thrived amid the creative throng, presiding over noisy gatherings around his dining table, and cajoling the artists into musical and theatrical performances with his characteristic ebullience and panache.

Serov first visited Abramtsevo in 1875 at the age of ten, and discovered an environment that contrasted sharply with his lonely, uprooted childhood often spent solely in the company of a mother who was intense, focused and emotionally reserved. While Valentina Serova prayed at the altar of diligence and austerity, Abramtsevo was a world of noise and sunlight, of comfort and companionship, of boisterous parties and heated debate, all of which spilled from the house into its riverside meadows and wooded glades. It was an avowedly cheerful and productive place that offered the young artist his first truly stable and sociable home. Serov repaid the Mamontovs' hospitality with works of great beauty, among them *Girl with Peaches*, a portrait of their daughter Vera, which he painted in the Abramtsevo dining room in 1887

(Fig. 4.5). Serov here provides a masterclass in painting texture and light, evoking with consummate skill the velvety skin of the peaches and sharp gleam of the knife, the casual softness of Vera's hair and dress, the foliage glimpsed through the window, and the reflective glaze of the plate on the wall. With its radiant colour and artless brushwork, the painting is seen as one of Russia's greatest Impressionist works, and bears affectionate testament to the loving and buoyant atmosphere in which it was produced.

While Abramtsevo was a particularly notable crucible of the arts, many other country estates in Russia provided fertile ground for the efflorescence of cultural life. Serov found a similarly sympathetic creative haven at Domotkanovo, the estate of his schoolfriend Vladimir Derviz, who had studied with Serov at the Academy of Arts and married the artist's cousin, Nadezhda Simonovich. Shielded from practical necessities in the peaceful seclusion of the Derviz home, Serov became ever more adventurous in his artistic practice, as an 1888–9 portrait of Nadezhda holding her baby daughter brilliantly demonstrates (Fig. 4.6). Painted experimentally on iron plate, the unfinished work lays bare a mesh of fragmented, almost frenzied brushstrokes, as form dissolves into a haze of cream and slate grey around the figure of the sleeping child. The *plein air* painting practice that Serov had developed at Abramtsevo also became an increasingly important component of his practice, culminating in a portrait of his wife Olga in the grounds of Domotkanovo in 1895 (plate 16).

Serov's early portraits were invariably of family and friends, but by the mid 1890s he had established a reputation as a portraitist of unusual versatility and flair, and attracted the attention of society's elite. In 1896 he was invited to the coronation of Nicholas II in the Cathedral of the Dormition in the Kremlin to record the event (Fig. 4.7), which led to a flock of commissions from other members of the imperial family. There were also sittings with the prime of Russia's cultural talent, as when Serov painted Rimsky-Korsakov in 1898 (plate 17). A member of the Five, Rimsky-Korsakov had been particularly close to Mussorgsky, with whom he devised an ingenious piano-sharing arrangement in the apartment they shared in St Petersburg in the early 1870s. Mussorgsky had daily use of the instrument until he left for his civil service job at noon, whereupon Rimsky-Korsakov would take over, with evening access agreed in advance. The schedule worked amicably enough, and Mussorgsky served as Rimsky-Korsakov's best man when he married in 1872. Their friendship and collaboration prompted Tretyakov to buy the portrait of Rimsky-Korsakov directly from the artist, recognising its importance as a complement to the painting of Mussorgsky that Repin had completed some fifteen years before.

Tretyakov had now been suffering ill health for several years, but remained a dynamic and demanding patron. In 1897 he commissioned a portrait of the writer Anton Chekhov from Iosif Braz, but when artist, patron and sitter were all dissatisfied with the result, he charged Braz with painting another version in Nice the following year (plate 18). This would be the last portrait that Tretyakov commissioned, for he died on 4 December 1898 at the age of sixty-six. Serov drew him in his coffin and painted three watercolour sketches for a planned posthumous portrait that was never realised, while Repin expanded on an earlier portrait of the collector to produce a celebrated image of him in his gallery in 1901 (plate 19).

Tretyakov's death marked the end of an era. While the collector lay dying in Moscow, Sergei Diaghilev and his colleagues were busy founding a new artistic journal and exhibition society in St Petersburg known as the World of Art, which would showcase innovative developments and changing priorities in Russian art. Tretyakov lived long enough to see the journal's first issue, for which he had little but contempt: 'The appearance is good, but it has been compiled in a terribly muddled and stupid way.'[1] He may have turned in his grave two years later when his daughter Liubov married Lev Bakst, a breathtakingly original stage and costume designer, who worked closely with Diaghilev on both the World of Art enterprise and the Ballets Russes that took Europe by storm from 1909.

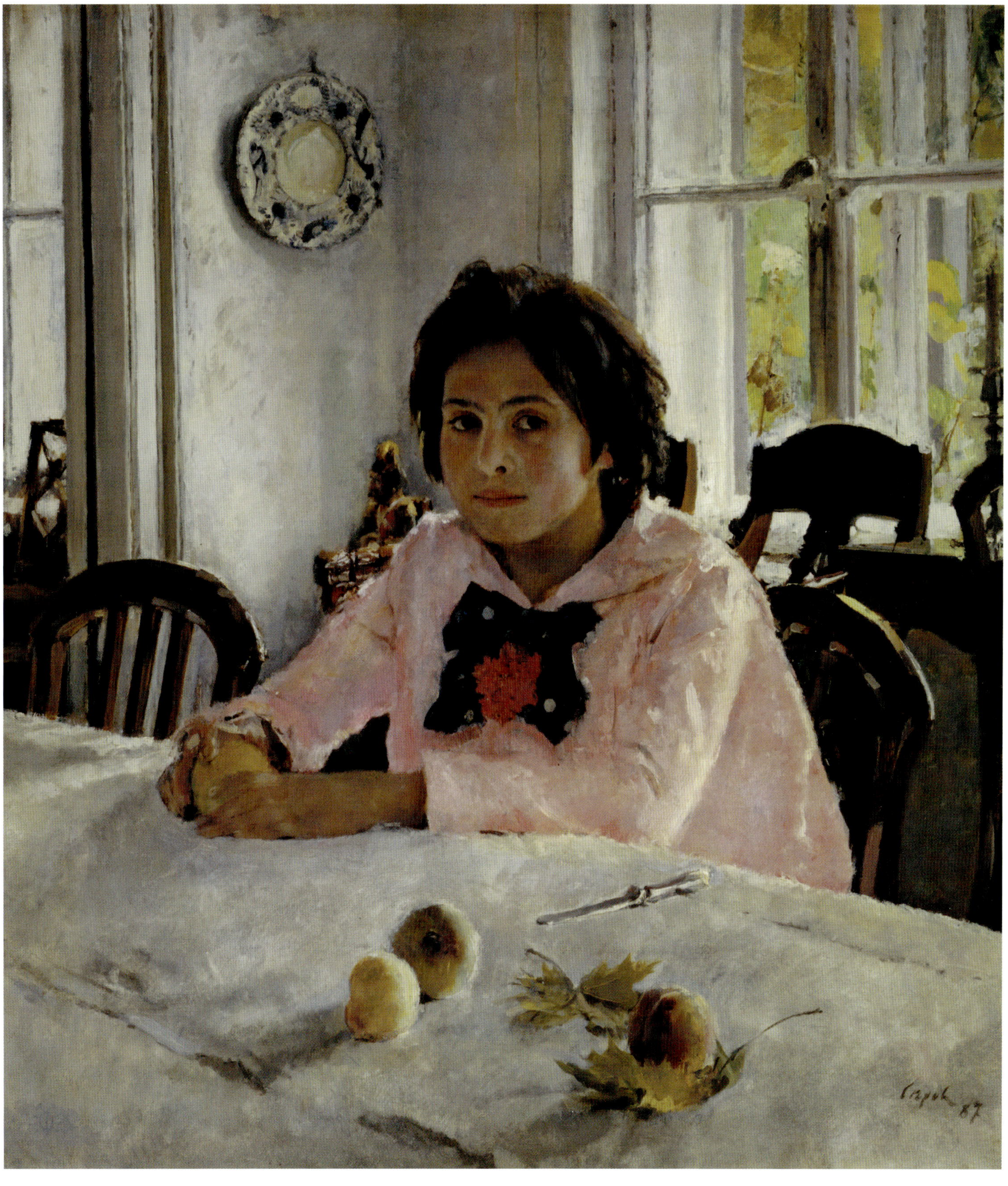

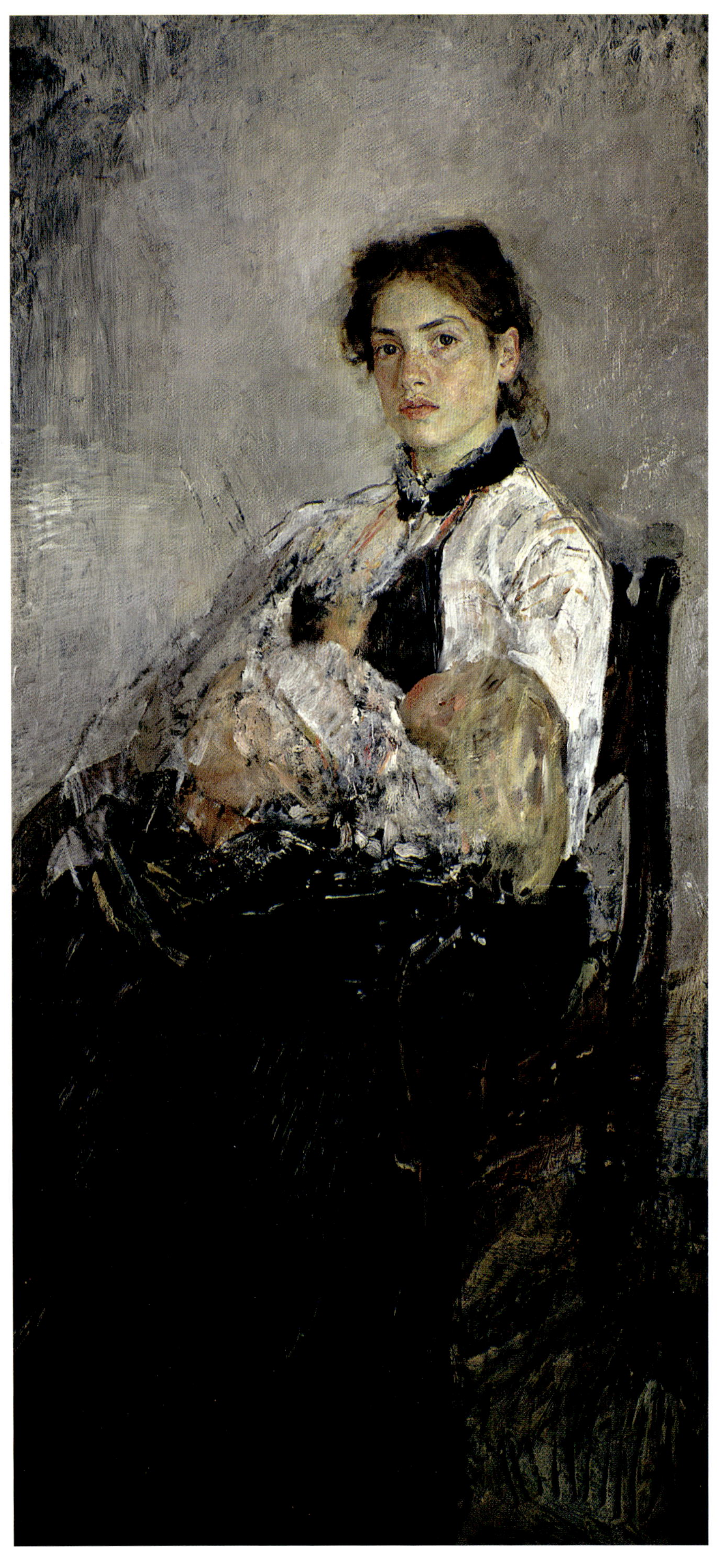

Fig. 4.6
*Nadezhda Derviz
with Her Child* (unfinished)
Valentin Serov, 1888–9

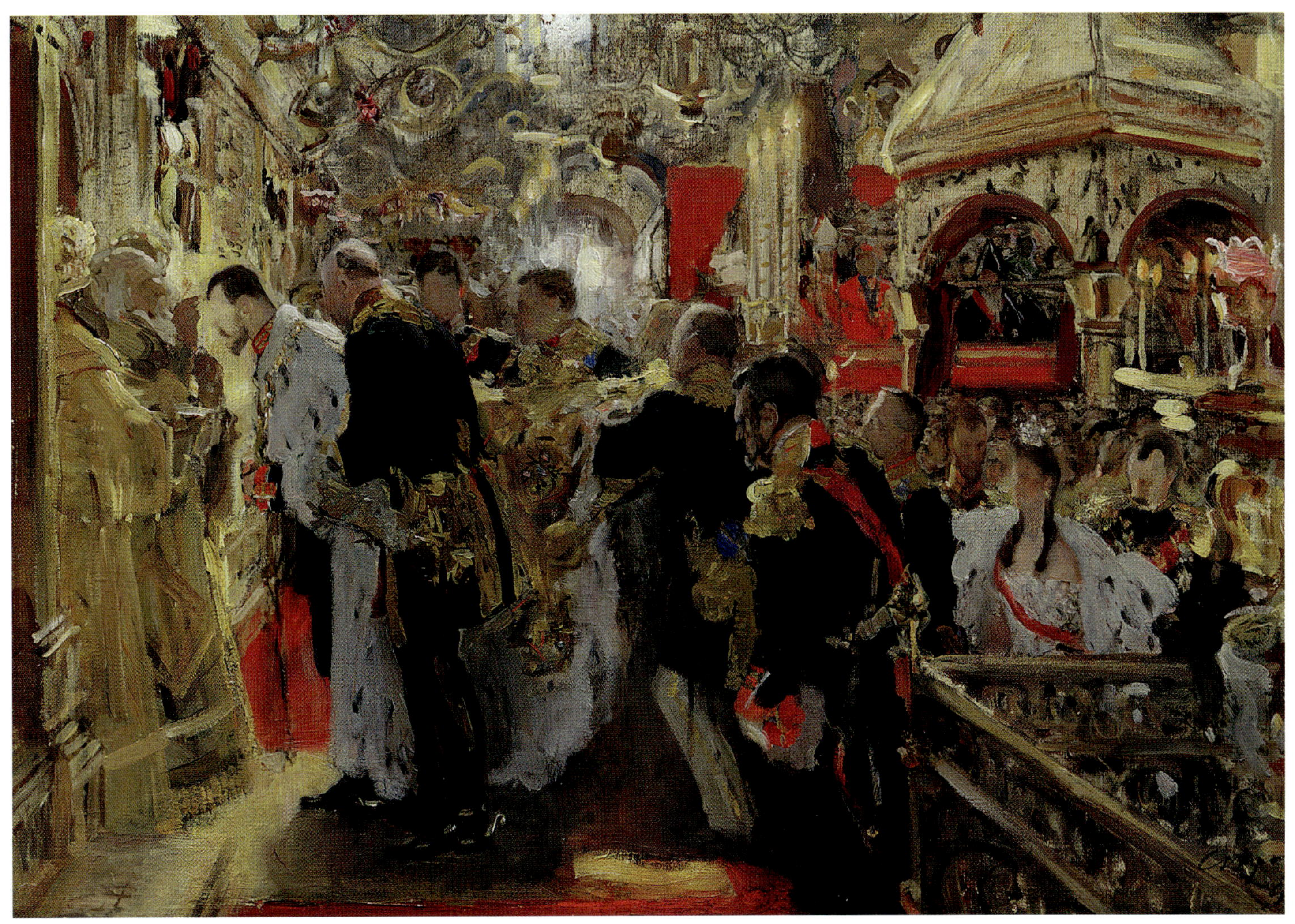

Radical new artistic languages were afoot too, as illusionism began to be replaced by flat surfaces or distorted volumes, and brushwork was deployed in ever more stylised and self-conscious ways. These and other developments would irrevocably change the attitudes of progressive young artists towards three-dimensional form and pictorial space. The naturalism of the Peredvizhniki and the Impressionism of Serov had life in them still, but they would be buffeted by waves of experimentation and innovation that carved new contours and textures into Russian art. Figurative painting would soon be eroded into different shapes and iterations, or washed away entirely to make space for something new.

Fig. 4.7
Coronation: the Anointing of Nicholas II in the Cathedral of the Dormition
Valentin Serov, 1896

Note

1   A.P. Botkina, *Pavel Mikhailovich Tretiakov v zhizni i iskusstve*, 5th edn (Iskusstvo, Moscow, 1995), p.294.

Plate 14

Baroness Varvara
Ikskul von Hildenbandt
Ilia Repin, 1889
Oil on canvas, 1965 x 717mm

The wife of the Russian ambassador to Rome from 1876 to 1891, Baroness Varvara Ikskul von Hildenbandt (1850–1929) was a notably cultured and well-travelled figure, and the salon that she hosted in her St Petersburg home from the 1880s attracted eminent writers and artists. Among them was Ilia Repin, who took to sketching portraits of other visitors and was commissioned by Tretyakov to paint the salonnière in 1889. 'The Baroness is in raptures at the thought that her portrait will be in such a famous gallery,' Repin wrote to his patron. 'She is an interesting model, and poses like a statue.'[1] Repin repeated the stark use of red and black that gave his portrait of Vladimir Stasov such impact the same year (plate 12). In contrast to the small scale of Stasov's portrait, however, the baroness is portrayed nearly life-size on a canvas almost two metres high.

Repin captures the detail of Hildenbandt's remarkable attire with great éclat, from the ruched skirt and tightly cinched blouse with its high-necked bow, to the curious points and folds of the headdress. Then there is the mesmerising effect of flesh concealed and flesh revealed. The all-encompassing outfit leaves only the face and hands bare, and even then the face is partially veiled, with the dark, shielded eyes and arched brows contrasting with the bright dimple of the exposed chin. The pose may be static but the image is a dynamic one, encouraging the eye to move from the deep sweep of the overskirt to the pinnacle

of the headdress, and from a background differentiated only by faint shadow to the brilliant sheen of Hildenbandt's bracelet, rings and brocaded cuff. The result is a painting par excellence of hauteur and slightly quizzical detachment, imbued with this stylish and self-possessed woman's consciousness of what it was to have one's portrait adorn Tretyakov's walls. The baroness was forced to leave her mansion in St Petersburg after the Revolution of 1917, and eventually emigrated to Finland and then Paris, where she settled in 1922.

1 Letter to Tretyakov, 16 March 1890, in _Repin: Perepiska s P.M. Tretiakovym, 1873–1898_, ed. M.N. Grigoreva and A.N. Shchekotova (Iskusstvo, Moscow and Leningrad, 1946), p.143.

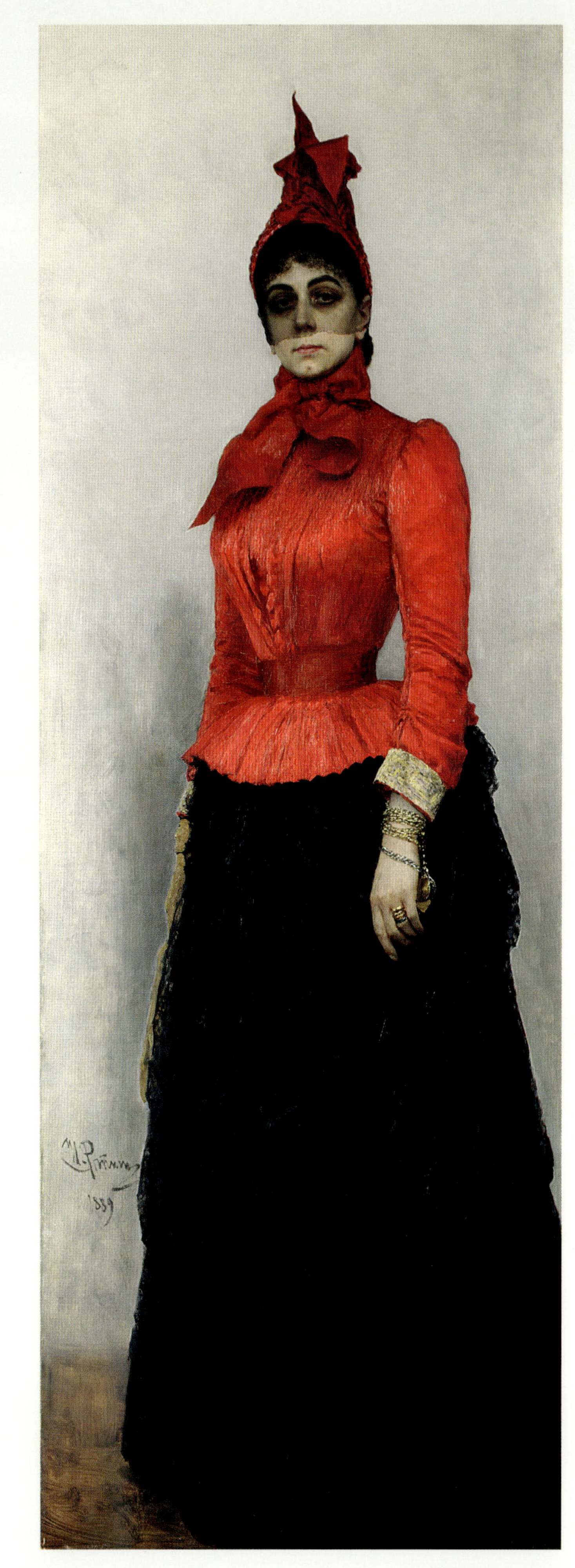

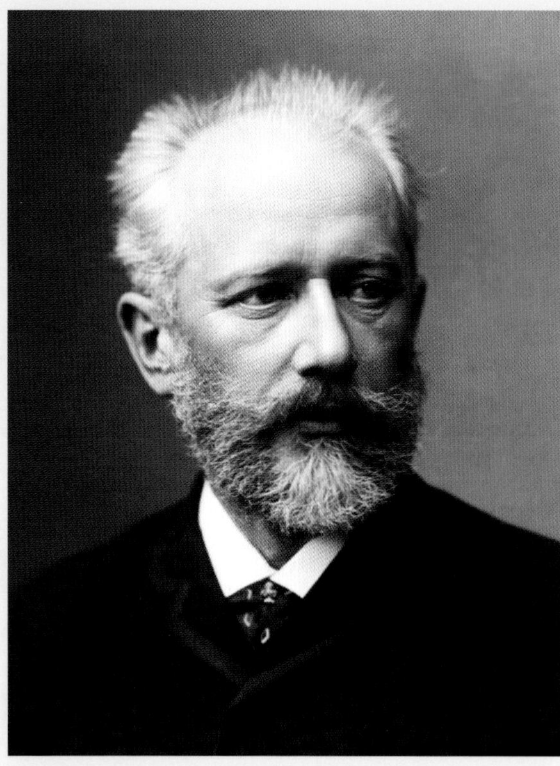

Plate 15

Petr Tchaikovsky
Nikolai Kuznetsov, 1893
Oil on canvas, 960 x 740mm

Petr Tchaikovsky (1840–93) was part of the first intake of students at the St Petersburg Conservatoire in 1862, while Anton Rubinstein, its founder and first director, was teaching instrumentation and composition there (plate 8). Recognising Tchaikovsky's lucent talent, Anton's brother Nikolai then appointed him the inaugural professor of music theory at the Moscow Conservatoire when it opened in 1866. The post became something of a poisoned chalice, as Tchaikovsky found himself caught in the crossfire between the conservative factions of the Conservatoire and the nationalists who congregated around Stasov and the Five. He continued to compose regardless, and eventually came to represent a conciliatory middle ground between the two opposing camps, believing Russian music to be neither servile nor superior to that of the West, but part of an international culture that transcended national divides.

Nikolai Kuznetsov (1850–1929) painted Tchaikovsky in Odessa in 1893, when the composer was touring with the Russian Philharmonic Society. Tchaikovsky had by then acquired national and international fame. In 1884 he had been granted the Order of St Vladimir, fourth class, which conferred hereditary nobility and won Tchaikovsky an audience with Alexander III. A keen admirer of the composer, the tsar followed this with the award of a lifetime pension of 3,000 roubles a year. Tchaikovsky had also toured Europe and the United States as a guest conductor with some of the world's leading orchestras, including an appearance at the inaugural concert of the Carnegie Hall in New York City in 1891.

For all his success, Tchaikovsky was a deeply unhappy man, living apart from a wife whom he had married to mask his homosexuality, and loathing the public spotlight that celebrity had brought. Kuznetsov captured this unease in a tense, almost hostile pose, with Tchaikovsky clamping his hand on a musical score as he fixes the viewer with a chary gaze. Particularly striking is the facture of the background, in which broad, loose brushstrokes create a symphony in brown that contrasts with the more meticulous painting of Kuznetsov's early career (Fig. 3.2). This is an artist on the cusp of a bold new aesthetic, abnegating detail and finesse in favour of an exhilaratingly energetic and untrammelled approach.

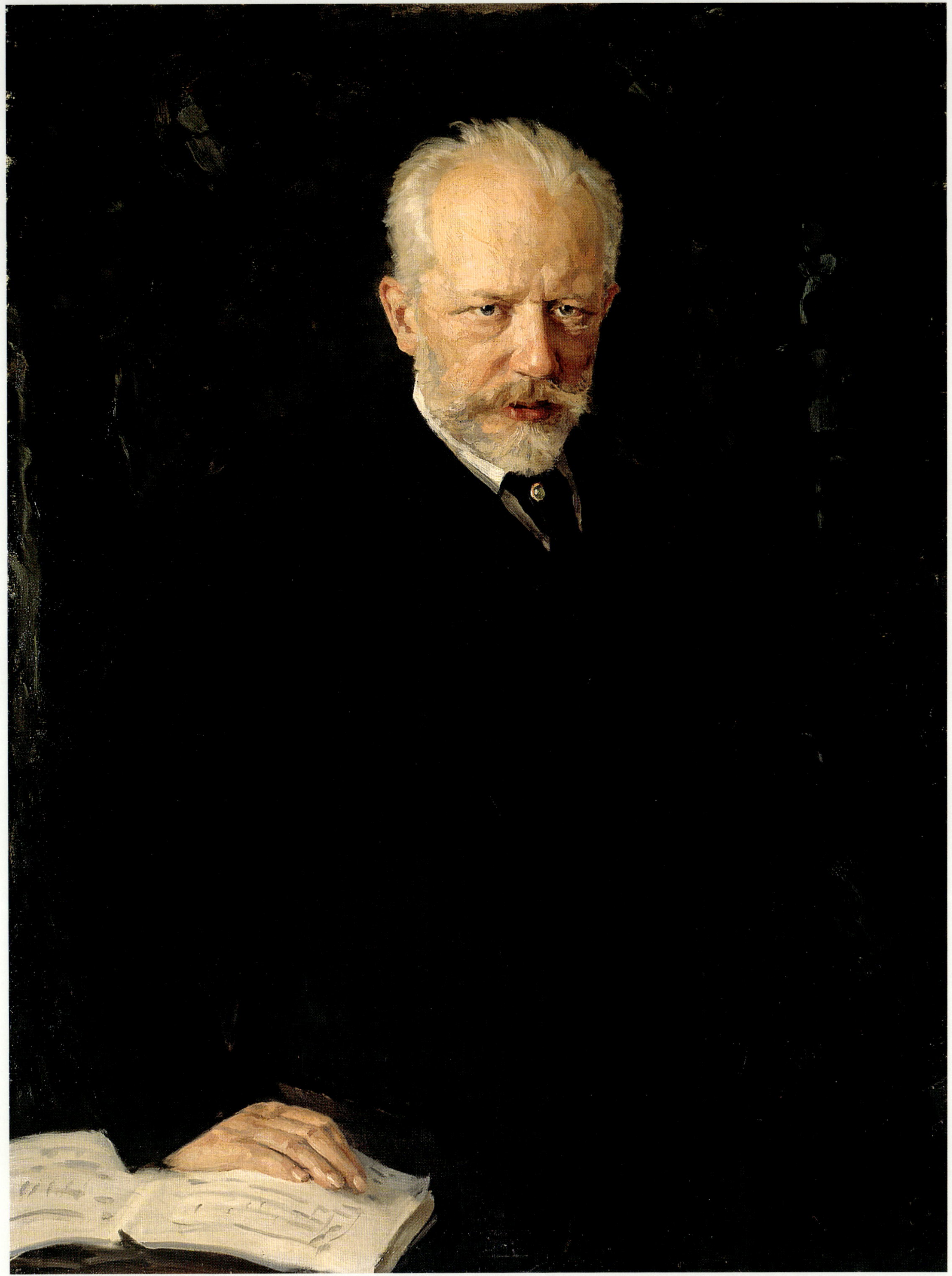

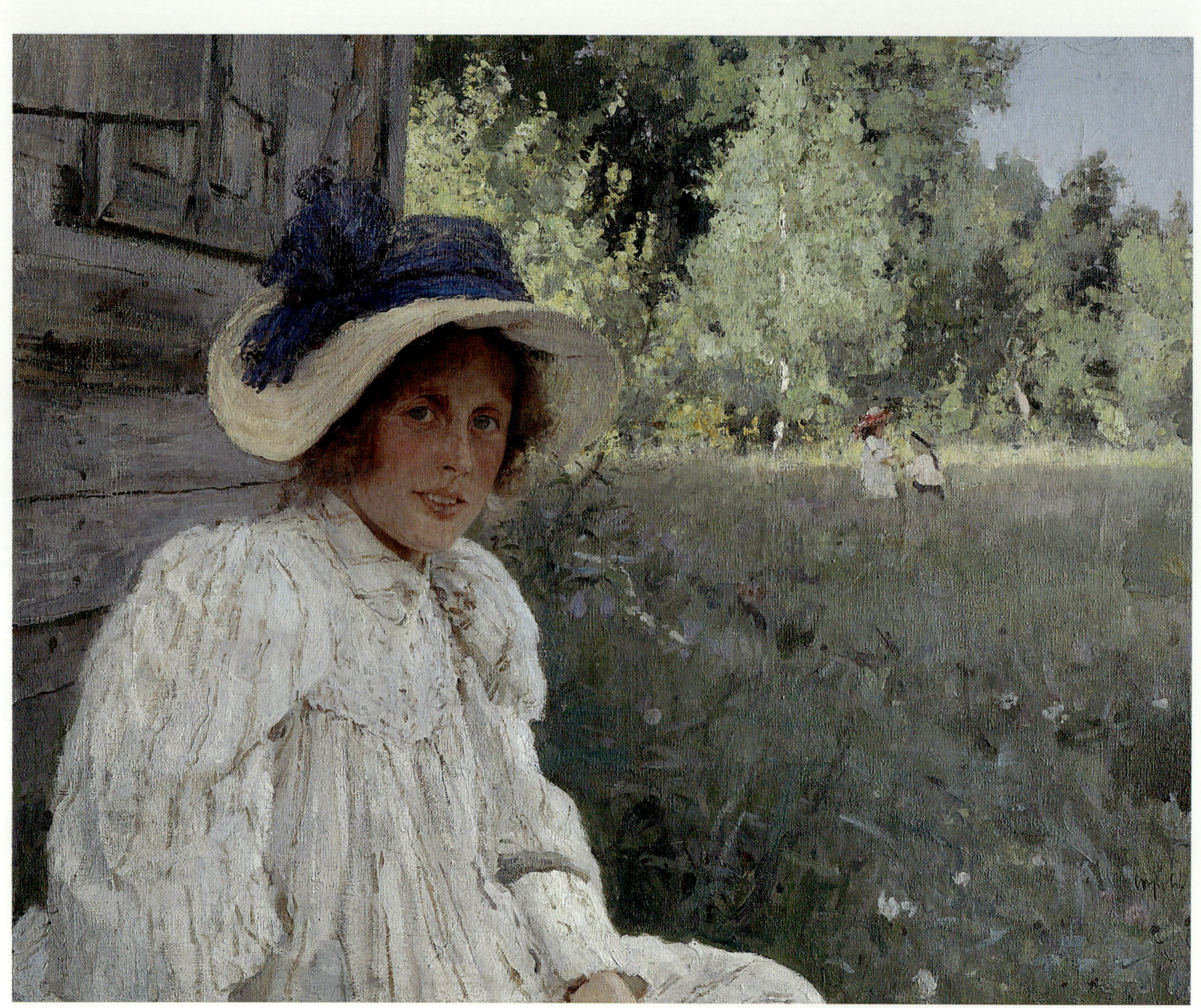

Plate 16

In the Summer
Valentin Serov, 1895
Oil on canvas, 740 x 940mm

This portrait depicts Serov's wife, Olga Serova (née Trubnikova, 1864–1927), an orphan who had been raised in his aunt's house. She and Serov knew each other for many years before they married in 1889, with Repin, one of Serov's long-standing mentors, serving as a witness. Olga was a quiet and reserved woman, described shortly after her wedding as 'a petite, pleasant blonde with beautiful eyes, simple and very modest'. The same commentator noted crisply that as Olga was not a particularly strong personality, she would not exert 'influence over her husband'. The marriage was nonetheless long and happy, and produced six children.[1]

In Olga, Serov found a sympathetic listener with whom he could discuss his aspirations as an artist. Associating the brilliance of Renaissance painting with a relaxed way of life, he confided in her in 1887 that 'I want to be just as carefree. At present they all paint heavily, without joy. I want joy and will paint only joyfully.'[2] This credo seems to be fully realised in this portrait of Olga that he painted eight years later at Domotkanovo, the country estate of his friend Vladimir Derviz. Serov often stayed at Domotkanovo, where he felt liberated from the pressures of commissions and professional networking that plagued him in urban society, and painted some of his greatest *plein air* work.

The portrait stakes its modernist credentials in many ways. The fact that Olga is unnamed in the painting's title elevates the ambiguities of visual effect over the strictures of fixed identity, while the unblended brushstrokes and bright accents of blue and white betoken an Impressionist exploration of colour and light. The composition, for its part, is novel in its framing and asymmetry, with the figure of Olga, placed off-centre and close to the picture plane, countered by the two children playing in the sunshine. The result is an anthem to family intimacy, which equally hymns the Arcadian delights of Russian estate life.

1   Letter from Ilia Ostroukhov to Elizaveta Mamontova, 8 March 1889, in *Valentin Serov v perepiske, dokumentakh i interviu*, ed. I.S. Zilbershtein and V.A. Samkov (Khudozhnik RSFSR, Leningrad, 1985), vol. 1, p.152.

2   Letter to Olga Trubnikova, 17 May 1887, ibid., p.90.

Plate 17

Nikolai Rimsky-Korsakov
Valentin Serov, 1898
Oil on canvas, 965 x 1132mm

The son of an aristocratic family with a proud tradition of naval and military service, Nikolai Rimsky-Korsakov (1844–1908) long combined a musical and military career, having studied at the School for Mathematical and Navigational Sciences in St Petersburg before entering the Imperial Russian Navy, and making his first tentative attempts at musical composition around the same time. In 1861 he was introduced to Mily Balakirev, César Cui and Modest Mussorgsky, who exerted a powerful influence. 'I … absorbed the tastes of Balakirev, Cui and Mussorgsky without reasoning or examination,' the composer later confessed.[1] Joining them and Alexander Borodin to form the Five, he shared their quest to develop a classical Russian repertoire by incorporating folk song and other traditional motifs in his work.

In 1871, however, Rimsky-Korsakov's allegiance to the Five faltered when he was appointed professor of practical composition and instrumentation at the St Petersburg Conservatoire, at the age of just twenty-seven. Still in the navy, he taught his classes in uniform, which military officers were required to wear at all times. The new post exposed him to a Westernised academic training for which he developed great respect, and which provided a powerful counter to the nationalistic orientation of the Five. Rimsky-Korsakov never disavowed the work of his early collaborators, and devoted many hours to editing and orchestrating compositions by the Five in later years (though the edits he made were not without controversy). His grounding in academic practice nonetheless caused him to appreciate and seek inspiration in Western as well as native musical styles, and he became a devoted servant of the St Petersburg Conservatoire, which has borne his name since 1944.

As had been the case in Ge's portrait of Tolstoy (plate 11), Serov elected to portray Rimsky-Korsakov immersed in his work, with books and musical scores piled high around his desk. The composer seems to be on the verge of conducting with his right hand, while the other grips a score so tightly as to cause the veins to protrude. It is a composition of ordered chaos and focused activity, reflecting the balance of creativity and professionalism that underpinned the success of Rimsky-Korsakov's career.

1   Nikolai Rimsky-Korsakoff [*sic*], *My Musical Life*, trans. J.A. Joffe (Martin Secker, London, 1924), p.19.

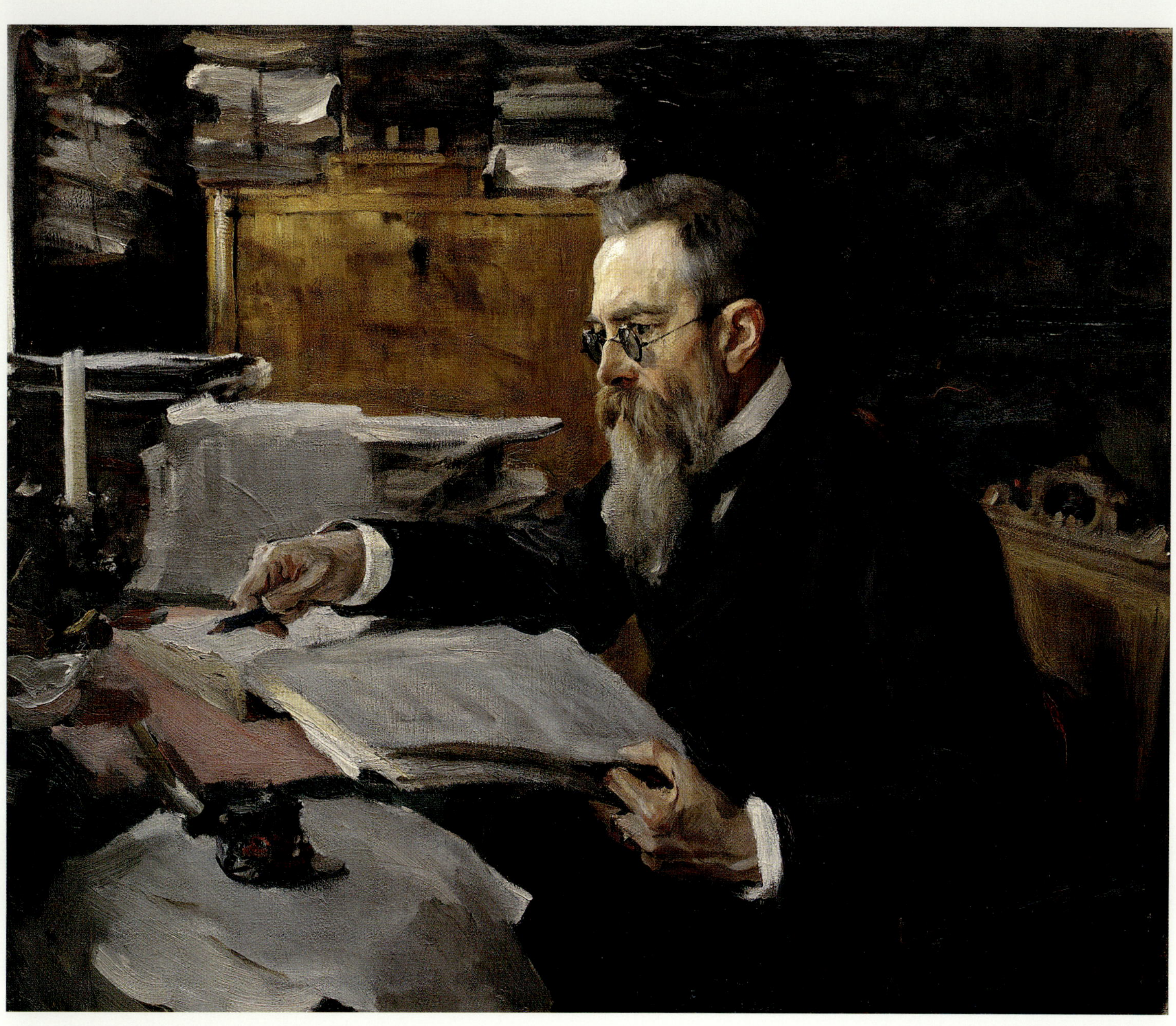

Plate 18

Anton Chekhov
Iosif Braz, 1898
Oil on canvas, 1020 x 800mm

A trained and practising doctor, Anton Chekhov (1860–1904) first came to attention with the exquisite language and terse economy of his short stories, and was widely seen as a master in the genre. By contrast, his play, *The Seagull*, was panned by critics when it premiered in 1896, causing the wounded playwright to renounce any further theatrical work. In 1898, however, the director Konstantin Stanislavsky staged a revival of *The Seagull* in his experimental Moscow Art Theatre to enthusiastic applause. This portrait therefore marks an unsettling but exciting moment in the writer's life, as he encountered unexpected approbation for a work that had previously been dismissed out of hand. The Moscow Art Theatre would later produce *Uncle Vanya* (1899) and premier *Three Sisters* (1901) and *The Cherry Orchard* (1904), completing the quadrivium of plays that established Chekhov as the most elegiac chronicler of the landed gentry's demise.

Iosif Braz (1873–1936) was a well-educated and cosmopolitan artist, having studied in Holland, Munich and Paris as a young man. These foreign sojourns gave him wide exposure to stylistic innovations in modern Western painting. He then studied in Repin's studio in the Academy of Arts in St Petersburg from 1895 to 1896, which gave him a solid grounding in the sort of portrait techniques that had enjoyed wide popularity in Russia in recent years. Collectively, these experiences enabled Braz to produce a powerful and nuanced image of Chekhov when Tretyakov commissioned him to paint the playwright in Nice in 1898. Braz reprised the convention of posing his sitter in relatively formal mode in an armchair, as had been the case in Perov's portrait of Dal and Repin's portrait of Turgenev (plates 3 and 5). The relatively conservative composition is leavened, however, by broad, sweeping brushstrokes that capture the way in which the deep tones of Chekhov's suit changed like the feathers of a mallard's head in different lights. Reproductions of the portrait have become ubiquitous in editions of the writer's work, and in 1960 it occupied pride of place at an exhibition in Moscow that was dedicated to the centenary of his birth.

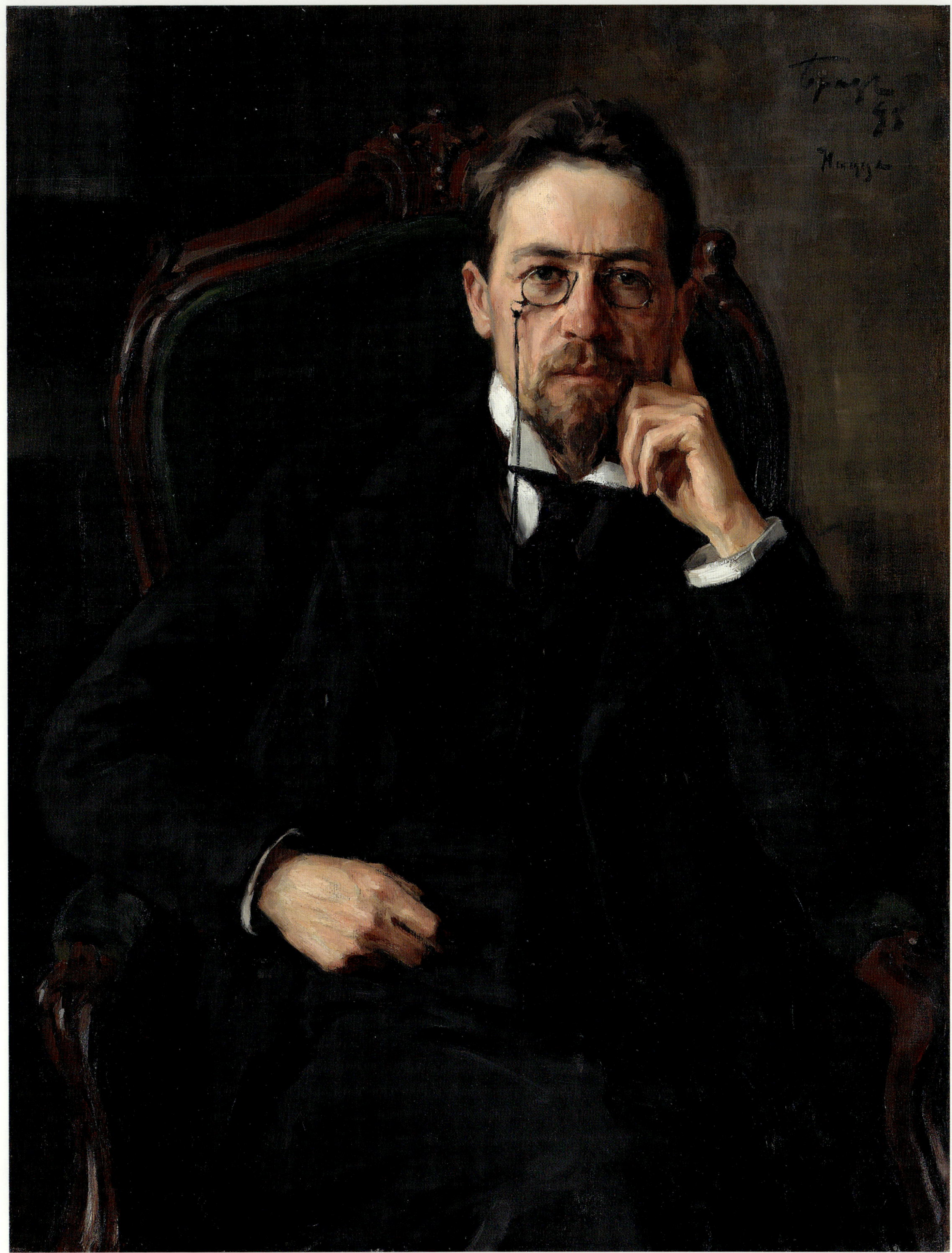

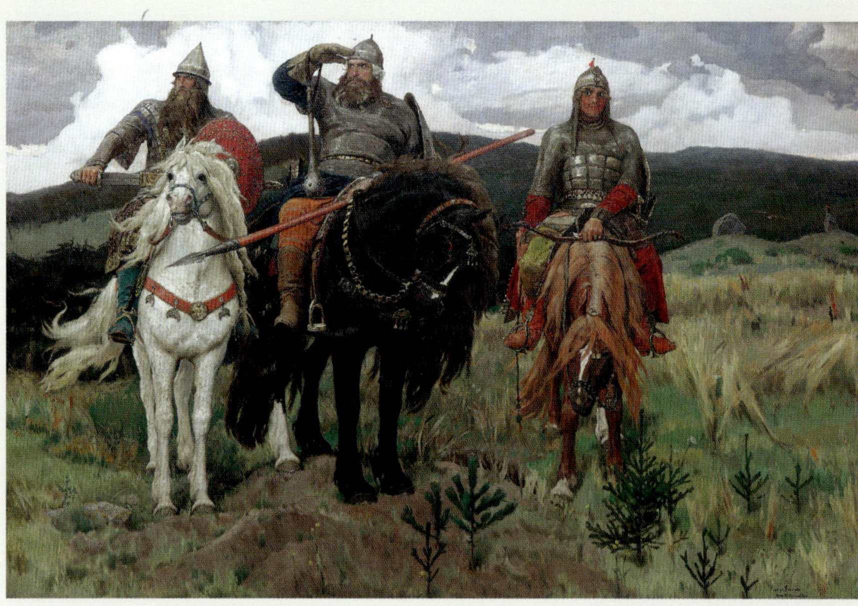

Plate 19

Pavel Tretyakov
Ilia Repin, 1901
Oil on canvas, 1110 x 1340mm

Repin and Tretyakov first met in the early 1870s and developed a long and productive working partnership. Tretyakov was by a distance Repin's most important patron, and eventually acquired fifty-two oil paintings and eight drawings by the artist. Repin was not only one of the first painters whom Tretyakov turned to when he was looking to commission a new portrait, but also advised the collector on which other artists' works to buy. These included paintings by leading artists of the first half of the nineteenth century, which ensured that Tretyakov's collection was representative of a broad sweep of Russian art, rather than contemporary painting alone. The two men became extremely close and traded gossip, opinion, confidences and advice in a correspondence that lasted twenty-five years.

Repin painted Tretyakov on several occasions, including a seated portrait of the collector in his gallery that the artist began in 1882 and completed the following year. This served as a model for the 1901 portrait, which Repin painted three years after his subject had died. The collector here seems characteristically shy and withdrawn, disinclined to engage with any prurient observer, and contemplating instead the art collection that constituted his life's greatest work.

Tretyakov stands in front of many recognisable paintings in his collection. These include *Bogatyrs* (Fig. 4.9), a vast image of the heroic warriors of medieval Russian legend that Viktor Vasnetsov had started seventeen years previously in a specially equipped studio at Abramtsevo. This can be glimpsed through the doorway where Tretyakov hung it, and where it still hangs today. Hailed as a high point of the national revival movement that had been gathering momentum in painting, architecture and the decorative arts, *Bogatyrs* was central to Tretyakov's project of celebrating and promoting Russian art. It was the final painting that the patron bought.

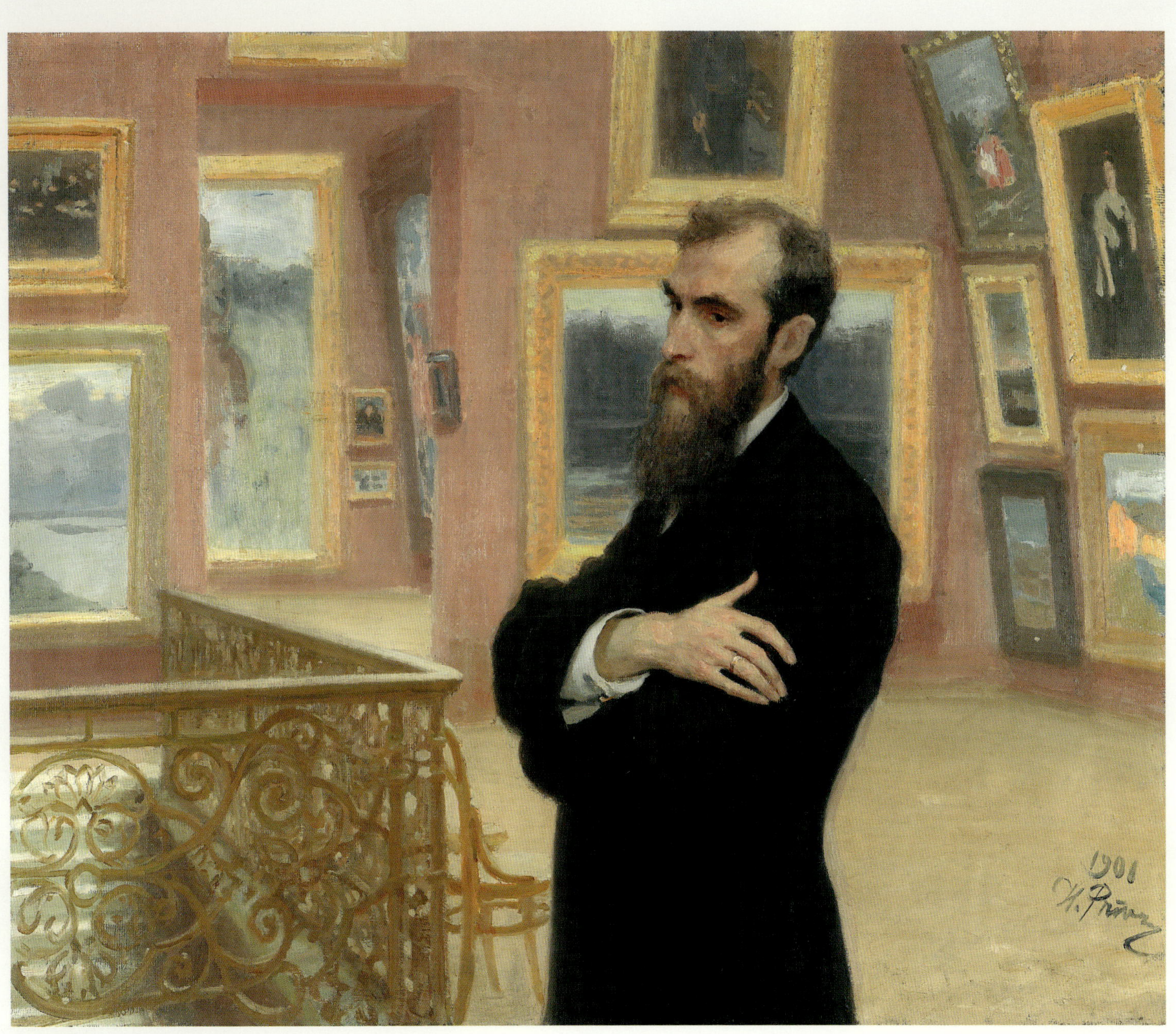

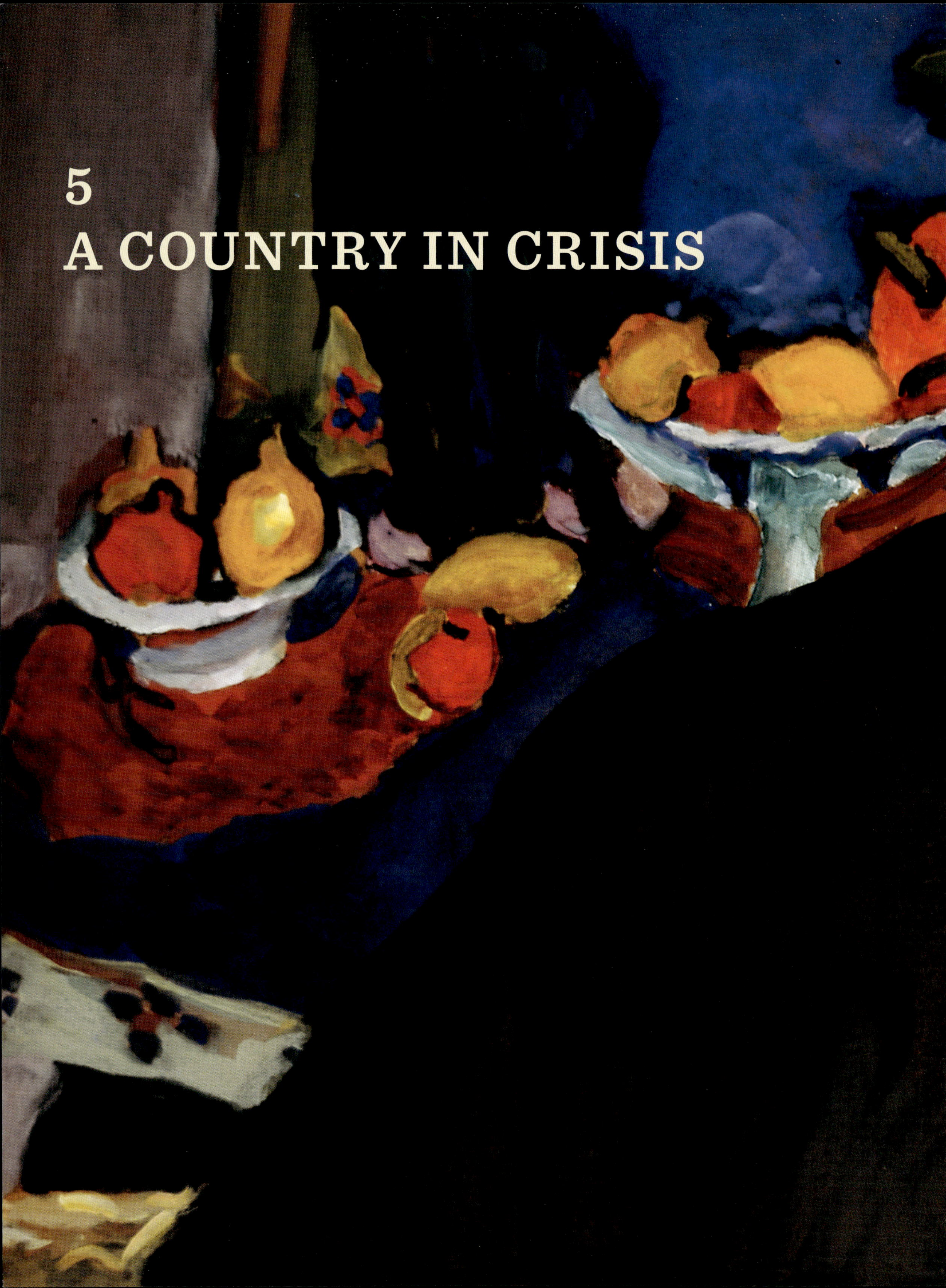

5
A COUNTRY IN CRISIS

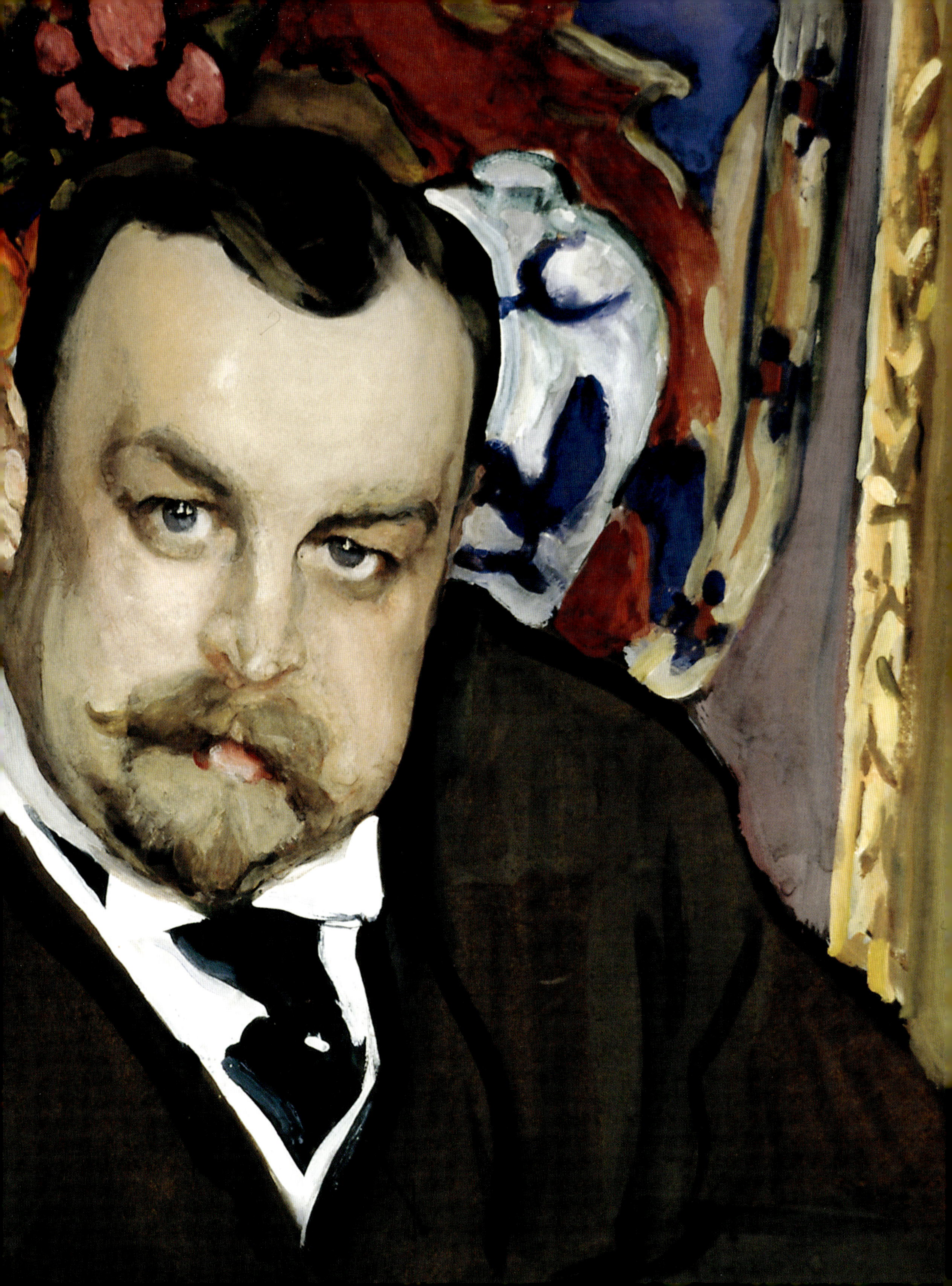

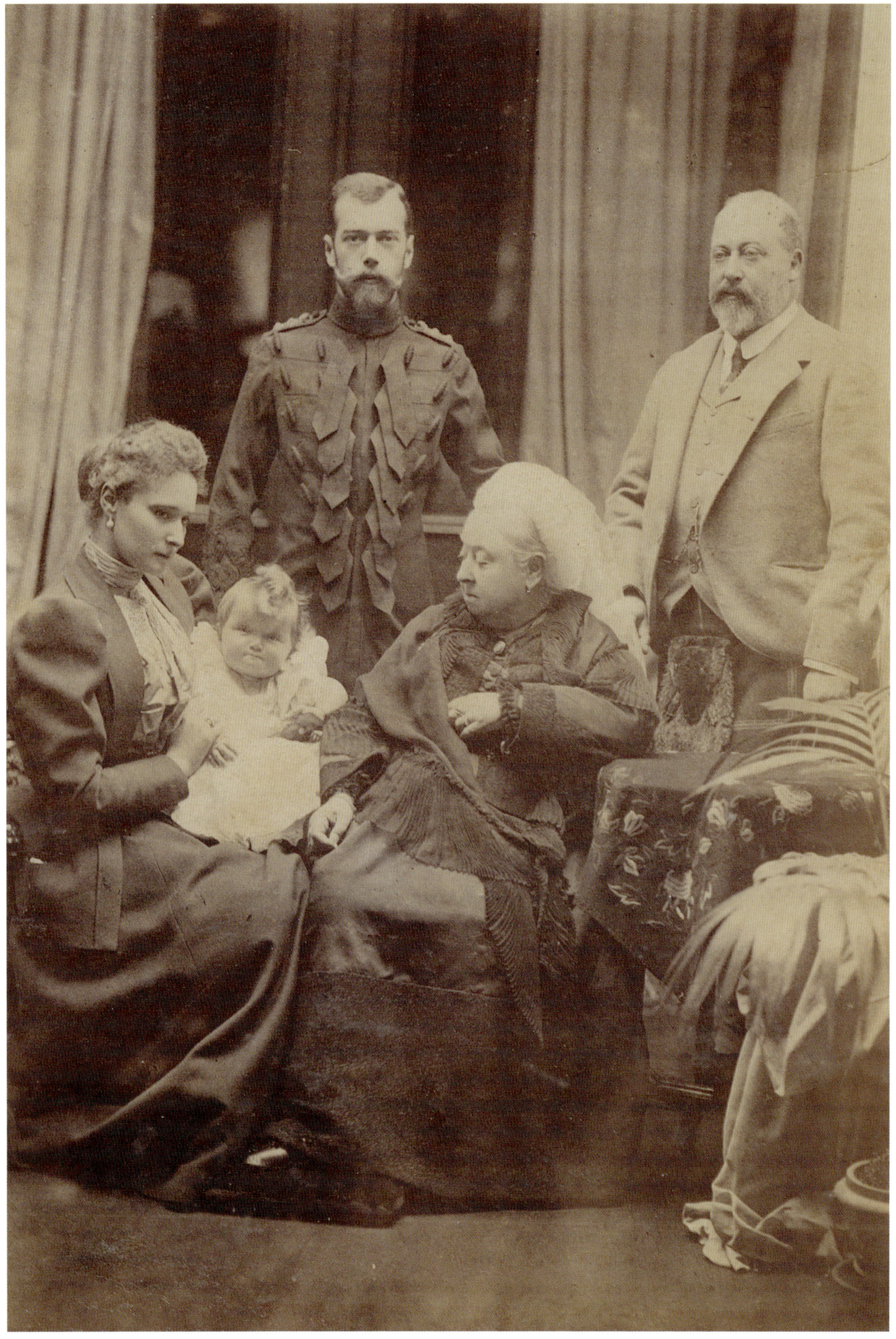

Fig. 5.1
Royal group at Balmoral (left to right:
Tsarina Alexandra Fedorovna, Grand
Duchess Olga Nikolaevna, Tsar
Nicholas II, Queen Victoria, Edward,
Prince of Wales)
Photographed by Robert Milne, 1896

RARELY HAS A RULER EXPERIENCED greater extremes of family happiness and political strife than Nicholas II, who succeeded his father, Alexander III, in 1894, and doggedly held on to the throne until the Revolution of 1917. As a young man, Nicholas had fallen deeply in love with Princess Alix of Hesse and by Rhine, a granddaughter of Queen Victoria, to whom he was related through the labyrinthine entanglements of European royalty. There were anxieties about the match on both sides, but the pair withstood alternative suggestions and married in the Winter Palace in St Petersburg on 26 November 1894, less than a month after Tsar Alexander's death at the age of just forty-nine. Alix took the name of Alexandra Fedorovna on her admission to the Russian Orthodox Church. Her first child, Grand Duchess Olga, was born in 1895, and was subjected to Queen Victoria's imperious scrutiny during a trip with her parents to Balmoral the following year (Fig. 5.1).

For all the initial reservations about Nicholas and Alexandra's marriage, it proved to be one of great ardour. The couple made no attempt to conceal their devotion to each other, and maintained a loving, almost cloying correspondence when they were apart. They were never happier than when ensconced with their four daughters and much longed-for son and heir, Alexei, who arrived in 1904. The family albums bulged with photographs of jaunty outings and boating trips, of matching outfits and parlour games (Fig. 5.2). Behind it all, though, lay the unspeakable sadness of Alexei's haemophilia, a condition that was passed through the maternal line and afflicted many of the royal houses of Europe. The empress's trauma at her son's illness, which was kept hidden from the public, led her to form desperate liaisons with anyone who offered hope of a cure. That with the self-styled peasant mystic Grigory Rasputin later played no small part in the imperial family's rising unpopularity and eventual demise.

While Nicholas derived stability and contentment from his loving family life, his natural reserve caused him untold anxieties in the public sphere. The tsar was haunted by a horrific event that marred the celebrations of his coronation in May 1896, when tens of thousands of revellers gathered to enjoy free refreshments at a vast military training ground on the

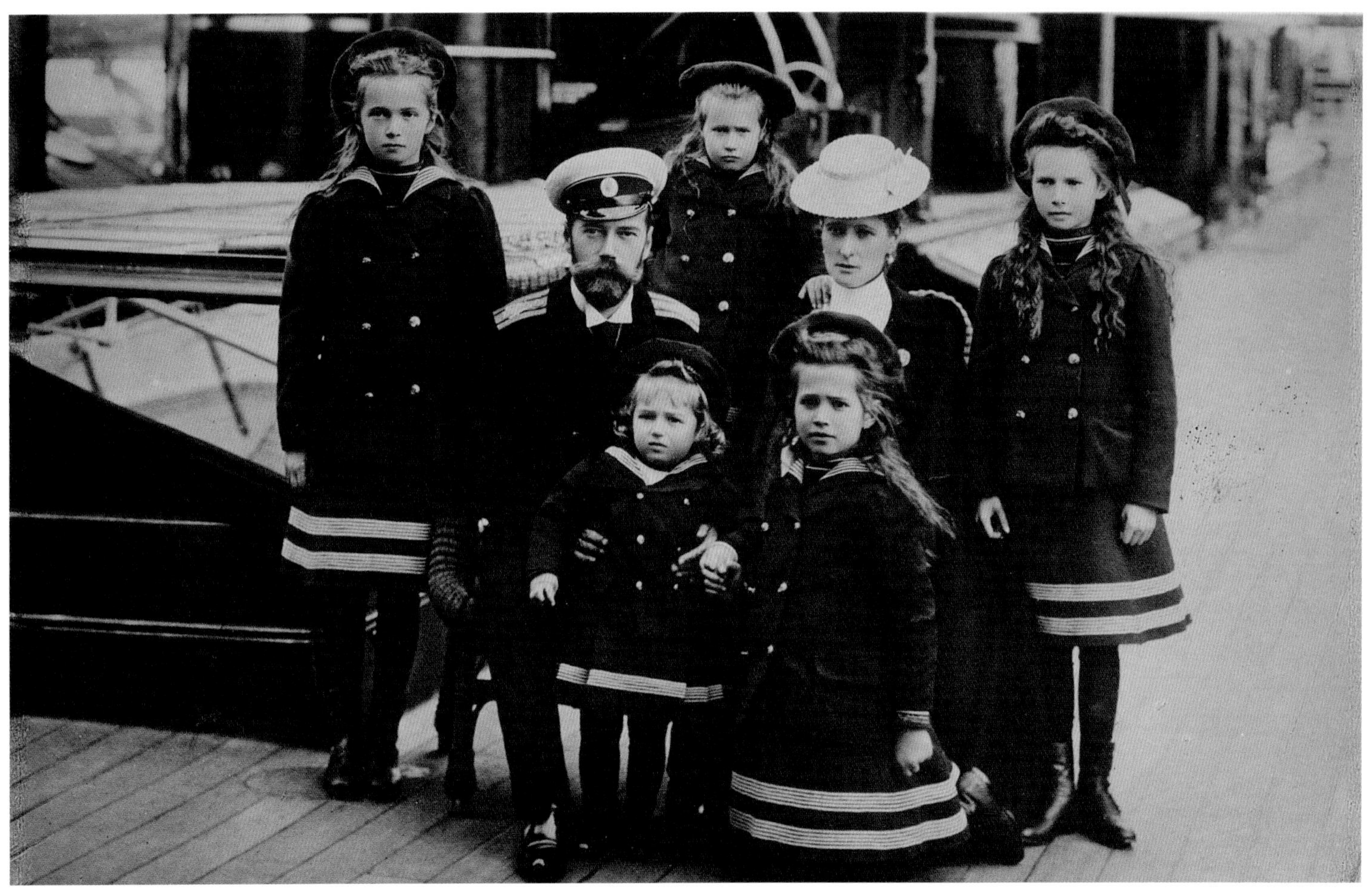

outskirts of Moscow known as Khodynka Field. As the crowds intensified, boards that had been placed over the field's ditches and trenches collapsed, and over 1,300 men, women and children were crushed or trampled to death. Against his better judgement, Nicholas was persuaded to continue with the official ceremonies, but would live to rue the day. Khodynka Field became shorthand for an ill-fated reign in which military might crumbled and dynasties collapsed, as the established order of one of Europe's greatest empires was irrevocably overturned.

Among those who suffered a dramatic change of fortune in the early years of Nicholas's reign was Savva Mamontov, whose passion for creative experimentation had proved such a catalyst for the visual and theatrical arts. Mamontov's recent protégés included Mikhail Vrubel, a friend of Serov's, who had joined him in the colourful community of artists that gathered at Abramtsevo. There Vrubel modelled quixotic pots and clay heads that he fired in iridescent glazes in his own ceramics studio. He also developed a stunningly original painting style in which Symbolist ideas were expressed in saturated colours and tessellated brushwork inspired by the textures and forms of medieval and Byzantine art. Vrubel's first major painting in this vein, *Seated Demon* (Fig. 5.3), was roundly reviled by critics, but Mamontov was fascinated by it and Vrubel's other explorations of the demon theme, and offered the artist his full support. Vrubel not only painted his patron's portrait (plate 20), but also provided stage sets and costume designs for the Russian Private Opera that Mamontov had founded in 1885.

The Russian Private Opera played a major role in the development of Russian music by staging and popularising the work of the more radical composers of the previous quarter century – Borodin, Mussorgsky, Tchaikovsky and Rimsky-Korsakov among them (plates 7, 15 and 17). It also launched new stars, including the opera singer Nadezhda Zabela (plate 21), whom Vrubel married in 1896, and the renowned bass Fedor Shaliapin (plate 22). The composer and pianist Sergei Rachmaninov joined the company as assistant conductor the following year. Mamontov, ever the hands-on if not meddlesome patron, not only funded the enterprise but trained the singers and actors, and often even conducted the orchestra himself. Such was his appetite for artistic innovation that he was also one of the first two sponsors of the *World of Art* journal that the circle of Sergei Diaghilev launched in St Petersburg in 1898.

Sadly, Mamontov's cultural philanthropy was not to last, for in 1899 the impresario was arrested and tried for embezzling funds during the construction of the Moscow-Yaroslavl railway. He was acquitted but went bankrupt, unable to recover from the financial and reputational damage that the court case had caused. His visionary patronage came to an ignominious end, although the Russian Private Opera (renamed the Private Opera Society) continued to operate without Mamontov until 1909.

If Mamontov's demise sounded the death knell for various cultural initiatives in Moscow and St Petersburg, others hit full stride as the twentieth century dawned. Leading the way was the Moscow Art Theatre, which had been conceived by the director Konstantin Stanislavsky and the critic and playwright Vladimir Nemirovich-Danchenko during a legendary eighteen-hour lunch that lasted from 2 o'clock on the afternoon of 22 June 1897 until 8 o'clock the next morning.[1] Their brainchild opened in rented premises the following year with an eclectic season of plays by writers from Ibsen to Shakespeare. But it was the theatre's staging of works by Chekhov (plate 18), starting with *The Seagull* in 1898, that established its reputation as Russia's most innovative and risk-taking theatrical space. Adopting the seagull as its emblem, the company became the prime breeding ground for Stanislavsky's famous techniques later known as 'method acting', which required the total immersion of an actor in his or her role. The qualities and capabilities of the performers were firmly prioritised. As Nemirovich-

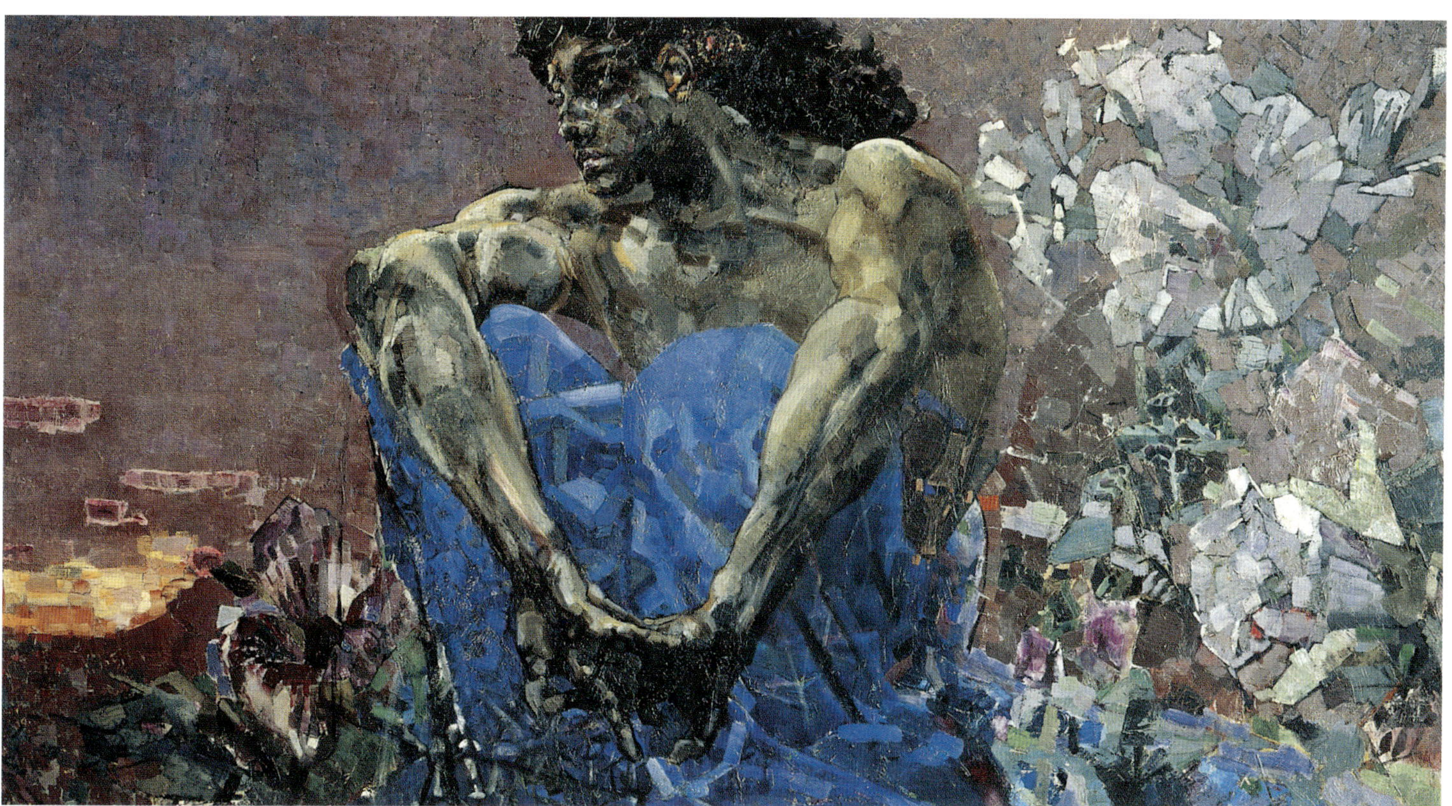

Fig. 5.3
Seated Demon
Mikhail Vrubel, 1890

Danchenko wrote to Stanislavsky, 'you may meet with stubbornness on my part when it comes to spending spare thousands of roubles on decorating the theatre, but you will never encounter obstacles to the invitation of a useful actor, or the removal of a useless one.'[2]

In 1901, the leaders of the Moscow Art Theatre commissioned the great Art Nouveau architect Fedor Shekhtel to undertake the complete reconstruction of an old theatre in central Moscow. This incorporated the latest in lighting equipment and a sensational revolving stage, and from 1902 became the company's permanent home. The theatre's forward-looking aspirations were expressed by a striking modernist bas-relief by the brilliant young sculptor Anna Golubkina that topped one of its stage doors. With its state-of-the art facilities, startlingly raw and emotive performances, and young audiences hungry for visual and dramatic stimulation, the Moscow Art Theatre left the city's other theatre companies in the shade.

This is not to say that the older theatres ceased to make an impact. The spectacular scale and auditorium of the Bolshoy Theatre, some ten minutes' walk away, continued to allow for vast operatic productions and ballets. The Maly Theatre, next door to the Bolshoy, also maintained its reputation for intense, often melodramatic plays by the likes of Ostrovsky, Turgenev and Pisemsky (plates 2, 5 and 6), and provided a stage on which established actors continued to shine. These included the doyenne of Russian drama, Maria Ermolova, whom Serov immortalised in an unforgettable portrait in 1905 (plate 23). The difference that the Moscow Art Theatre made, however, was to provide a venue for the sort of experimental and untested work that these more conservative, state-sponsored institutions were far less likely to support.

The transformation of the Moscow Art Theatre from creative vision to functioning reality depended on responsive and committed patrons. Among them was Savva Morozov, who came from a staggeringly wealthy industrialist family that had made its fortune in cotton before investing in banks and railways. The Morozov family's businesses were extensive enough to employ 8,000 workers in the 1890s, and its scions lent their support to the arts in diverse ways.[3] For Savva, it was theatrical initiatives that persuaded him to open his purse-strings. A major, sometimes sole, shareholder of the Moscow Art Theatre, he single-handedly funded Shekhtel's new home for the theatre, virtually living on the building site while the reconstruction was under way. He also commissioned a sublime Art Nouveau mansion from Shekhtel, where guests were ushered by 'a big moustachioed man with a Circassian dagger in his belt' into a salon adorned with vast panels by Vrubel.[4] Sadly, Savva's sympathies with the likes of the left-wing political activist and writer Maxim Gorky, and his enlightened treatment of employees, caused a rift with his mother, who ousted him from the family business in 1905. Savva shot himself in the south of France a month later, at the age of forty-two.

Savva's suicide was not the only one to blight the family, for his cousin Arseny put a revolver to his head in 1909 while waiting for the artist Maurice Denis to come and supervise the hanging of some paintings.[5] Cultural engagement and personal tragedy in this generation of the Morozov clan seemed to be incredibly, fatally intertwined. The family's investment in the arts did not end there, however, for Savva's brother Sergei founded and endowed the Moscow Museum of Handicrafts and devoted his energies to the preservation of peasant crafts – a preoccupation of many wealthy Russian patrons at the time.

Arseny's brothers Mikhail and Ivan, for their part, shone a spotlight on modern French art in ways that the country had not yet seen. Ivan (plate 24) was the more adventurous collector, with a superb eye and progressive taste that made him one of the world's greatest patrons of Impressionist and Post-Impressionist painting. Mikhail in turn amassed a much smaller but still impressive collection that began with works by the Barbizon school, but eventually encompassed pastels by Degas and portraits by Renoir, a seascape by Van Gogh, Tahitian landscapes by Gauguin and a bistro scene by Manet. It is entirely possible that Mikhail would have rivalled his brother Ivan as a patron had he not died in 1903, at the age of thirty-three.

Serov painted Mikhail's son Mika in a blaze of Impressionist virtuosity in 1901 (Fig. 5.4), as well as a portrait of Mikhail in far sterner guise the following year (Fig. 5.5). While Mika is tousled and liquid-eyed, emblematic of the guileless absorption of a child, his father is ham-handed and severe, fixing the viewer with his bespectacled and unsettling gaze. With these two contrasting portraits, Serov confirmed the range of moods and characteristics that he was able to conjure with his sweeping, loaded brush, and retained his status as the pre-eminent portraitist of Russia's Silver Age.

The Morozov family epitomise the contribution of merchant and industrialist patrons to Russia's cultural efflorescence at the turn of the century, albeit on a particularly lavish scale. Fifty years previously, merchants and businessmen had been derided in the plays of Ostrovsky for their boorishness and self-serving attitudes. Now, by contrast, they were often open-minded, altruistic and prepared to invest in cultural initiatives that might otherwise never have seen the light of day.

Fig. 5.4
Mika Morozov
Valentin Serov, 1901

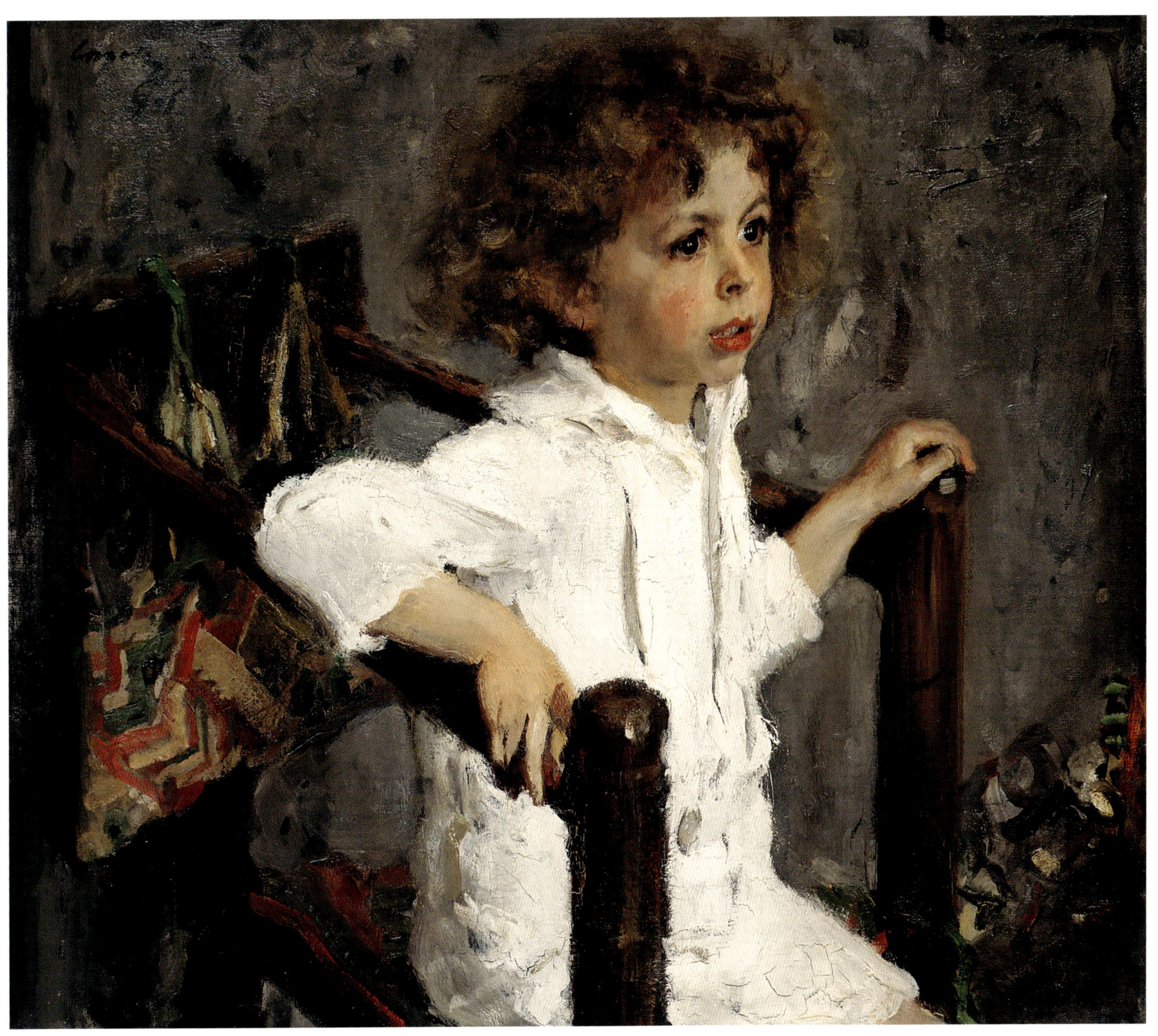

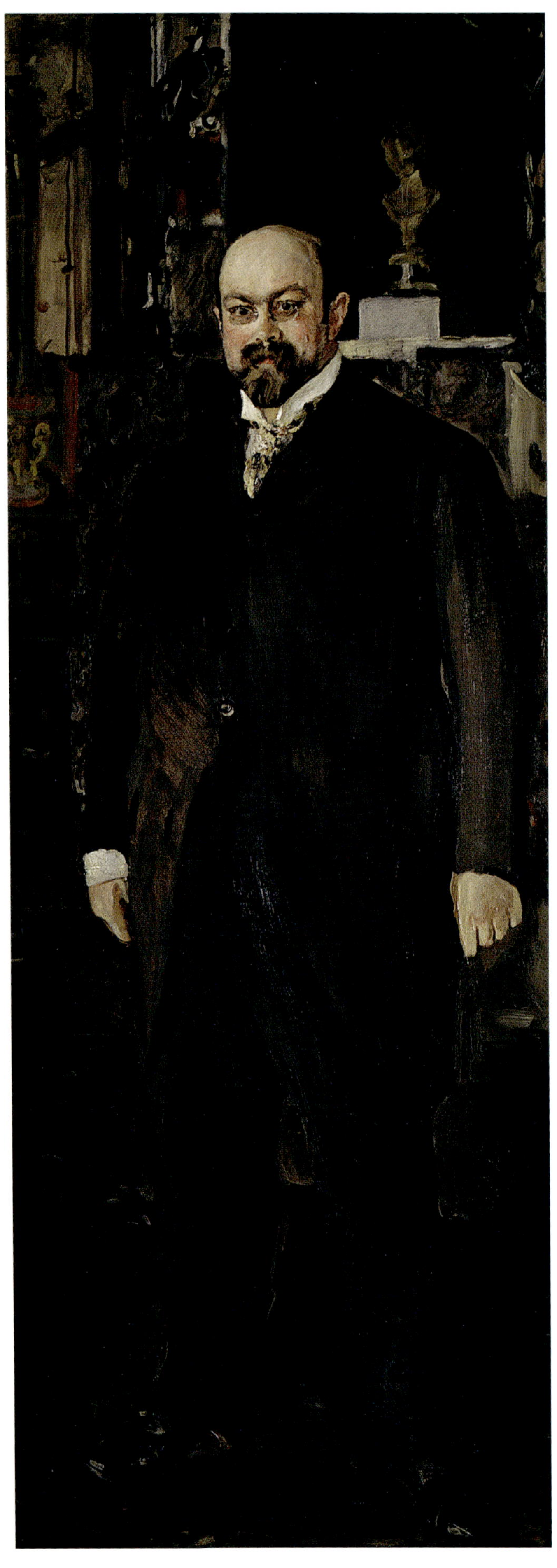

Fig. 5.5
Mikhail Morozov
Valentin Serov, 1902

Unfortunately, patrons such as these were navigating increasingly troubled waters, for Russia was entering a period of turmoil on both the international and the domestic stage. The Russo-Japanese War, which stemmed from rival territorial claims in East Asia, opened with Japan's surprise attack on the Russian Eastern Fleet at Port Arthur on 8 February 1904, and ended in a humiliating defeat for Russia some twenty months later. Meanwhile at home, discontent with long working hours, low wages and unsafe conditions in factories had led to a number of strikes for some years, culminating in a period of intense disaffection and major strike action in late 1904. By January 1905, there were walk-outs at several hundred factories in St Petersburg, the city was without electricity and public areas were closed.

On 22 January 1905, several thousand demonstrators marched towards the Winter Palace to present a petition to the tsar that called for, among other requests, universal suffrage, improved working conditions, fair wages and an eight-hour working day. Amid scenes of unbelievable confusion and miscommunication, they were attacked with sabres and fired upon by soldiers of the Imperial Guard in various parts of the city, leading to scores of fatalities and hundreds of casualties (exact figures vary widely) on a day that became known as Bloody Sunday. In an almost grotesque understatement, the tsar, who was safe from the atrocities at a palace outside the city, is said to have described the shocking episode as 'painful and sad'.[6]

The demonstration had been peaceful and largely apolitical in intent. But the actions of the authorities, with their callous disregard for freedom of speech and human life, prompted understandable public outrage and stoked the flames of a revolutionary movement that was already under way. Social and political unrest escalated into what became known as the 1905 Revolution, and eventually persuaded the tsar to agree to a series of reforms. The October Manifesto established basic human rights, allowed for the formation of political parties, extended suffrage and instated an elected parliament, the State Duma of the Russian Empire, as the main legislative authority. Nicholas II deliberated for two days before signing it, but took solace in the hope that 'this grave decision will lead my dear Russia out of the intolerable chaos she has been in for nearly a year'.[7] The Manifesto was followed by the Russian Constitution, which established a limited constitutional monarchy in 1906. For the time being, the tide of dissent was stemmed.

The events of 1905 had both immediate and long-term effects on the visual and performing arts. One of the massacres of unarmed demonstrators on Bloody Sunday took place directly outside the Academy of Arts and was witnessed by Serov, who was working in the building that fateful day and would later recall the horror in a painting and some terse illustrations for a satirical magazine. He and fellow artist Vasily Polenov wrote a letter to the directorate of the Academy expressing their dismay that the Academy's president, Grand Duke Vladimir Aleksandrovich, was in command of troops that 'killed defenceless people' and 'spilled our brothers' blood'.[8] Serov lobbied other artists to signal their protest as well, but ended up being something of a lone voice. He resigned from the Academy the following month, unable to countenance affiliation of any kind with an institution that had such firm links to the imperial military elite. Rimsky-Korsakov, for his part, sided with demonstrating students at the St Petersburg Conservatoire, for which he was dismissed from his post.

More broadly, the turbulence of 1905 augured a period of fevered activity as Russians agonised over the future of their country and questioned the nature of their own social, political or creative role. A new generation of Russian writers caressed their beloved language into poetry and prose of stunning sonority and lexical elegance. They included the peerless poet Anna Akhmatova (plate 26) and her husband Nikolai Gumilev (plate 25), who would later come to symbolise a moral and intellectual steadfastness in the face of the arbitrary executions of the secret police during the early Soviet period, and the purges and terrors of Stalin's reign.

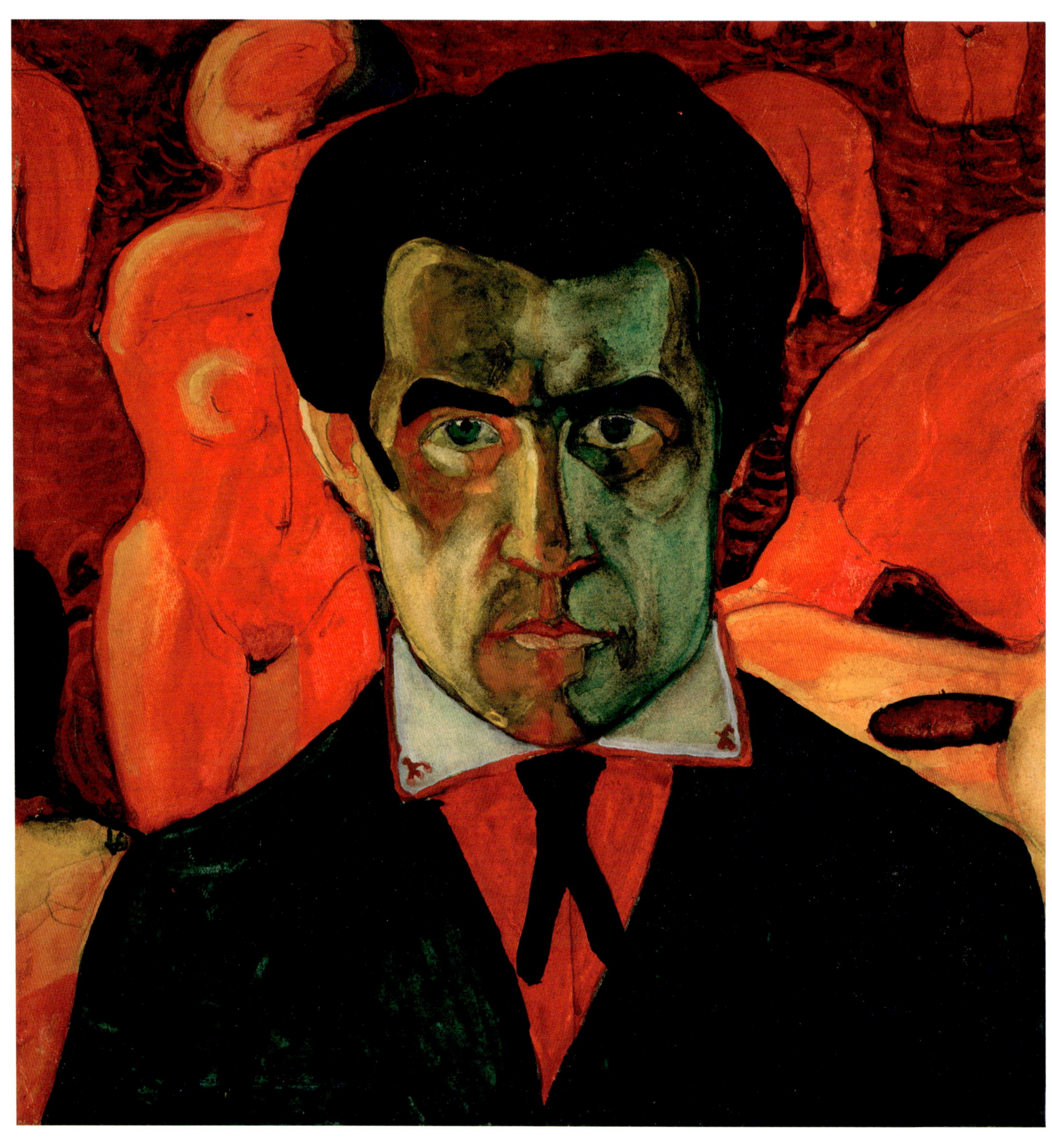

Fig. 5.6
Self-portrait
Kazimir Malevich, 1910

128

At the same time artists grouped and regrouped around a dizzying succession of publishing and exhibiting ventures that provided prominent platforms for the emergent avant-garde. Some of these projects sought to extend the dialogue with Western art. In 1908, for example, Mikhail Larionov organised his famed Golden Fleece exhibition in Moscow, which displayed the works of Gauguin, Van Gogh, Matisse, Derain and Braque alongside the likes of Tatlin, Malevich and Chagall. Others, including Larionov's partner Natalia Goncharova, foreswore their early fascination with Western innovation and trained their sights on the East.

Whatever their personal orientation, these and other members of the avant-garde increasingly turned away from naturalistic and mimetic figuration, and delved instead into a range of styles that veered from the cheerful exuberance of neo-primitivism and the agitated fragmentation of cubo-futurism, to forms of abstraction that bore no relation whatsoever to the visual world. These developments did not preclude portraiture. As Malevich's *Self-portrait* of 1910 demonstrates (Fig. 5.6), portraits could offer unusual and productive opportunities for the bold coloration and formal reductionism that many of these artists were so keen to explore.

The ground-breaking experiments of the avant-garde have acquired an international following and tend to overshadow the work of their predecessors. Yet they formed part of a Russian painting tradition of some two centuries' standing, in which portraiture had always played a vibrant role. From the deferential portraits of the early imperial rulers to the expressive images of the early twentieth century, portraitists not only advanced visual languages of great complexity, but provided a window on to Russia's sense of self. Never was this more true than in the half century that preceded the Revolution of 1917, when Russian portraitists reached an apogee of intellectual and aesthetic ambition, and recorded an astonishing spectrum of talent that Tretyakov gathered with such prescience on his gallery walls. Their paintings give the lie to perceptions of Russian art as imitative of Western painting, or as some alien entity that the foreigner can never truly understand. Indeed, Russian portraiture allowed for the articulation of values and achievements that demonstrated Russia's transcultural curiosity, and at the same time set her gloriously, self-confidently apart.

Notes

1   Jean Benedetti, *The Moscow Art Theatre Letters* (Methuen Drama, New York, 1991), p.3.

2   Vladimir I. Nemirovich-Danchenko, *Izbrannye pis'ma* (Iskusstvo, Moscow, 1979), vol. 1, p.123.

3   Nick Worrall, *The Moscow Art Theatre* (Routledge, London, 1996), p.68.

4   Beverly Whitney Kean, *French Painters, Russian Collectors: Shchukin, Morozov and Modern French Art 1890–1914* (Hodder & Stoughton, London, 1983), p.88.

5   Arseny's suicide took place in the home of the brother of the art dealer Ambroise Vollard, who recalled the shocking event in *Souvenirs d'un marchand de tableaux* (A. Michel, Paris, 1948), pp.158, 168.

6   Robert K. Massie, *Nicholas and Alexandra* (The Folio Society, London, 2002), p.103.

7   Ibid., p.106.

8   Letter from Serov and Polenov to the Council of the Imperial Academy of Arts, 18 February 1905, in *Valentin Serov v perepiske, dokumentakh i interviu*, ed. I.S. Zilbershtein and V.A. Samkov (Khudozhnik RSFSR, Leningrad, 1989), vol. 2, pp.12–13.

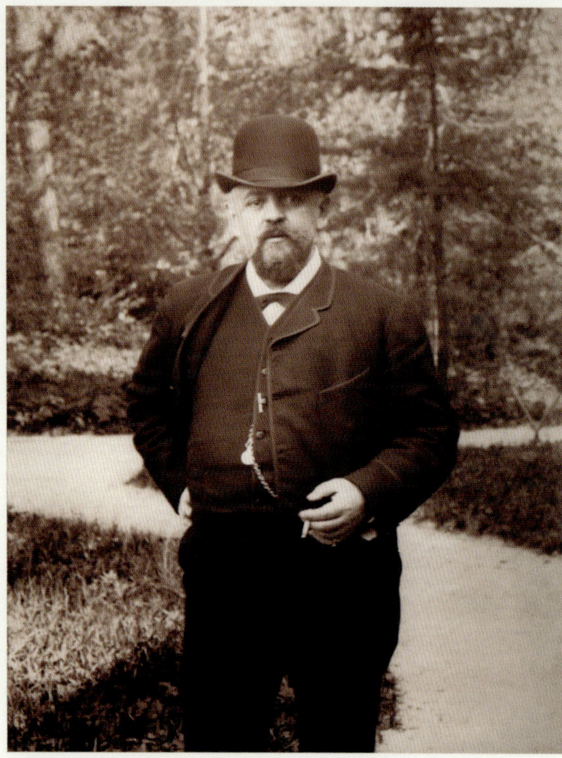

Fig. 5.7
Savva Mamontov
Unknown photographer, 1880s

Plate 20

Savva Mamontov
Mikhail Vrubel, 1897
Oil on canvas, 1890 x 1435mm

Mikhail Vrubel (1856–1910) graduated from the law faculty of St Petersburg University before studying in the Academy of Arts in the early 1880s, where he shared a studio with Valentin Serov and Vladimir Derviz. He then worked on frescoes and restoration work in St Sophia Cathedral and the twelfth-century Church of St Cyril in Kiev, which gave him a lasting love of Byzantine art. He also travelled to Venice, where he studied the technique and aesthetic impact of mosaics. These experiences, combined with a fascination in Symbolist thinking, led Vrubel to develop a highly individual style characterised by small blocks of colour arranged like tesserae, and the fragmentation of form into faceted planes. This was deployed in fantastical paintings and portraits, as well as decorative schemes for some of Moscow's most lavish mansions and public buildings, and led to Vrubel's election as an academician of the Academy of Arts in 1905.

Savva Mamontov (1841–1918), the railway magnate and artistic impresario, met Vrubel in the late 1880s and became his most loyal supporter for the next decade. Vrubel not only ran a highly experimental ceramics studio at Mamontov's estate of Abramtsevo and contributed designs to his Russian Private Opera, but joined the patron and his family on several trips to Europe. Mamontov also commissioned Vrubel to produce two vast mosaic panels for the All-Russian Exhibition in Nizhny Novgorod in 1896. When these were rejected by the selection committee, the incensed patron exhibited them in a specially built pavilion just outside the exhibition grounds, the sensation of which greatly popularised Vrubel's work.

Vrubel's portrait of Mamontov the following year carries no hint of gratitude or obeisance, however, but conveys the steely persistence with which the patron often bent artists to his will. Particularly striking are the powerful hands and formidable gaze, which form three points of a triangle around the bold white front of Mamontov's dress shirt. Even the painting of the still life on the table to Mamontov's left seems agitated and frenzied, as if mediating the irrepressible energy of this most dynamic of men whose interventions led to entirely new departures in Russia's visual and theatrical arts.

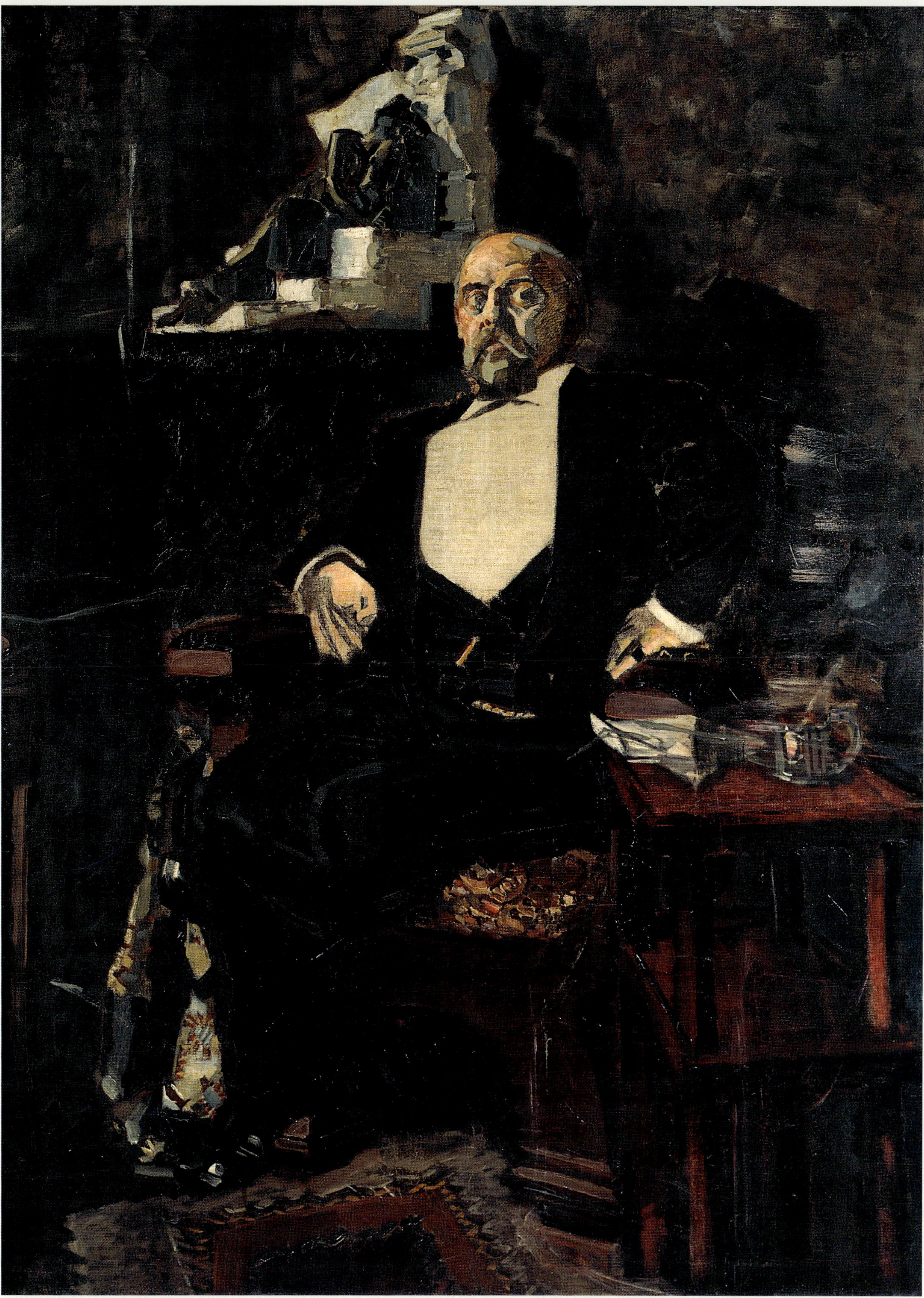

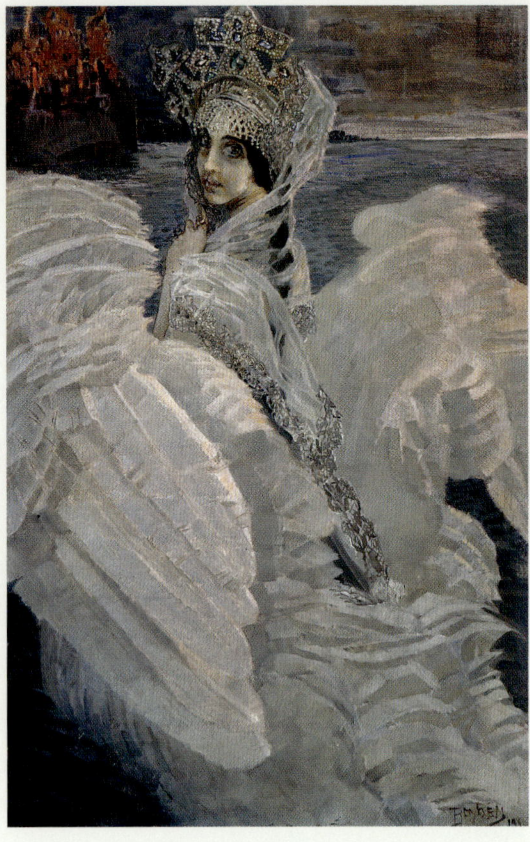

Plate 21

Nadezhda Zabela-Vrubel
Mikhail Vrubel, 1898
Oil on canvas, 1253 x 765mm

Fig. 5.8
The Swan Princess
Mikhail Vrubel, 1900

Mikhail Vrubel met Nadezhda Zabela (1868–1913), a talented soprano, in 1896, the year of his sensational association with the All-Russian Exhibition in Nizhny Novgorod (see page 130). They were married in Geneva later the same year and settled in Moscow, where Zabela-Vrubel joined the company of Mamontov's Russian Private Opera. Her performances included starring roles in the operas of Rimsky-Korsakov (plate 17), for which Vrubel often produced the set and costume designs.

Vrubel painted his wife on many occasions, including this luminescent portrait of 1898. The artist is at his eccentric best in the rendition of the outfit, with its outsize bonnet, pince-nez and primrose sash captured in thick, multidirectional brushstrokes. But he avoids any such effervescence in the portrayal of Nadezhda's face, which, in contrast to the expressive bravura of the outfit, is gentle and restrained. The portrait was painted on a farmstead belonging to Nikolai Ge, who took the troubled younger artist under his wing.

Despite Mamontov's downfall following charges of embezzlement in 1899, Zabela-Vrubel's career went from strength to strength, and Vrubel often painted her in role. In 1900, for example, he painted his wife as the Swan Princess in Rimsky-Korsakov's opera *The Tale of Tsar Saltan*, which premiered on the stage of the Russian Private Opera with sets and costumes to Vrubel's designs (Fig. 5.8). From 1904,

Zabela-Vrubel also performed with the Mariinsky Theatre in St Petersburg. Sadly, Vrubel's health was in sharp decline by this time. He was hospitalised for mental illness in 1902, and painted demons inspired by the poem *The Demon* by Mikhail Lermontov in an increasingly obsessive and frenzied manner. The following year his son died, leading to a howling anguish that often surfaced in the artist's work. In March 1910 he sat bare-chested at an open window throughout the freezing winter night, and died of pneumonia a week later, at the age of fifty-four. His wife followed him three years later, dying scarcely a month after giving her last concert in 1913.

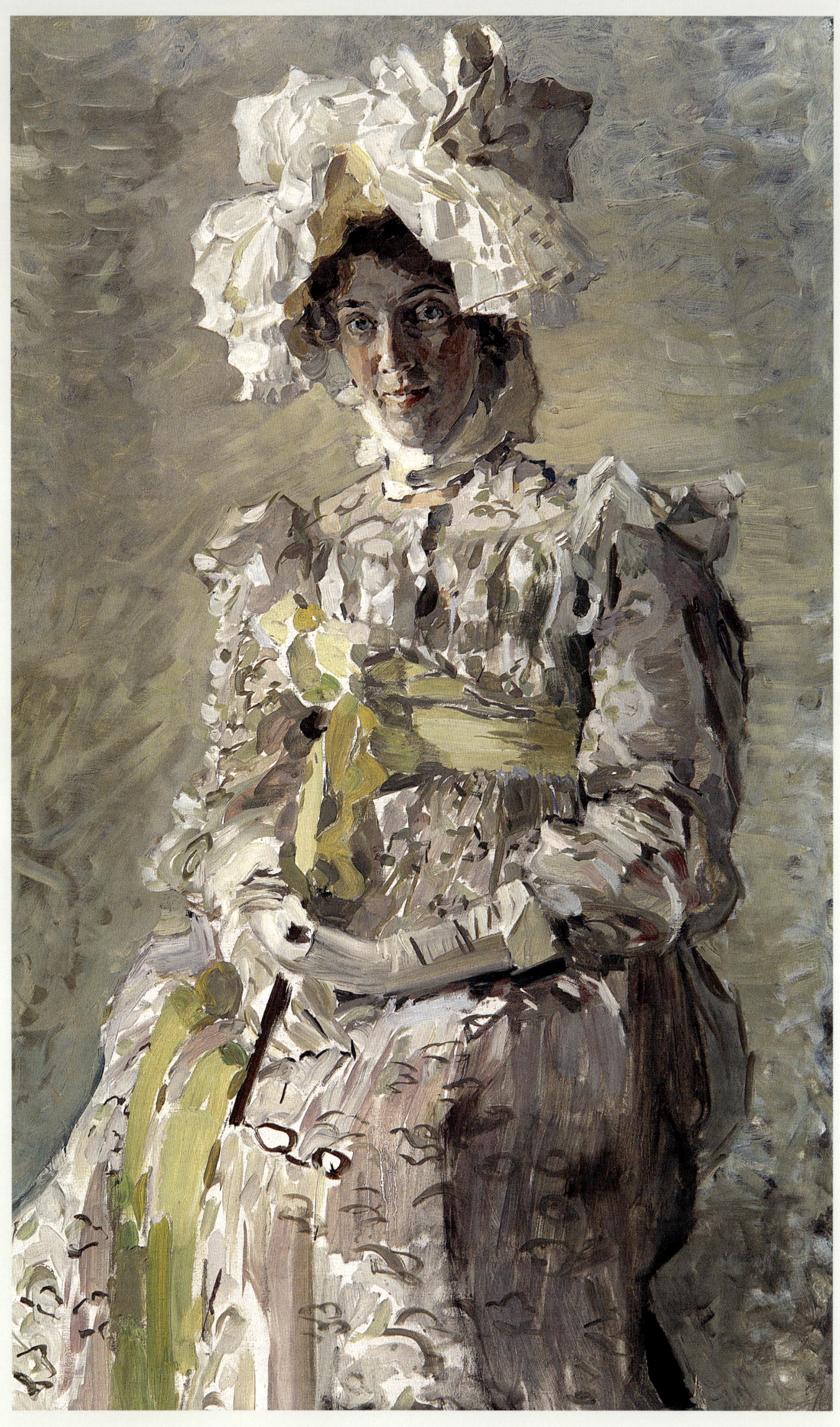

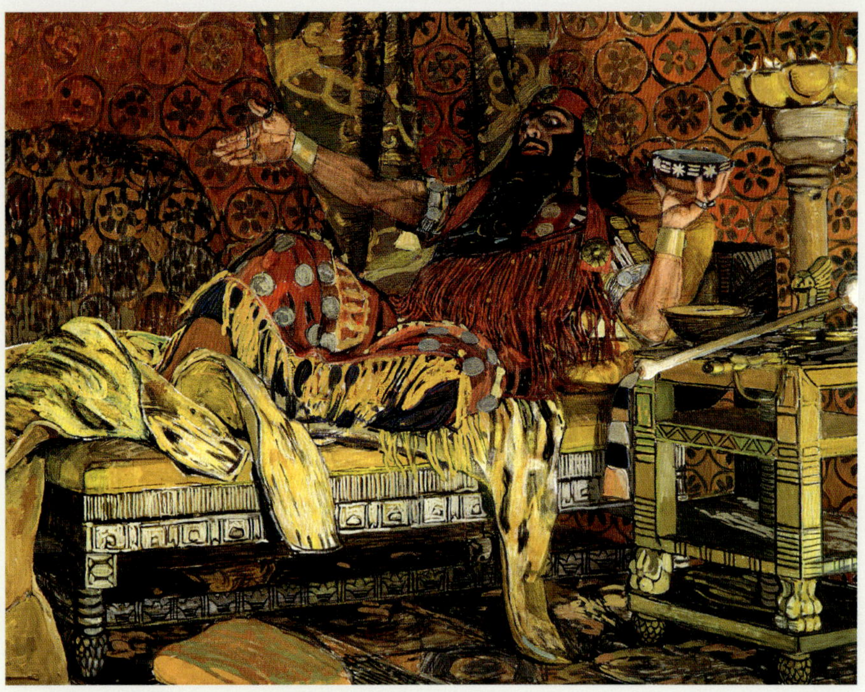

Plate 22

Fedor Shaliapin
Konstantin Korovin, 1905

Oil on canvas, 650 x 461mm

Fedor Shaliapin (1873–1938) was one of the greatest bass singers of his generation. He began his career at the Imperial Opera in St Petersburg in 1894 before joining Mamontov's Russian Private Opera, where he played *Faust's* Mephistopheles to great acclaim. Through Mamontov he met the composer and pianist Sergei Rachmaninov (Fig. 6.8), who became a friend for life and coached Shaliapin in many roles, including that of Boris Godunov in Mussorgsky's eponymous opera. Shaliapin's spectacular performance in Diaghilev's landmark production of this opera in Paris in 1908 helped to ensure the success of Diaghilev's ventures in Europe, and established the part of Boris Godunov as the singer's signature role.

On the strength of his success in Mamontov's company, Shaliapin was employed by the Bolshoy Theatre in Moscow and the Mariinsky Theatre in St Petersburg, and was portrayed on many occasions, his mobile features and melodramatic gestures offering rich pickings for a painter's brush. In 1908, for example, the artist and theatre designer Alexander Golovin portrayed Shaliapin in declamatory mode in the role of Holofernes in Alexander Serov's opera *Judith*, which had been staged in the Mariinsky Theatre the previous year (Fig. 5.9). The artist Konstantin Korovin (1861–1939), however, chose a more intimate approach. As a contributor to Mamontov's opera company and an established designer for the imperial theatres, Korovin had known Shaliapin for

years. This small, informal painting of the singer reading by a window (plate 22) registers both that friendship and the Impressionist influences that Korovin had absorbed during his many trips to France.

Shaliapin went on to enjoy an international concert and operatic career, with performances at La Scala in Milan, directed by Arturo Toscanini, and as far afield as Australia and the United States. He also played a major part in establishing the reputation in the West of Russian operas by the likes of Mussorgsky and Rimsky-Korsakov (plates 7 and 17). He lived abroad, in Finland and France, from 1921, and was buried in Paris on his death in 1938, but such is his stature in Russia that in 1984 his remains were transferred with great ceremony to the Novodevichy Cemetery in Moscow, where they now constitute something of a national shrine.

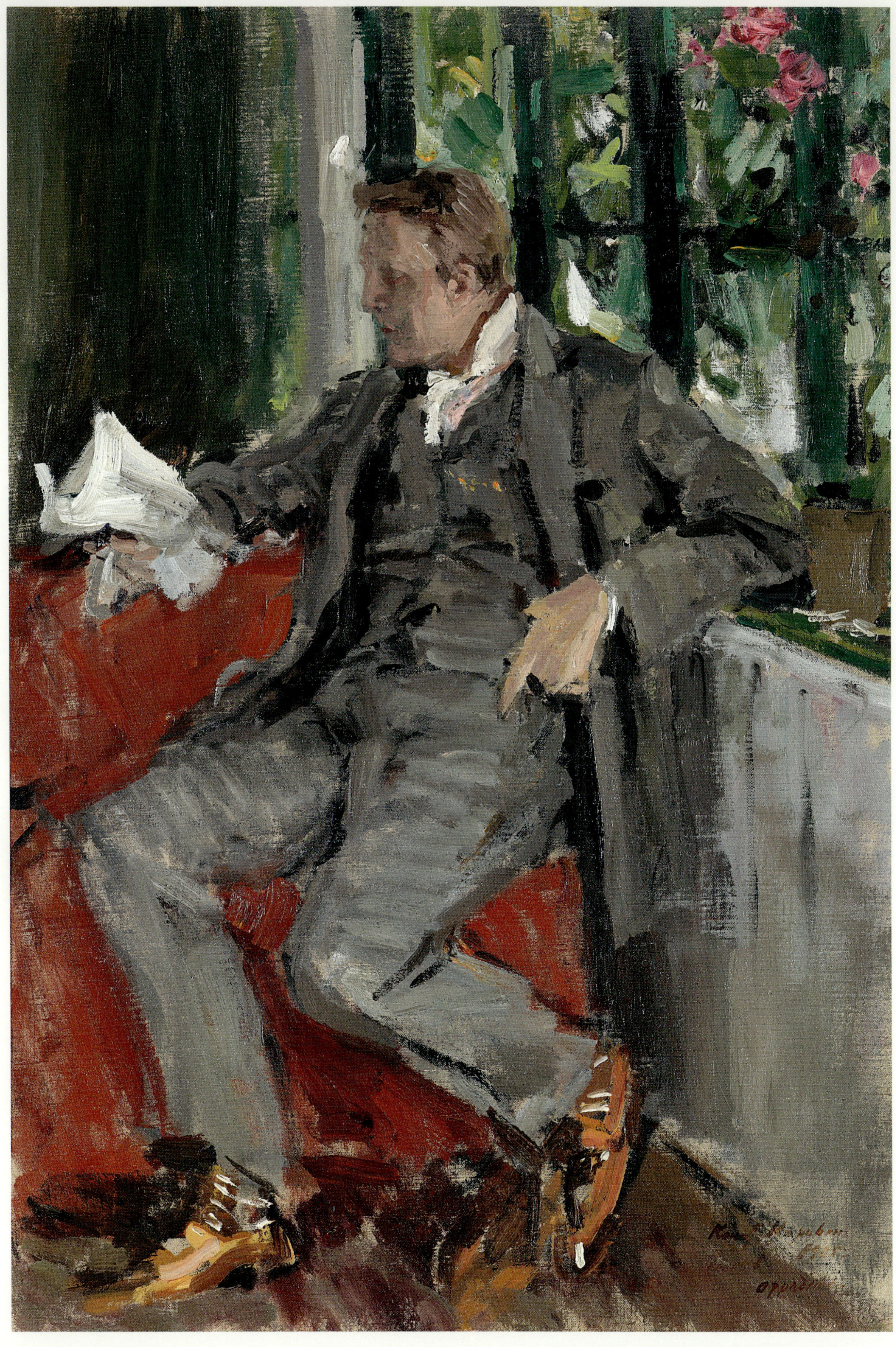

Maria Ermolova
Valentin Serov, 1905
Oil on canvas, 2240 x 1200mm

Maria Ermolova (1853–1928), the daughter of a theatre prompter, joined the company of the Maly Theatre in Moscow in 1871, where she was initially given relatively lowly if popular roles in vaudeville. In 1876, however, she was cast as Laurencia in Lope de Vega's _Fuenteovejuna_ (1619), which marked a turning point in her career. Ermolova's magnetic performance in this tale of popular uprising resonated powerfully with the younger and more progressive members of her audience, leading to demonstrations and the closure of the play by the authorities.[1] It nonetheless established Ermolova as the company's leading actress and led to acclaimed performances that spanned a period of some fifty years. Her greatest triumph was in Friedrich Schiller's _The Maid of Orleans_ (1801), which she played for eighteen years from 1884 to 1902. Other roles and plays were written specially for her, among them _Platonov_ (1878), Anton Chekhov's first major drama (plate 18). In this instance Ermolova rejected the offering from a relatively unknown newcomer, and it was not published until 1923.

Serov's portrait of 1905 was commissioned by the Moscow Literary and Artistic Circle, possibly to mark the thirty-fifth anniversary of Ermolova's career. It was painted in the drawing room of her apartment on Tverskoy Boulevard, one of Moscow's most elegant and fashionable addresses at the time. Striking in the first instance is Serov's audaciously low viewpoint, which accentuates the actress's commanding presence. Then there is his inventive treatment of the background, in which the dado and the frame and reflection of the mirror are reduced to a cool geometry of circles, arches and squares, all of which is dissected by the sweeping black of Ermolova's gown. The result is a powerful painting in a strongly modernist vein, as the articulation of walls and bodies is reduced to a brilliant pattern of intersecting shapes and lines. It confirmed the self-assurance of artist and sitter alike. Such was Ermolova's eventual stature that a theatre, a planet and a crater on Venus were named after her, and the director Konstantin Stanislavsky declared her to be the greatest actress that he had ever seen.

1   Martin Banham, _The Cambridge Guide to Theatre_ (Cambridge University Press, Cambridge, 1995), p.346.

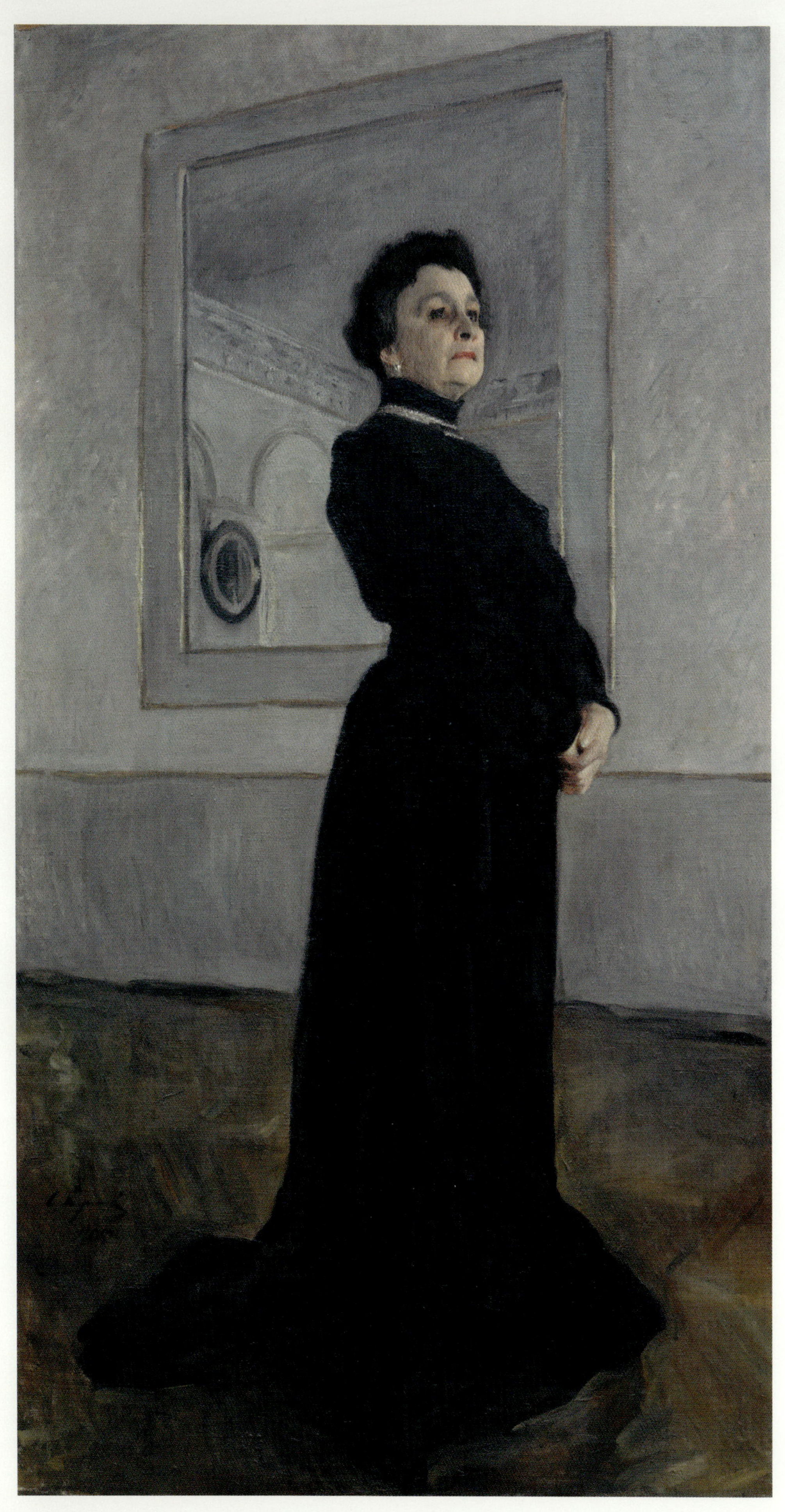

Ivan Morozov
Valentin Serov, 1910
Tempera on cardboard,
635 x 770mm

Ivan Morozov (1871–1921) was the most remarkable of an inordinately wealthy family of merchant-industrialists who established a distinguished record of patronage in theatre and the visual arts. He was tutored in painting by Konstantin Korovin, and as a young man began to collect Russian art. This included paintings by Serov, Vrubel, Larionov, Goncharova and Chagall, and eventually numbered well over a hundred Russian works. In 1903, however, Ivan's older brother Mikhail died and left Ivan his own collection of modern Western art, marking a watershed in Ivan's patronage. From then on Ivan acquired modern French paintings, including five by Monet, six by Renoir, eleven by Gauguin, thirteen by Bonnard, and no fewer than eighteen by Cézanne. He also owned twelve bronzes by Aristide Maillol and five paintings by Van Gogh.

When Serov painted Morozov in 1910, the patron's collecting activities were at a peak. His latest passion was for Matisse, by whom he eventually owned eleven paintings. In 1910 he acquired *Fruit and Bronze* (1910, Pushkin Museum of Fine Arts, Moscow) from the artist for 5,000 francs. Serov duly included this painting in the background of his portrait to acknowledge Morozov's trail-blazing patronage. The flattened forms and strong outlines of Serov's technique by this time stand witness to the impact that the paintings in Morozov's collection had on modern Russian art.

Morozov and his fellow collector Sergei Shchukin (1854–1936) led the field of patrons of Impressionist and Post-Impressionist painting. Their collections were nationalised after the Revolution, and were later divided between the Hermitage Museum in St Petersburg and the Pushkin Museum of Fine Arts in Moscow. The Shchukin and Morozov families have nonetheless never forsaken their right to the collections, and over the decades have made several unsuccessful attempts to have them returned.

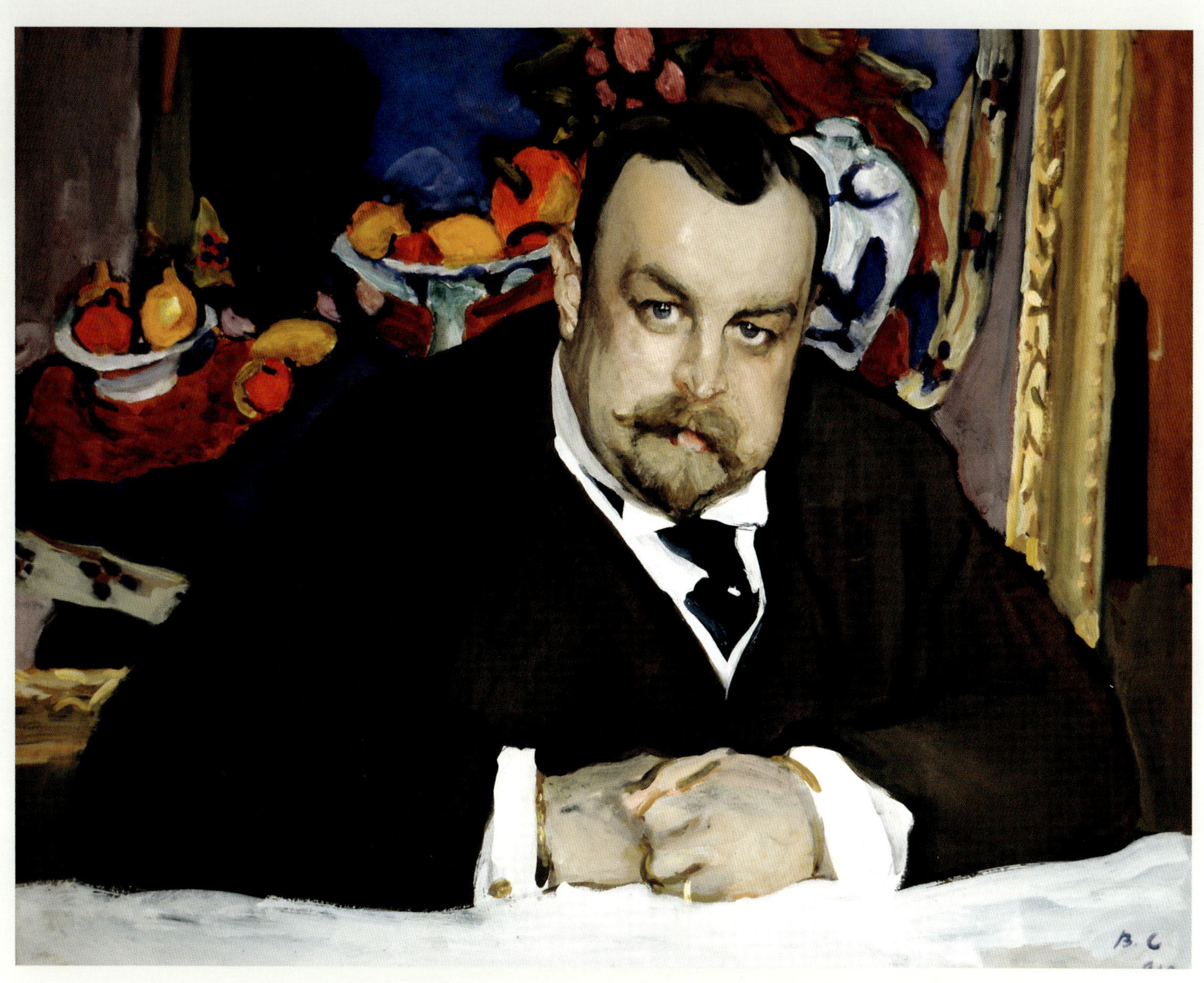

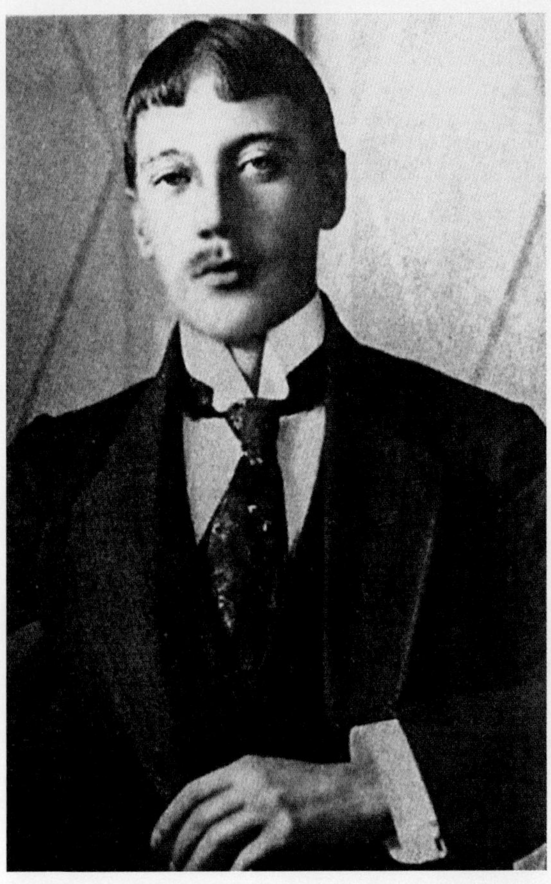

Plate 25

Nikolai Gumilev
Olga Della-Vos-
Kardovskaia, 1909
Oil on canvas, 1045 x 795mm

Olga Della-Vos-Kardovskaia (1875–1952), the daughter of a civil servant, studied in Kharkov and then in Repin's studio in the Academy of Arts, where she coincided with Iosif Braz (plate 18). Following her marriage to fellow artist Dmitry Kardovsky in 1899, she left the Academy and lived in Munich and the Crimea, before settling in St Petersburg in 1902. The following year she set up her own studio at Tsarskoe Selo, a small town outside the city, where one of the most magnificent imperial palaces is situated. She was also a founder-member of the New Society of Artists, an initiative launched by alumni of the Academy to organise exhibitions in St Petersburg and other towns of the Russian Empire, and to offer 'moral and material support' to students and graduates of the Academy.[1]

Della-Vos-Kardovskaia painted the poet and literary critic Nikolai Gumilev (1886–1921) at an exciting point in his career. Gumilev had recently published two thought-provoking collections of Symbolist poetry, *The Path of the Conquistadors* (1905) and *Romantic Flowers* (1908), and spent a year studying at the Sorbonne in Paris from 1907 to 1908. In 1909, the year of his portrait, he also founded the magazine *Apollon*, which became a seminal vehicle of Symbolism as both a literary and an artistic movement. Della-Vos-Kardovskaia intimates this Symbolist orientation in her portrait, in which an elongated and dandified Gumilev, with his immaculately parted hair, elegant moustache and Panama hat, adjusts a flower in his buttonhole in front of an ethereal landscape of mountains and trees.

The year after this portrait was painted, Gumilev married Anna Akhmatova (plate 26), with whom he began to question the legacy of Symbolism. Together they and a handful of other poets developed a new literary movement known as Acmeism, which developed notions of the 'poet-craftsman' who had a duty to express aesthetic, emotional and philosophical ideas with greater clarity and precision than had been the case in the mystical language of the Symbolists. Gumilev also travelled extensively in Europe and Africa, and enlisted in the Imperial Army one month after the Russian declaration of war in 1914, even though he had a medical exemption. 'The voice of war calls me,' he declared. His marriage with Akhmatova did not survive the lengthy separations, and they divorced in 1918. His stylistic complexity, cosmopolitan background and rhetorical flair found no favour with the new Soviet government, and he was executed for alleged counter-revolutionary activities in 1921.

1   Dmitry Severiukhin, *Staryi khudozhestvennyi Peterburg: rynok i samoorganizatsiia khudozhnikov* (Mir, St Petersburg, 2008), p.377.

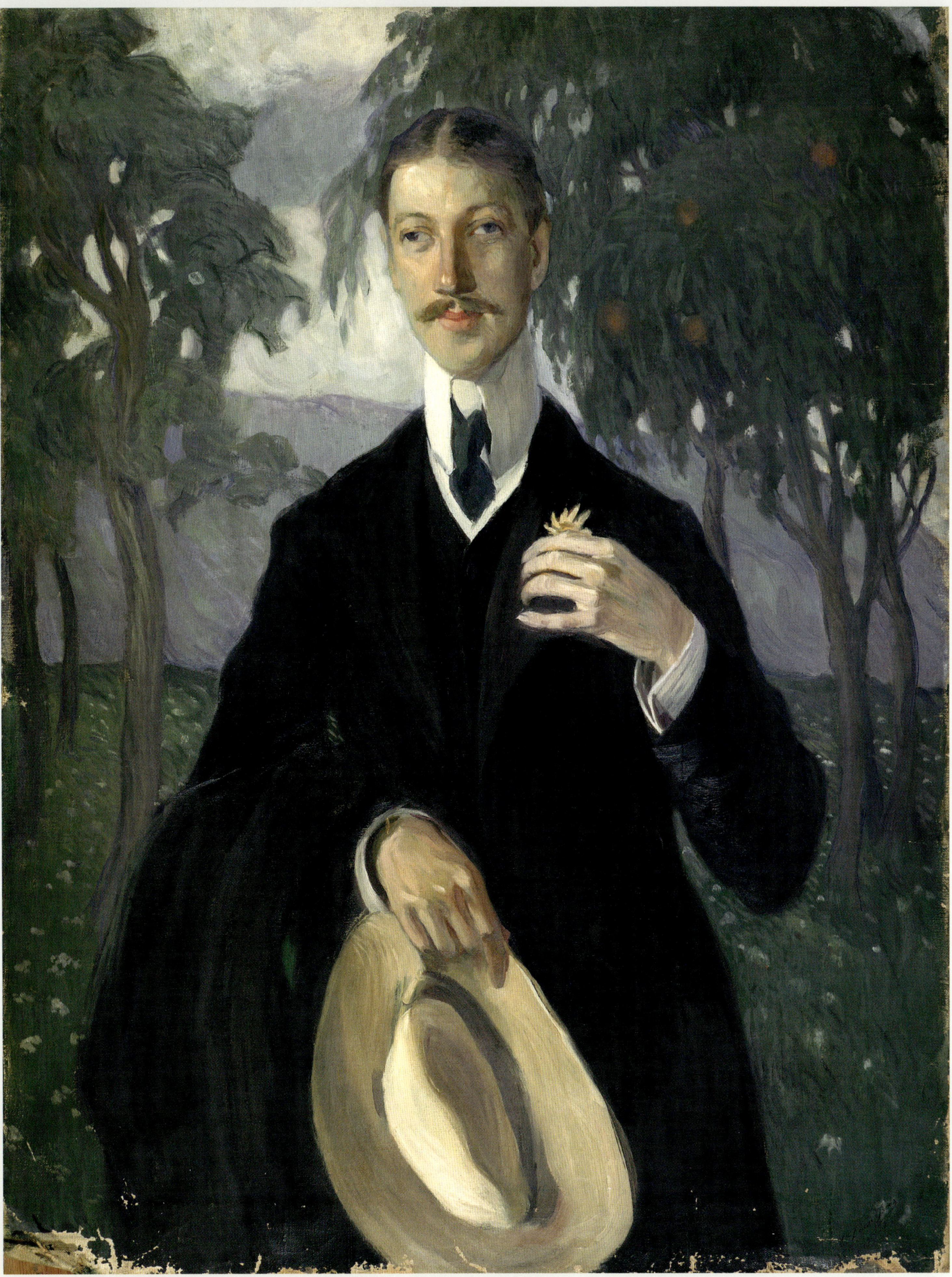

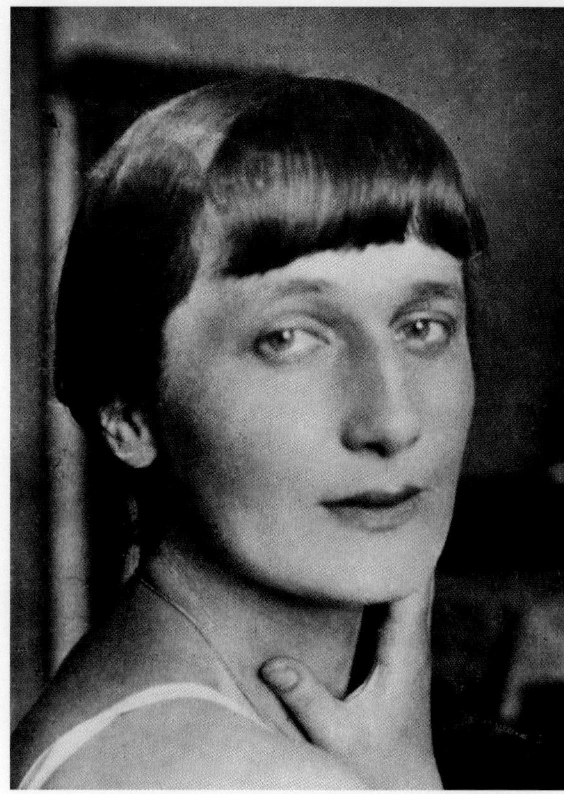

Fig. 5.11
Anna Akhmatova
Unknown photographer,
*c.*1925

Plate 26

Anna Akhmatova
Olga Della-Vos-
Kardovskaia, 1914
Oil on canvas, 860 x 825mm

Anna Akhmatova (1889–1966) was the daughter of a maritime engineer and an aristocratic mother who had once formed part of the violent revolutionary group that had orchestrated the assassination of Alexander II in 1881. Anna studied law at Kiev College for Women, but left to devote herself to literature. In a period that saw Russian poetry reach unprecedented heights, she became one of the most powerful poets of the century, forever loved by Russians for voicing horror at the atrocities of the Bolshevik and Stalinist regimes when so many were silenced. As she wrote in 1961:

> *No, not under the vault of alien skies,*
> *And not under the shelter of alien wings –*
> *I was with my people then,*
> *There, where my people, unfortunately, were.*[1]

Akhmatova met Nikolai Gumilev (plate 25) in 1903, and published her first poem in his journal *Sirius* in 1907. Following their marriage in 1910, they travelled abroad, in Paris befriending Amedeo Modigliani, who drew Akhmatova in the guise of Egyptian dancers and queens. A son, Lev, was born in 1912. The same year her first collection of poems, *Evening*, was hailed for the elegance and economy of its style. By 1914, the year of Della-Vos-Kardovskaia's portrait, Akhmatova was already established as one of Russia's most arresting young poets. In a composition that captures her unforgettably beautiful profile, she is stylish and self-

contained, a figure of stillness and contemplation amid the sweeping ochre shawl and rolling hills beyond.

The following years were ones of political persecution and personal anguish. After Akhmatova's divorce from Gumilev in 1918, her second husband tried to stop her writing by burning her poems. She bitterly mourned Gumilev's summary execution in 1921. Labelled an 'internal émigré', she was unable to publish her work after 1922, but continued writing, living with the art critic Nikolai Punin from 1926. Punin and Lev were both imprisoned during the mass arrests of the 1930s, in Lev's case simply for being Gumilev and Akhmatova's son. Under constant surveillance, Akhmatova burned her manuscripts and queued every day for months at a jail where Lev was held, among others desperate for news of their loved ones. Years later – although possibly as a literary device to confirm that she had been a witness to these events – Akhmatova claimed that a woman had recognised her in the queue one day and had whispered, 'Can you describe this?' 'Yes I can,' Akhmatova had responded, and recalled, 'something that looked like a smile passed over what had once been her face'.[2] The result was *Requiem* (1935–40, first published in Munich, 1963), the self-professed 'mouth through which a hundred million scream'.[3] Both a mother's anguished cry and a cycle of lament for Stalin's victims, *Requiem* became Akhmatova's best-known work.

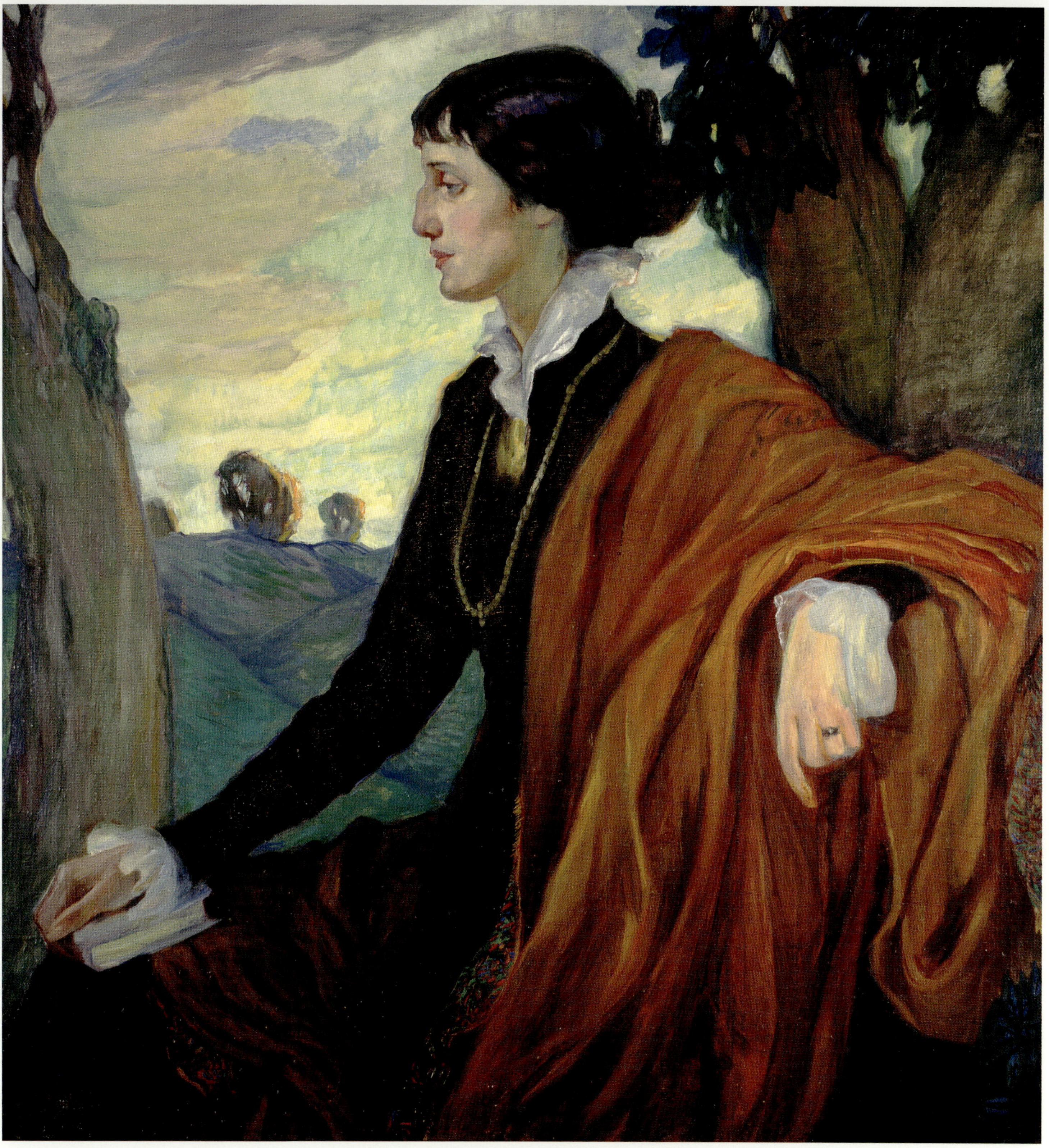

Punin died in the Gulag in 1953. After repeated arrests and incarcerations, Lev was finally released in 1956, during the Thaw. The ban on Akhmatova's poetry was gradually relaxed at the same time. She won the Taormina Prize for Poetry in 1964 and was awarded an honorary degree by Oxford University in 1965.

1   *The Complete Poems of Anna Akhmatova*, trans. Judith Hemschemeyer, ed. Roberta Reeder (Canongate Press, Edinburgh, 1992), p.384.

2   Ibid.

3   Ibid., p.393.

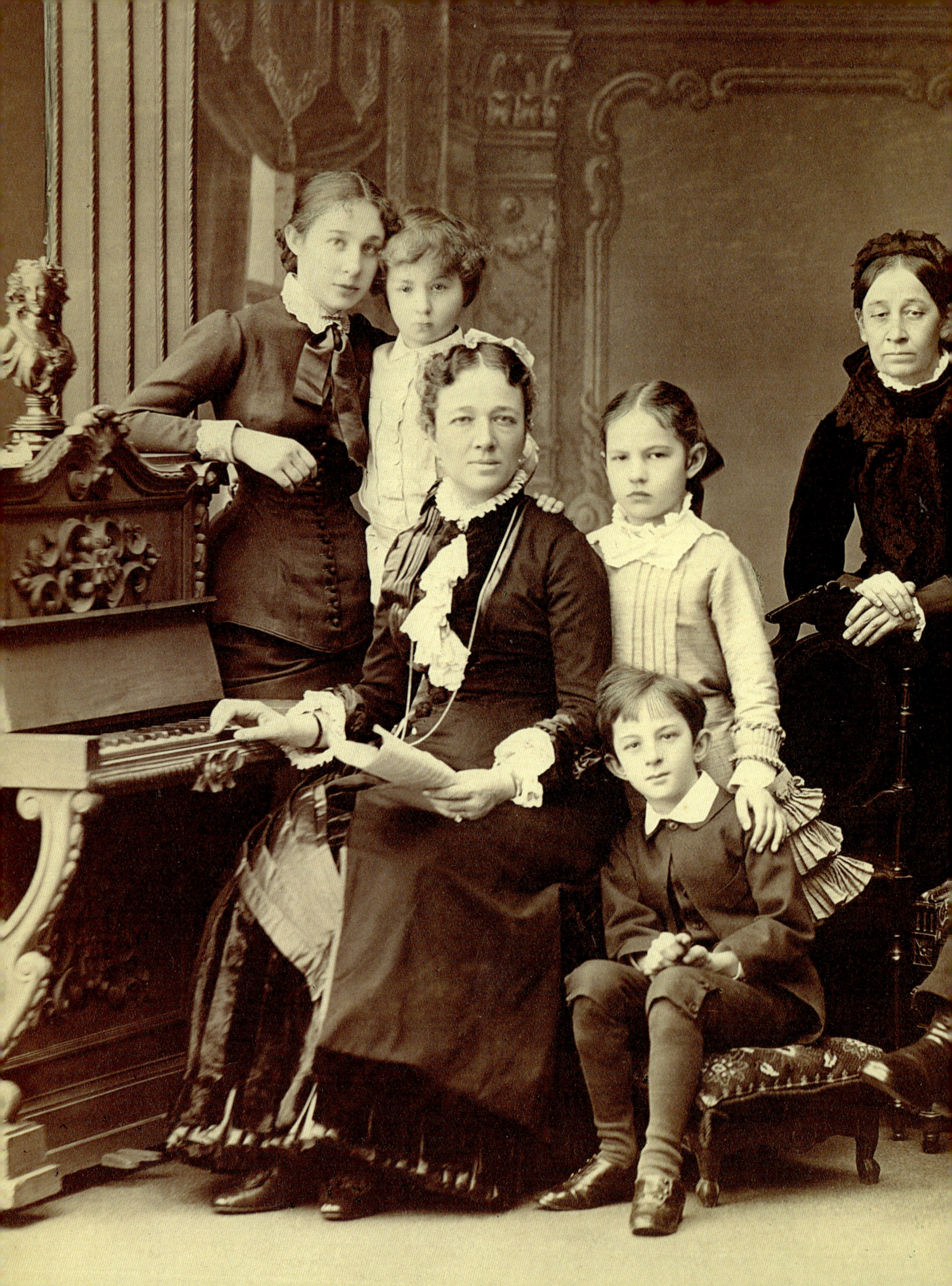

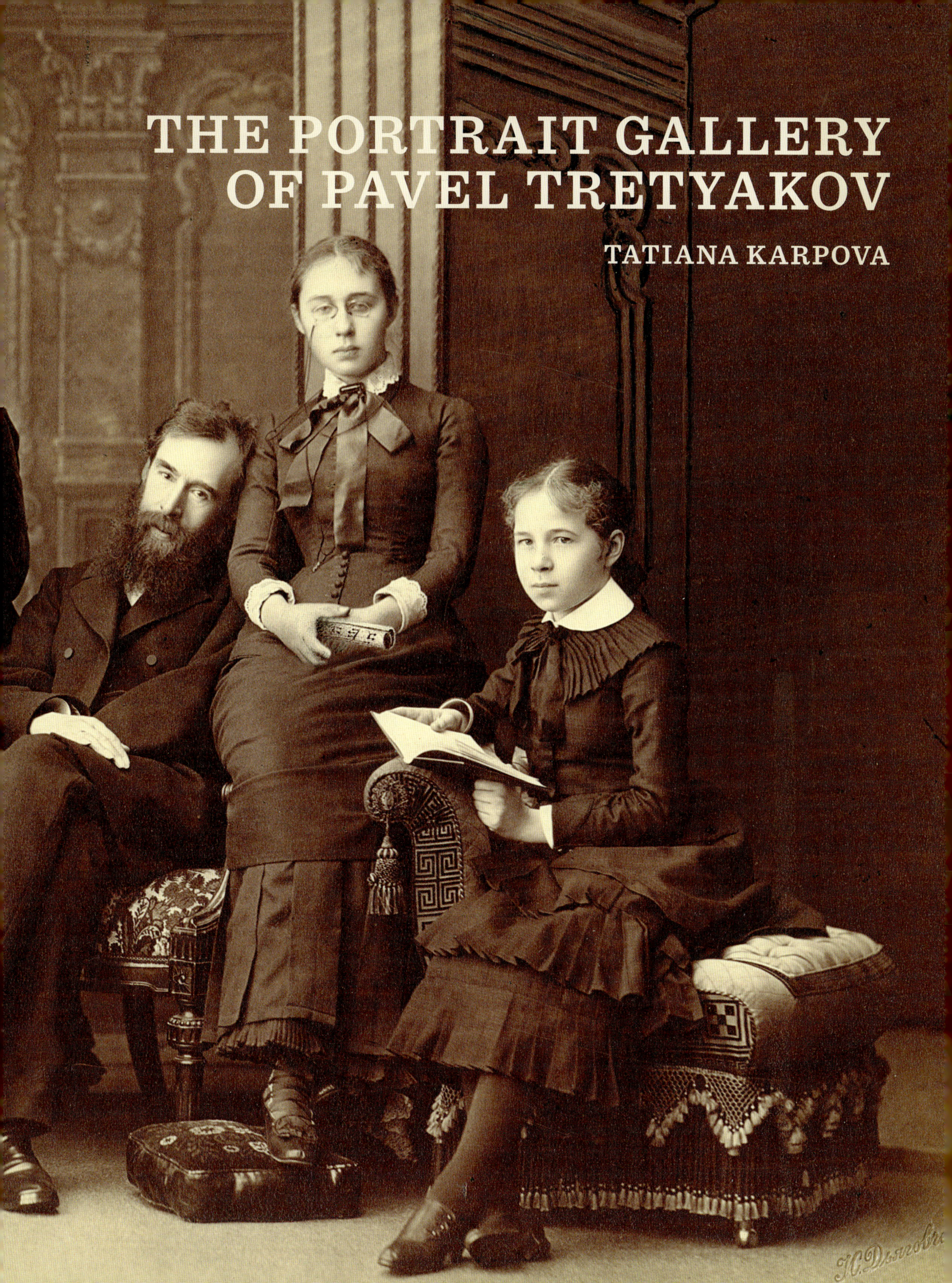

THE PORTRAIT GALLERY OF PAVEL TRETYAKOV

TATIANA KARPOVA

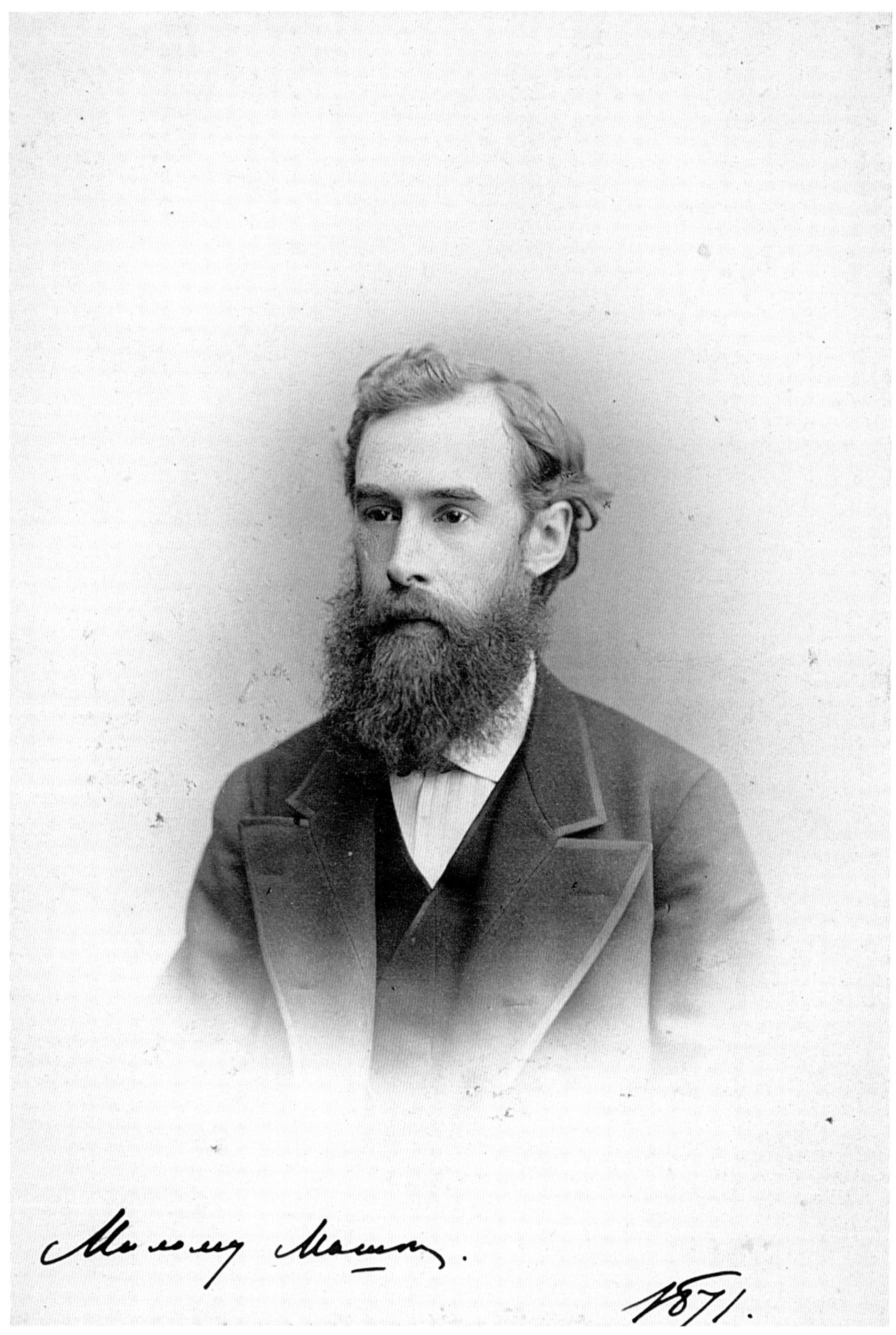

THE TRETYAKOV GALLERY owns a portrait collection that is unique in quality and historic significance. Its foundations were laid by the creator of the museum, Pavel Tretyakov (Fig. 6.1), who from the late 1860s began to commission and acquire portraits of outstanding figures in Russian culture: in his own words, he was interested in 'Russian writers, composers and, in general, figures from artistic and scholarly spheres'.[1] He was guided by two principles – the historical role of the sitter and the artistic value of the portrait – an approach that was continued after the collector's death. Tretyakov imagined his portrait collection as a museum within a museum – a national portrait gallery within a national gallery of art. With this aim in mind, the portraits were originally hung together. In the early 1880s, however, the rows of portraits were reconfigured and integrated into the halls devoted to individual artists.

Tretyakov's portrait collection had special significance in Russia in the second half of the nineteenth century, as it emerged alongside growing preoccupations with history, identity and spiritual growth. His initiative greatly stimulated the development of portraiture at the time, as many portraits were not commissioned by Tretyakov, but were painted with his collection in mind. The portrait gallery of the nation's most esteemed spiritual leaders, political thinkers and national consciences functioned as something of a moral landmark and reflected the nature of the Russian intelligentsia, with its stoic and messianic nature. The individual was seen as a beacon, a teacher of life, and the portrait as an icon of materialist and positivist thought. Collectively, the portraits acquired by Tretyakov thus formed a unique portrait-like iconostasis – a church screen on which icons were displayed – that expressed the notion of an ideal individual. Responding to the quest for self-awareness, the portrait gallery equally became a milestone in Russia's understanding of its own identity. As Russians endeavoured to grasp their distinctive national character, eager to see the country's history, art and science reflected in the lives of the people, so the portrait advanced the notion of an ideal citizenry in ways that had profound ramifications for the development of art and society alike.

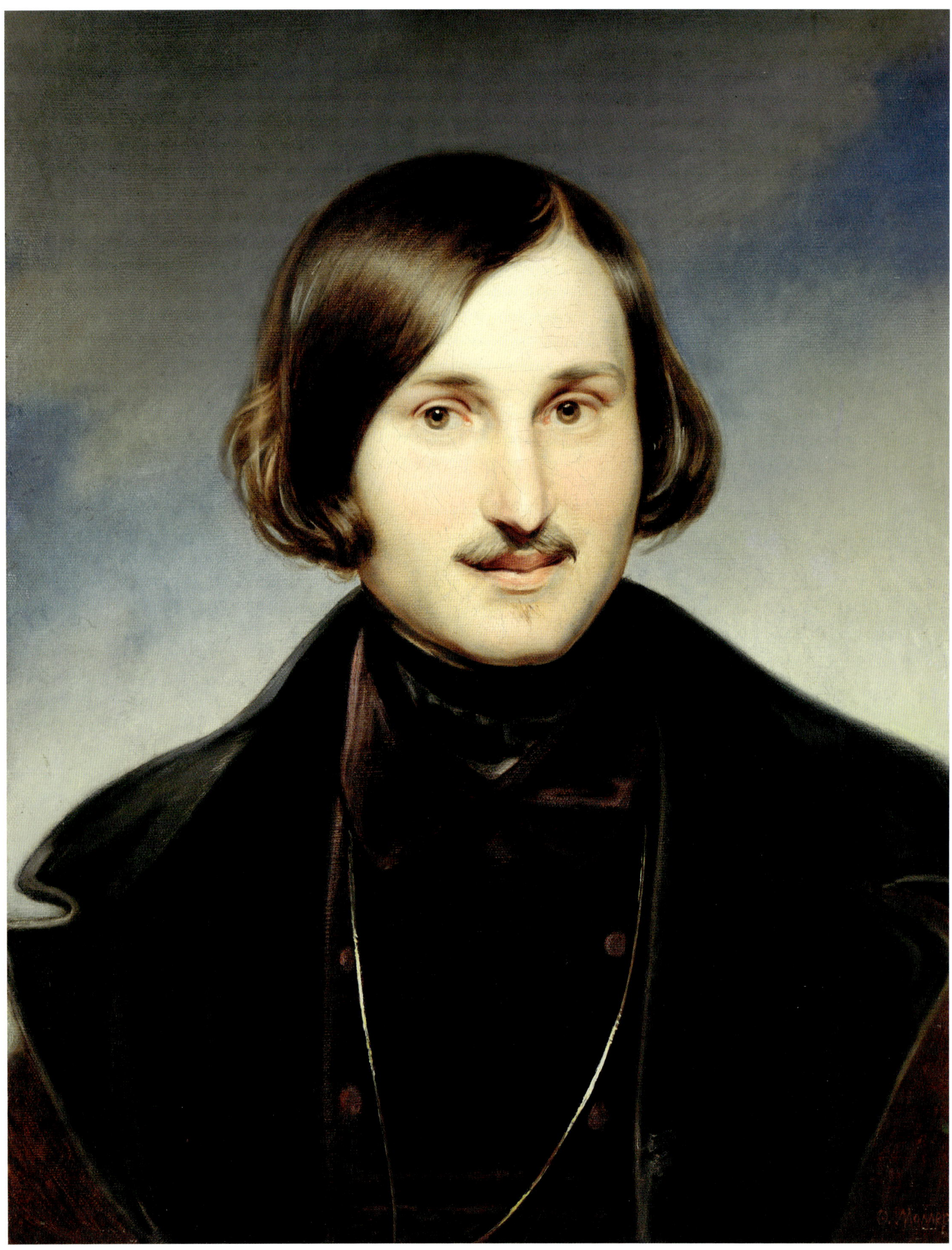

Tretyakov first commissioned a portrait in 1862, when he asked the artist Nikolai Nevrev to capture for posterity the character of the renowned actor Mikhail Shchepkin.[2] But it was not until the late 1860s and early 1870s that the collector began his explicit project to acquire and commission portraits of 'individuals whom the nation hold dear'. He paid particular attention to portraits made during the sitter's lifetime, and was fortunate to acquire the portrait of Nikolai Gogol by Fedor Moller (Fig. 6.2), and that of Alexander Pushkin painted by Vasily Tropinin in 1827 following a request from one of the poet's friends.

Tretyakov's gallery included portraits of those who were close to the collector in their views and convictions, and shared his idea of the socially significant figure who had made an exceptional contribution to Russian culture, science and public life. Pride of place was given to portraits of writers, for they were seen to be the nation's most representative teachers and bearers of truth, and dominated public attention. Their significance was confirmed in Tretyakov's gallery by paintings of Dostoevsky, Turgenev, Tolstoy and Chekhov (plates 4, 5, 11 and 18). Portraits of historians and writers with Slavophile leanings were also prominently displayed, including Alexander Ostrovsky (plate 2), Alexei Pisemsky (plate 6), Mikhail Pogodin and Nikolai Leskov. These writers devoted themselves to the search for national ideas by exploring the foundations of Russian culture and its intrinsic roots. Many of those portrayed, such as Pogodin and Dostoevsky, were members of the Moscow Slavophile Society, which the brothers Pavel and Sergei Tretyakov joined in the late 1860s, illustrating the closeness of the circles in which they and many of Pavel's sitters moved.[3]

In the Tretyakov family (Fig. 6.3), a passion for literature and art was matched by that for theatre and music. It was no coincidence that the first portrait that Tretyakov commissioned was of the actor Shchepkin, who had taken part in the first productions of works by Griboedov and Gogol, and captivated Tretyakov with his performances. Other masterpieces in the collection included portraits of the dramatic actress Pelageia Strepetova, who was painted by Repin (Fig. 6.4) and Iaroshenko (plate 10), and images of famous musicians and composers such as Modest Mussorgsky, Nikolai and Anton Rubinstein and Petr Tchaikovsky (plates 7, 8 and 15). Among the last portraits of a composer to enter the collection, in the year of Tretyakov's death, was Valentin Serov's portrait of Rimsky-Korsakov (plate 17). One of the most beloved composers in Russia, he developed the national theme in music, not least in operas on the subject of Russian folk tales and fables, such as *Snow Maiden* and *Sadko*.

The preponderance of male sitters in Tretyakov's collection is striking. This was particularly the case in the 1860s–1880s, when philosophical and anthropological enquiry was pursued in portraits of men but rarely women. Contemporaries commented on this. For a reviewer in the journal *New Time* in 1873, 'It is impossible not to notice the extreme monotony at the portrait exhibition – not a single female face on which the eye can rest amidst constant contemplation of Russia's great men.'[4] If portraiture of the 1860s–1880s was primarily based on the male dominant, however, at the turn of the century it was the female who often stood to represent humankind, leading to outstanding portraits of women in the work of Serov and Vrubel (plates 16 and 21). Radical changes in the status of women in society were equally reflected in portraiture of the twentieth century, for example in the compelling self-portraits by Natalia Goncharova and Zinaida Serebriakova (Fig. 6.5), and the portraits of Anna Akhmatova by Olga Della-Vos-Kardovskaia (plate 26), and Vera Mukhina by Mikhail Nesterov.

A major preoccupation for Tretyakov was which artists to select to execute his commissions. He relied on his intuition to seek out those who could meet his aim of combining artistic quality with physical likeness and documentary authenticity. Striving for excellence in his collection, Tretyakov often commissioned portraits of the same figure from different artists. Pisemsky, for example, was painted for the collector by Perov and later by Repin (plate 6), and great effort was expended to secure a satisfactory portrait of Turgenev, which proved elusive. Tretyakov repeatedly commissioned his portrait from the likes of Perov,

Fig. 6.2
Nikolai Gogol
Fedor Moller, early 1840s

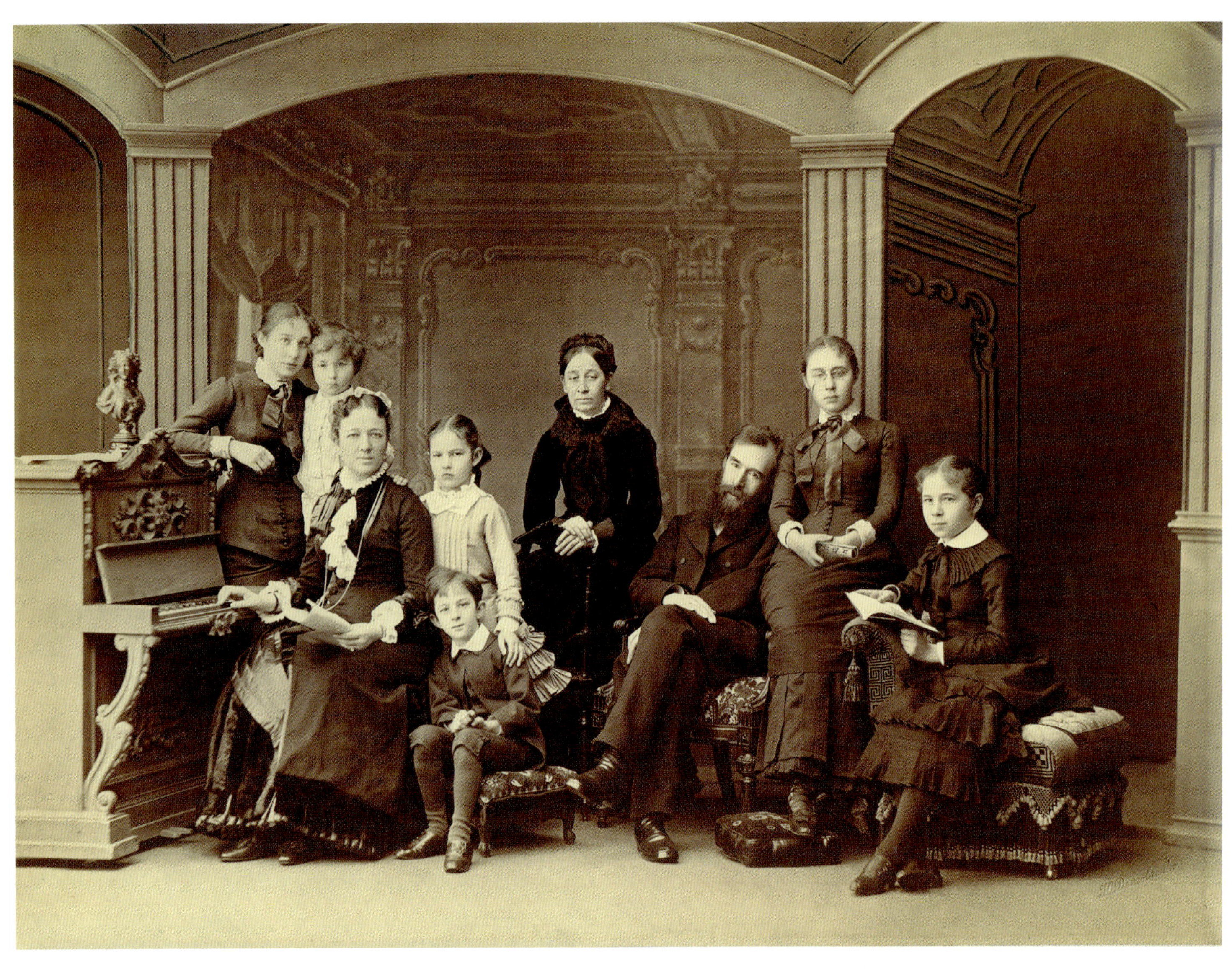

Fig. 6.3
Pavel Tretyakov and his family (left to right: Vera,
Ivan, Pavel's wife Vera, Maria, Mikhail (sitting in
the front), Maria Ivanovna, Pavel, Alexandra
and Liubov)
Photographed by I. Diagovchenko, 1884

Fig. 6.4
Study of Actress Pelageia Strepetova
Ilia Repin, 1882

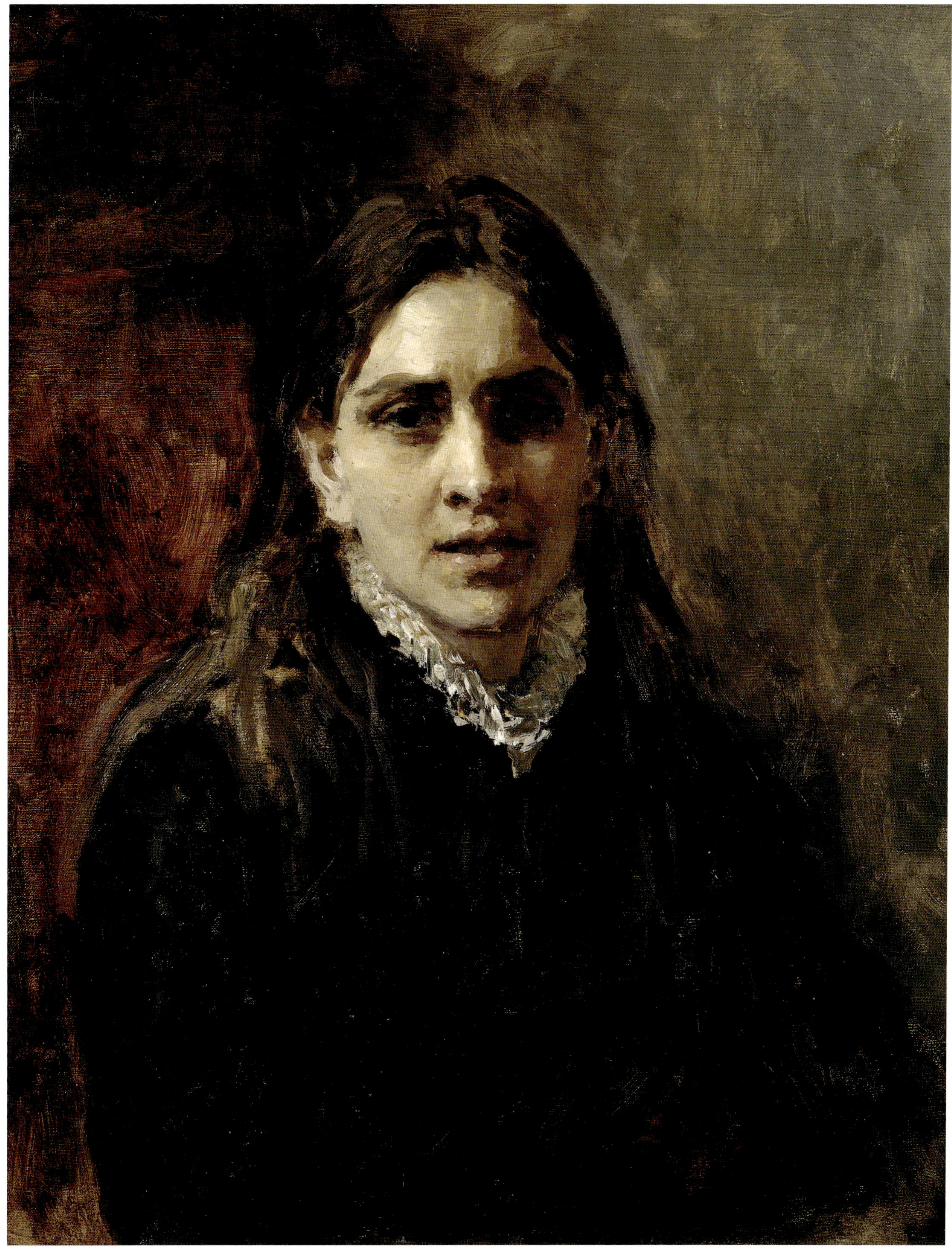

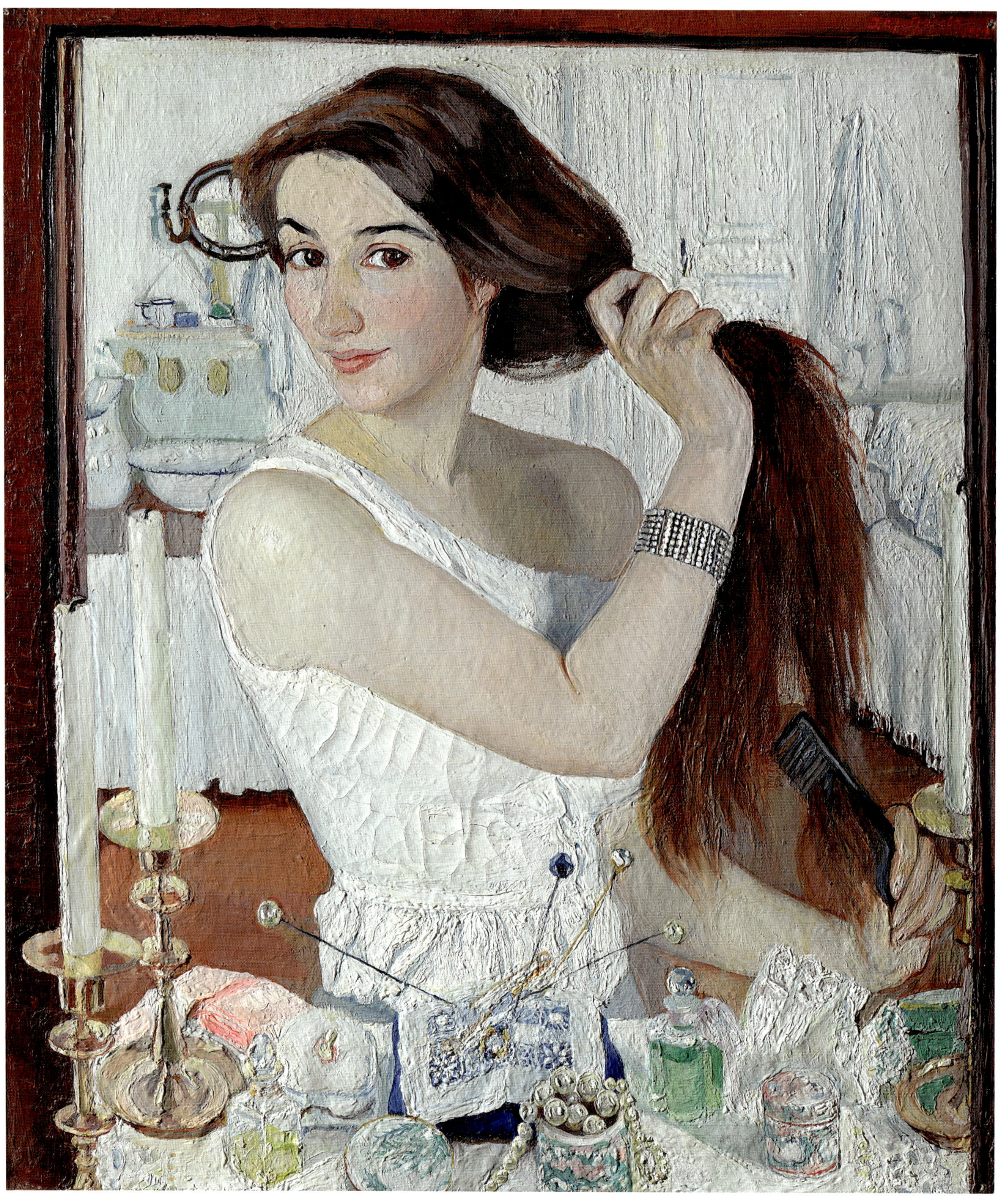

Repin (plate 5) and Kramskoy, aiming for a painting that caught the writer's internal and external qualities alike.

Tretyakov tried to avoid acquiring painters' copies, searching instead for original works of art. At times, though, he was forced to rely on copies. Perov made a copy for Tretyakov of a portrait of Mikhail Lermontov that had been painted from life by Petr Zabolotsky in 1837. Likewise, in 1873 Kramskoy painted a portrait of the playwright Petr Karatygin from a watercolour by Alexander Griboedov. On other occasions, Tretyakov sometimes commissioned portraits from photographs. These included Kramskoy's portraits of the writers Taras Shevchenko and Sergei Aksakov, and Repin's of Mikhail Glinka.

The second half of the nineteenth century marked an apogee of portraiture in Russia. This was a period of intense reflection on the question of individual identity and its relation to social and moral responsibility – a time that saw the rise of psychological enquiry into human nature in literature, theatre and the visual arts (it was no coincidence that in the 1870s, psychology became an independent scientific discipline). The art of portraiture reflected these developments, becoming one of the ways in which individuals were able to understand themselves and the society in which they lived.

Artists and critics in the 1860s–1870s agonised over the question as to who could and should be a sitter for a portrait. 'Who are the holy, the heroes, the knights and sympathisers of the nation, both now and in the recent past?' demanded Kramskoy.[5] As earlier authorities fell from grace, there was a driving need to find new moral exemplars, particularly in the aftermath of the reforms of the 1860s. 'Where is the universally acknowledged paragon now?' pondered Dostoevsky in *A Writer's Diary* (1876): 'What and whom should be honoured by society, and whom should it emulate? ... Who will now be considered exemplary, and, crucially, where will they come from, where will we find them, who will be responsible for naming them the best, and on which grounds?'[6] These questions preoccupied the intelligentsia of the 1870s. Vladimir Meshchersky even wrote an article called 'People, where are the people?' that appeared in *The Citizen* in 1873. The numerous public and private portrait exhibitions and collections that emerged at the time in their own way answered the questions raised by Dostoevsky, revealing an emergent philosophy of the individual, and the ways in which Russians could now identify those paradigmatic figures who exemplified modern Russian life.

In the wake of these developments, a new type of family portrait gallery arose during the 1860s–1870s. Previously, the rows of family portraits in city mansions and country estates had represented the social elite of Russia – the nobility – who for over a century and a half had stood at the head of the nation as, in Dostoevsky's words, the 'guardian and bearer of the rules of honour'.[7] As the nobility was gradually unsettled from its pedestal, however, Russians began to concern themselves less with status in order to focus on the virtue of the individual. This raised the question as to what should be done with the older collections of portraits – consign them to the attic, or augment them with portraits of new heroes? Tretyakov chose to resolve this problem by acquiring portraits from earlier generations, such as those of the poets Pushkin and Nikolai Karamzin (Fig. 6.6). The example that he set of incorporating old paintings with new commissions continued long after his death, for portraits from family collections greatly enlarged the holdings of the Tretyakov Gallery after the Revolution of 1917.

A second difference to emerge concerned the priorities of collectors. Typically, a noble portrait gallery had centred on family portraits, which were enhanced by depictions of imperial rulers and close friends. The collector of the second half of the nineteenth century, by contrast, was keen to represent himself alongside his historical predecessors and spiritual forebears. Collections of this type acquired a highly idiosyncratic character that reflected the personal history of the collector and his family within a broader social and cultural context. There was a need to identify forefathers within the broader history of humankind.

Fig. 6.5
At the Dressing-Table. Self-portrait
Zinaida Serebriakova, 1909

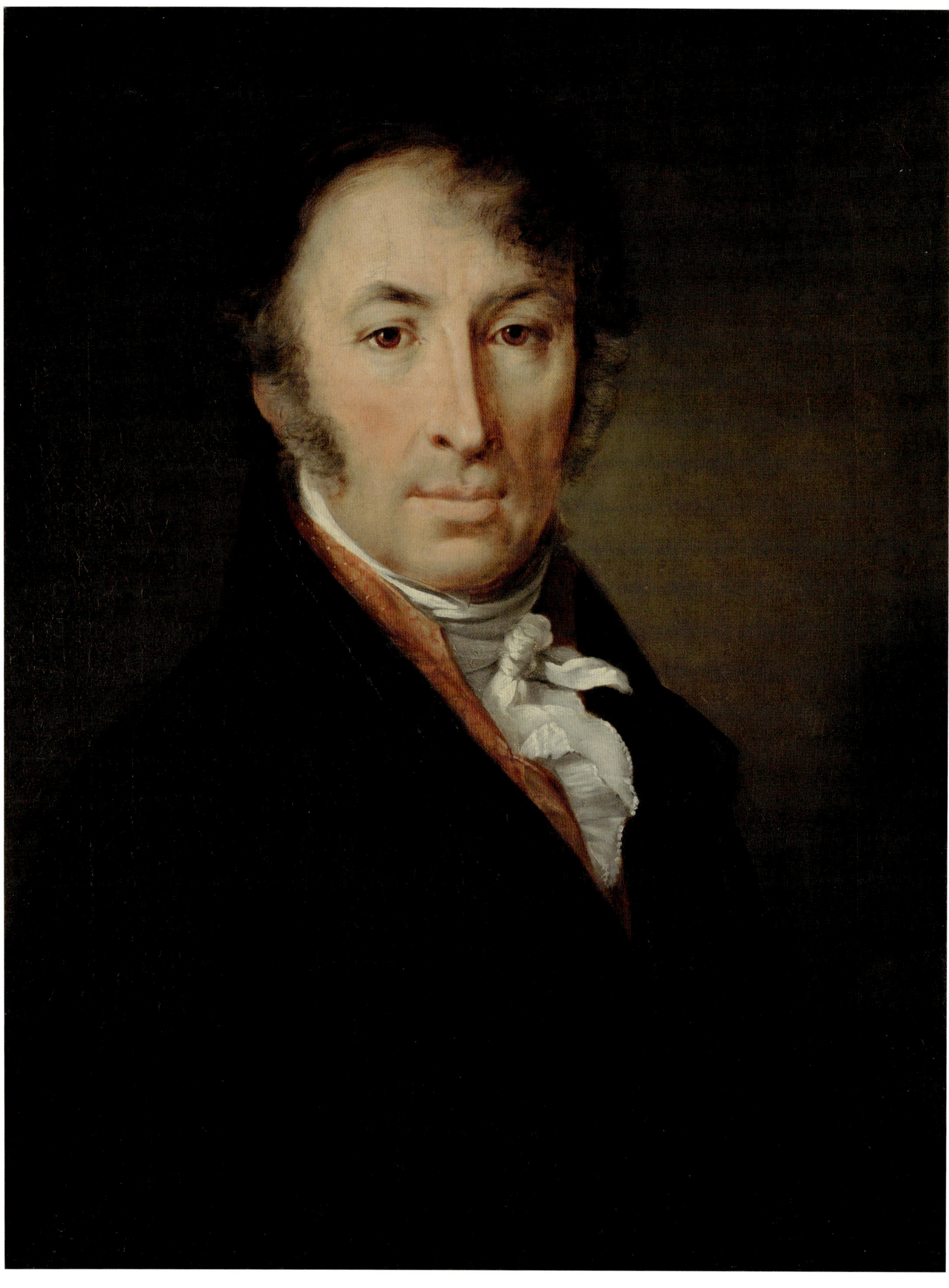

This desire was characteristic not only of the educated intelligentsia, who did not always have an extensive past genealogy, but of those of gentry origin too. Nikolai Ge, for example, surrounded himself with portraits of writers he had read, made a bust of the eminent critic Vissarion Belinsky, and copied Kiprensky's portrait of Pushkin (Fig. 2.3). He later offered these portraits to Tretyakov for his gallery, where they appealed as much to a wide audience as to the individual for whom they had been painted.

A final difference concerned the rate at which collections formed. The galleries of the eighteenth and the first half of the nineteenth centuries developed gradually, with each generation adding its own portraits to a family collection that grew slowly and organically. Now, however, man established his own historical and spiritual leanings by assembling what was seen to be a complete collection within one lifetime.

The private portrait galleries of the second half of the nineteenth century contained within them the embryo of a national portrait museum. The idea to found a national portrait gallery was further strengthened by exhibitions of historical portraits, of which there were four in Moscow and St Petersburg in the second half of the nineteenth and early twentieth centuries.[8] The family's portrait heirlooms left their ancestral estates to feature in these retrospective portrait exhibitions, thereby moving from the private to the public sphere.

The English tradition of exhibitions and museum displays of portraits, originating in the first third of the nineteenth century and culminating in the foundation of the National Portrait Gallery in London in 1856, had a significant impact on comparable initiatives in Russia. Notably, the first portrait exhibition held in Moscow in 1868 was the brainchild of L.N. Panin, secretary of the Moscow Society of Art Lovers, who in England had seen an exhibition of portraits of outstanding citizens comprising works by Hans Holbein the Younger, Anthony Van Dyck, Joshua Reynolds and Thomas Gainsborough. The idea of representing living history through images of people captivated Panin, and he tried to apply it to Russia. Tretyakov himself may have been inspired by the National Portrait Gallery, for he was in London on business in 1862, 1863 and 1865, is known to have visited exhibitions and museums, and began to commission and acquire portraits shortly after his return home.[9]

It is significant that England produced the first national portrait gallery, presenting the history of the nation through its people, uniting political figures of different persuasions, friends with their enemies, and creating a dialogue across generations. The Slavophile Alexei Khomiakov saw in Joseph Paxton's Crystal Palace the crux of English attitudes to the old-new paradox; he was struck by 'the ancient trees of Hyde Park, that no one dared to cut down' within the construction of the ultra-modern architectural structure.[10] The path of Russia's historic development, fraught as it was with harsh upheavals and the sense of a permanently fractured society, perceived England first and foremost as a country of good temperament and tradition, and as the owner of a stable middle culture whose absence in Russia was so acute.

Russia's public portrait displays owed much to the underlying desire to create a model that could transcend its divided society. In the late 1860s, for example, the director of the Rumiantsev Museum in Moscow, Vasily Dashkov, had used his private funds to commission from the likes of Kramskoy, Repin, Serov and Viktor Vasnetsov a 'gallery of portraits of historic Russian figures, in the style of monochrome copies from old original paintings, prints and photographs'.[11] Dashkov's subjects were primarily those who had served the empire with distinction and helped to strengthen the Russian state, yet his pantheon also included scientists, writers, artists and actors. The best-known publication of the lithographic studio of Alexander Miunster, the two-volume *Portrait Gallery of Russian Figures* (St Petersburg, 1865–9), similarly included famous writers and thinkers alongside monarchs and grand dukes. (Miunster's album, as well as Dmitry Rovinsky's *Detailed Dictionary of Russian Engraved Portraits*, was in Tretyakov's library.)[12] These initiatives reflected a basic human need for images of figures of public significance, and were equally in step with the field of 'historical iconography' that had emerged in the discipline of history in recent years.

The portrait galleries and publications that appeared in Russia in the middle of the nineteenth century were symptomatic of profound socio-political change. In the words of Dostoevsky, 'the gates of the social classes have only recently been opened here; it is now time to open them permanently. Let every act of honour, science and valour give anyone the right to join the highest ranks of people.'[13] Tretyakov founded his portrait gallery in similar vein, vowing not to include emperors, generals and other official figures, but leading lights in scientific, cultural and intellectual life, such as Dmitry Mendeleev (Fig. 6.7). The Tretyakov Gallery has maintained that practice to this day, and owns very few portraits of high officials, generals or church prelates.

Tretyakov's gallery and other new portrait galleries also responded to the search for national identity, as the French critic Eugène-Melchior de Vogüé recognised: 'one cannot praise enough the patriotic idea of ... M. Tretyakov to combine in his gallery portraits of those people who have acquired greatest fame over the last thirty years in literature and art. This collection will be a precious document for the future, and is already very instructive for a foreigner. These characteristic types belong to another era, and are driven by different ideas.'[14] In this respect the portrait galleries of the nineteenth century followed the fashion of the period to see history in terms of the biographies of great men. In the words of the Scottish writer Thomas Carlyle, founder and trustee of the National Portrait Gallery: 'Universal History, the history of what man has accomplished in this world, is at bottom the History of the Great Men who have worked here. They were the leaders of men, these great ones; the modellers, patterns, and in a wide sense creators, of whatsoever the general mass of men contrive to do or to attain.'[15] Carlyle's writings were widely known in Russia. In 1856, *The Contemporary* journal published a summary of his book *On Heroes, Hero-Worship and the Heroic in History*, and the book itself was later translated into Russian and reissued numerous times. Those whom Carlyle influenced included Petr Lavrov, who believed that the 'biographical element' was the foundation of all history, and the historian Pogodin, who similarly saw history as a summation of outstanding biographies. It should be noted, however, that there was also opposition to Carlyle and his followers' views from, among others, Leo Tolstoy.[16]

Let us return to the composition of Tretyakov's portrait gallery and the prominence of writers, which reflected an overriding preoccupation with literature at the time. 'Our century is the century of literature, of the novel,' declared the cultural historian Adrian Prakhov. For Tretyakov, the outstanding citizens of the era were indisputably writers. If for Carlyle hero-gods and hero-worshippers had featured in the past, heroes now appeared in the form of poets and men of letters. It became axiomatic that great literature was the path to immortality, and that the writer was the voice of the nation, the symbol that united it. Shakespeare and Dante thus rendered England and Italy superior to the silent grandeur of Eastern nations. For Carlyle, it was writing that gave great men the ability to express their 'inspired soul'.[17]

Carlyle's view on the role of the writer in modern life was shared by the Russian public, and resonated in the new portrait galleries. The myth of the writer would later be reassessed. In the early twentieth century, Vasily Rozanov argued that it generated a misleading hagiography: 'We are so spoiled by books ... that we no longer remember any generals ... What is needed is not "great literature", but a great, beautiful and useful life.'[18] In the second half of the nineteenth century, however, literary authority reigned supreme.

Interestingly, a writer's status was not necessarily dependent on the popularity of his fiction, but on the appeal of his polemical writings – yet another manifestation of the public's sense of the writer as a prophet and teacher. Literary historians, for example, have noted that, despite the public's undeniable interest in *The House of the Dead* (1861–2) and the success of

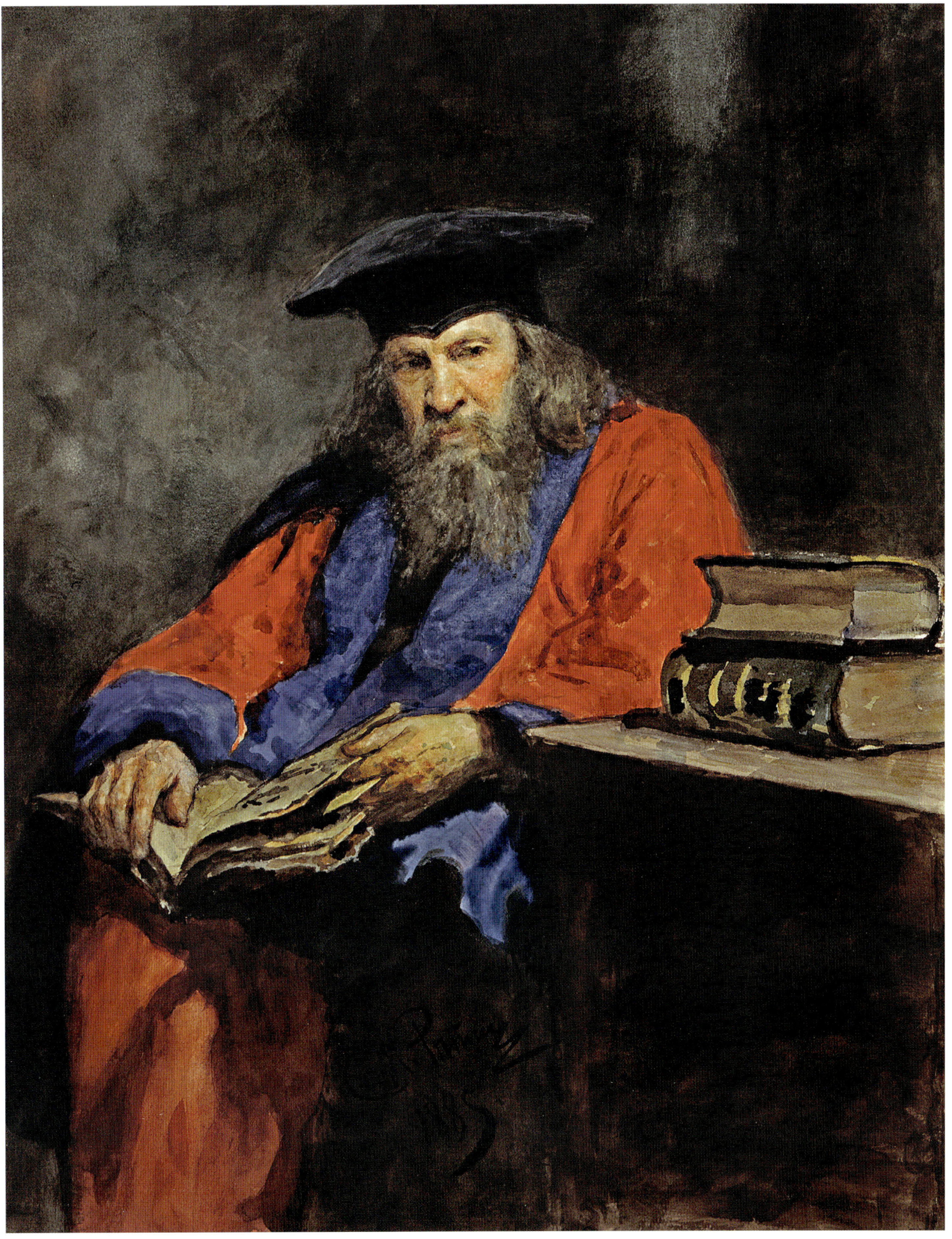

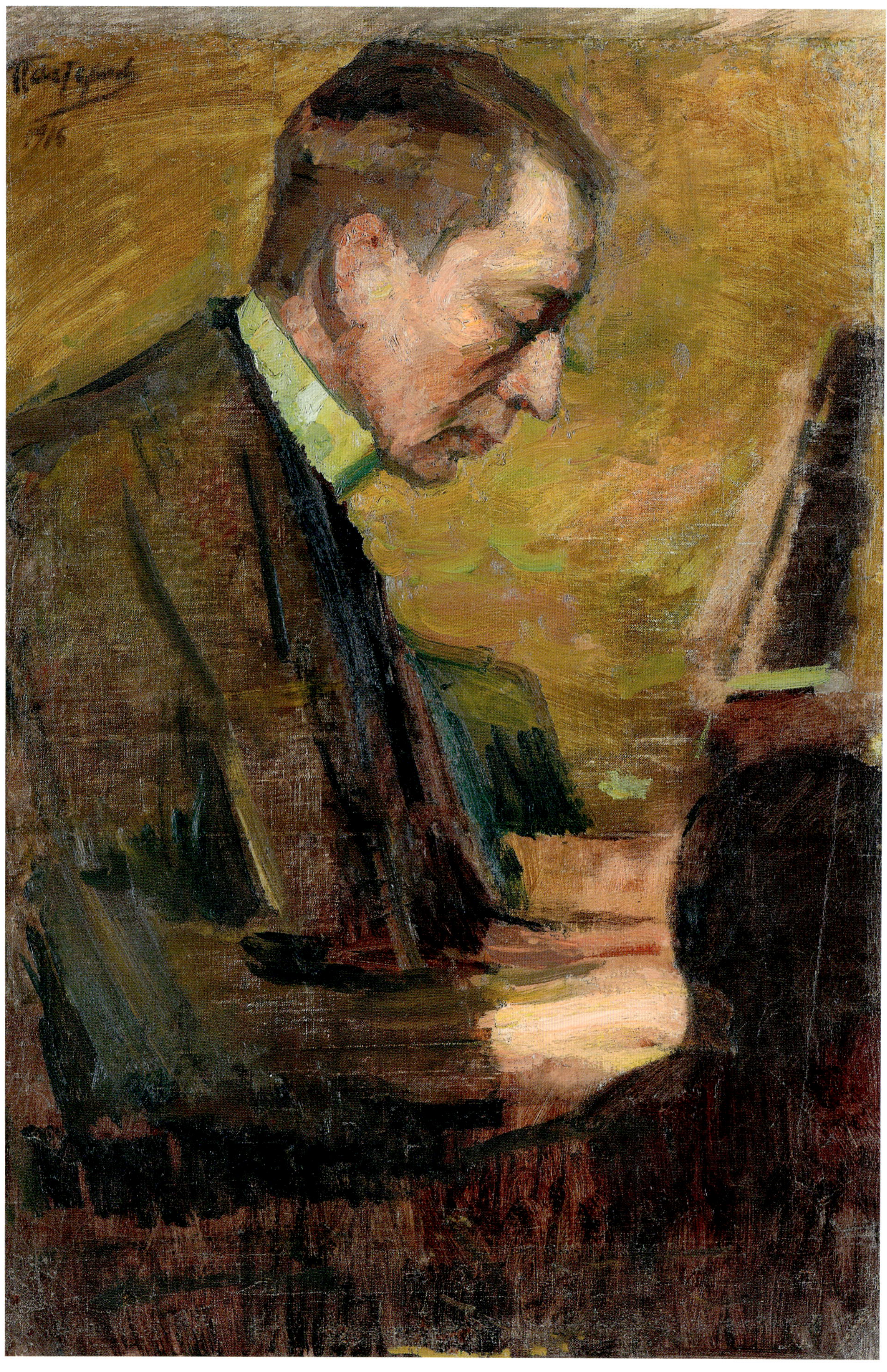

Crime and Punishment (1866), Dostoevsky's popularity grew relatively slowly, and only the socio-political *A Writer's Diary* pushed him into the realm of leading Russian writers.[19] Tolstoy's literary fate was similar. His popularity grew following *War and Peace* and *Anna Karenina*, but it was his socio-political writings of the 1880s–90s that secured his canonical place in the Russian public consciousness, as well as abroad. It was this decade that saw the largest number of portraits of the writer, including the famous Repin cycle (see Figs 3.8 and 3.9). Tolstoy was also painted by Ge (plate 11) and Iaroshenko, and sculpted by Ginzburg and Trubetskoy. Conversely, writers such as Leskov and Pisemsky, who did not adopt an educational mission, did not achieve a comparable level of authority, which often led to unbalanced perceptions of the artistic merit of their work.

As well as the question of who represented Russia's best citizens and were worthy models for a portrait, social and artistic commentators long deliberated on what kind of portrait constituted a true work of art. Writing in literature and socio-political tracts, they insisted that, in order to merit public attention, a portrait needed not only to provide a convincing likeness, but to capture the essence of the individual. Their debates echoed with the call to 'delve into the inner man' and convey the 'fundamental quality of an individual' which 'separates him from the crowds'. The notion of the portrait as not simply a description of the face but a summation of the sitter's ideal qualities was frequently stressed.

The public sense of the outstanding citizen in the second half of the nineteenth century was of someone who 'thought critically', to use a popular phrase of the time. The exemplary portrait of such an individual was Perov's 1872 portrait of Fedor Dostoevsky (plate 4), in which a pale, nervous face emerges from the dark background, while the hands locked tight over the knees serve as a metaphor for profound and ceaseless thought. Dostoevsky's portrait can be usefully compared with Kramskoy's *Christ in the Wilderness* that was painted the same year (1872, State Tretyakov Gallery), for both figures are immersed in some deep and preoccupying cycle of thought. Other sitters for portraits commissioned by Tretyakov were similarly seen as the embodiment of a public consciousness, with responsibility for the fate of the nation. Typical in this respect is the portrait of the writer, lexicographer and ethnographer Vladimir Dal, who was painted by Perov in the last year of his life (plate 3). Here the frail old man sits in a deep Voltaire chair, as if contemplating the depths of his past experience. The unusual seriousness evident here of the artist's relationship to the sitter, as well as the sitter's self-awareness, form a unique quality of Russian art.

Particularly rich is the iconography of Tolstoy, who attracted unparalleled public interest both in Russia and abroad. In his famous series of portraits of the writer, Repin conceived him as Tolstoy the ploughman, Tolstoy with a scythe, Tolstoy in the forest, Tolstoy in prayer. Repin's series culminated in the portrait *Leo Tolstoy Barefoot* (1901, State Russian Museum), which responded to Tretyakov's statement that 'Leo Nikolaevich [Tolstoy] is such an enormous personality that an image should be left for posterity of him full height and most definitely outside, in the summer'.[20] Repin's cycle of Tolstoy portraits in many respects resembles a detailed hagiographic icon, with the large portrait of the writer of 1887 in the centre, surrounded by episodes from his life.

In portraits of creative individuals, Repin achieved something that preoccupied many portraitists: he managed to evoke their creative gift without resorting to idealisation or abandoning realistic observation, and to translate their everyday appearance into an image of lasting significance. In one of his most brilliant portraits, that of the composer Mussorgsky (plate 7), Repin was merciless in depicting the human flesh destroyed by sickness and alcoholism: the stout figure, swollen face, red nose and tousled hair. However, the creative spirit within this large and diseased body is unmissable, as is Mussorgsky's stature and originality. Repin here creates a multi-dimensional image that exemplifies the coexistence of the creative and the everyday, and ensures that the former is never overshadowed by the latter.

Fig. 6.8
Sergei Rachmaninov
Leonid Pasternak, 1916

This fundamental rejection of hyperbole that might have seemed appropriate in depicting the great composer epitomises Repin's approach. The uncompromising portrait confirmed the artist's ability to comprehend and respect another's individuality without false modesty, sentimentality or hypocrisy, and to embrace the many complexities and contradictions of human nature that underpinned the culture of the time.

The confessional character of the portrait genre in the 1870s–1880s led to certain formal and stylistic tendencies. As a rule, portraits of this period did not strive for a great variety of poses, gestures, accessories or colour palettes. Rather, they often followed a uniform compositional scheme that exposed the face of the sitter and never concealed his gaze. In the 1890s–1910s, however, such qualities as likeness, objectivity and an analytical approach in portraiture gave way to greater liveliness in the subject, and greater attention to the artist's personal relationship with the sitter. Emotional immediacy, compositional variety and the facture of painting now came to the fore, at the expense of authentic likeness and accuracy. The multi-layered meanings of the Realist portraits of the second half of the nineteenth century would become a thing of the past.

An interest in Russian history on the one hand, and the question of the individual on the other, explain the fascination that gave rise to and continues to stimulate the art of the Russian portrait. A national portrait gallery creates a system of coordinates to construct both a philosophy of history and a history of distinct individuals. Tretyakov's portrait gallery may have been dispersed throughout the museum when it was reorganised on chronological and monographic lines, but its significance nonetheless remains. Visitors to the Tretyakov Gallery today are able not only to see works by renowned Russian painters and familiarise themselves with the masterpieces of a national school of art, but also to come face to face with those titans of Russian culture – writers, composers, artists, scientists and philosophers – whose spiritual enquiry and selfless service proved such a vibrant force.

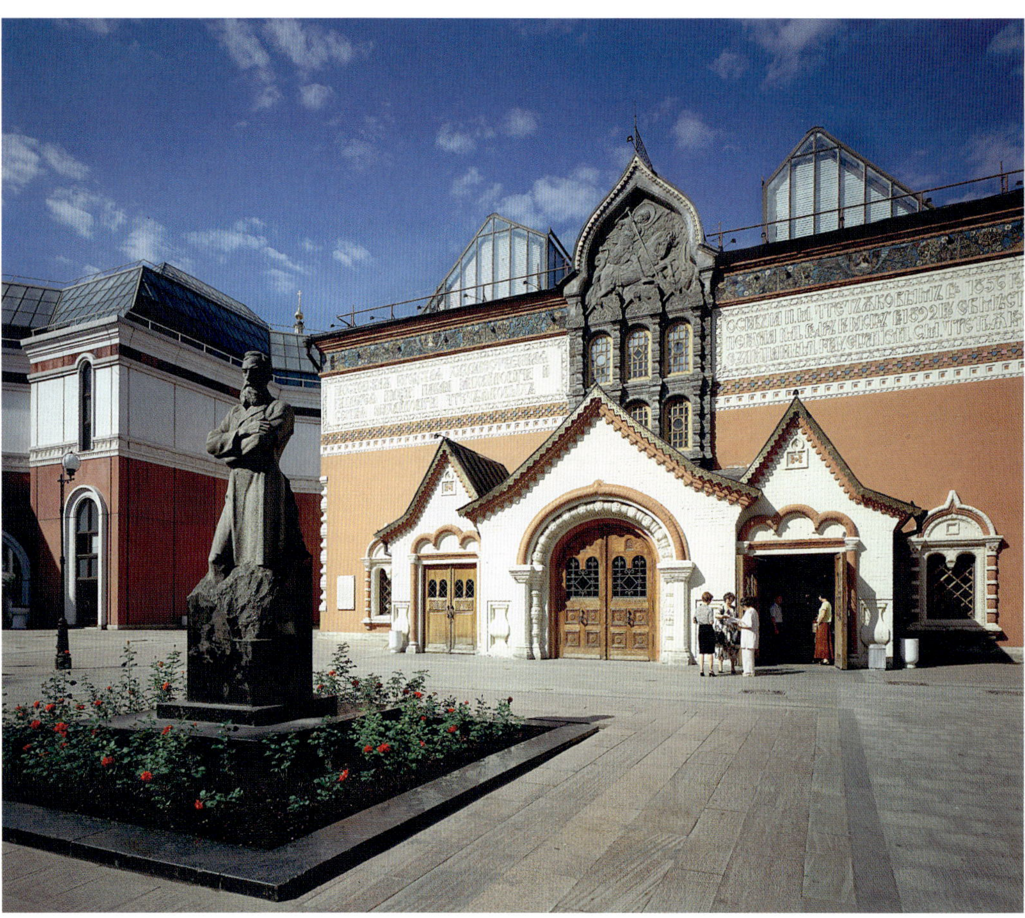

Fig. 6.9
The State Tretyakov Gallery, Moscow

Notes

1   Letter from Pavel Tretyakov to A.I. Rabotina, widow of Nestor Kukolnik, 16 August 1870, in Aleksandra Botkina, *Pavel Mikhailovich Tretiakov v zhizni i iskusstve* (Iskusstvo, Moscow, 2012), p.207.

2   In 1935 Nevrev's portrait of Shchepkin was transferred from the State Tretyakov Gallery to the State Museum of the Maly Theatre, Moscow.

3   T.V. Iudenkova, 'Problemy khudozhestvennogo sobiratel'stva P.M. i S.M. Tret'iakovykh vo vtoroi polovine XIX veka: mirovozzrencheskie aspekty: avtoreferat', unpublished doctoral dissertation (Moscow, 2014), p.17.

4   'Vtoroia peredvizhnaia vystavka kartin', *Novoe vremia*, no. 6 (1873).

5   Ivan N. Kramskoy, *Pis'ma, stat'i v dvukh tomakh*, vol. 2, ed. Sofia N. Goldshtein (Iskusstvo, Moscow, 1966), p.150.

6   Fedor Dostoevsky, 'Luchshie liudi', in *Dnevnik pisatelia: Izbrannye stranitsy* (Sovremennik, Moscow, 1989), p.330.

7   Ibid., p.329.

8   These included the *Exhibition of Portraits of Noteworthy Russians*, held in Moscow in 1868; the *Historical Exhibition of Portraits of the XVI–XVIII Centuries*, St Petersburg, 1870; the *Exhibition of Russian Portraiture over the Last 150 Years*, St Petersburg, 1902; and the famous exhibition of portraits in the Tauride Palace, St Petersburg, 1905.

9   See Tatiana Karpova, *Smysl litsa: Russkii portret vtoroi poloviny XIX veka. Opyt samopoznaniia lichnosti* (Aleteiia, St Petersburg, 2000); and Galina Andreeva, 'Pavel Mikhailovich pobyval kak obychno v Anglii…', *Tretiakovskaia galereia*, no. 1 (2004), pp.21–8.

10   Grigory Sternin, *Khudozhestvennaia zhizn' Rossii serediny XIX veka* (Iskusstvo, Moscow, 1991), pp.65–6.

11   Dashkov's portrait collection is now in the Pushkin Museum of Fine Arts, Moscow.

12   *Katalog biblioteki P.M. Tretiakova* (Tov. Tip. A.I. Mamontova, Moscow, 1905), p.3.

13   Fedor Dostoevsky, 'Podrostok,' *Polnoe sobranie sochinenii v 30 tomakh* (Nauka, Leningrad/St Petersburg, 1972–92), vol. 13, p.102.

14   Eugène-Melchior de Vogüé, 'Innostrantsy o Moskovskoi vystavke: Moskovskaia vystavka i russkoe iskusstvo', *Zagranichnyi vestnik* (1882), vol. 5, p.300.

15   Thomas Carlyle, *On Heroes, Hero-Worship and the Heroic in History* (George Routledge & Sons, London, 1903), p.5; translated as *Geroi, pochitanie geroev i geroicheskoe v istorii* (St Petersburg, 1908), pp.18–19.

16   Tolstoy's *War and Peace*, for example, took issue with Carlyle's theories. Tolstoy's initial unwillingness to pose for Tretyakov may well have been because the idea of a portrait gallery of historic figures representing 'great people' was contrary to his views. The artist Vasily Vereshchagin for his part published a small book in 1895 with the provocative title of *Illustrated Autobiographies of a Few Unremarkable Russian People*, which included an old butler and religious pilgrims. Vereshchagin's book, which stood in stark contrast to *The Exhibition of Portraits of Russian Noteworthy Individuals* (1868) and Dashkov's *Portrait Gallery of Historic Russian Figures*, was a reaction to his contemporaries' obsession with portraits of historical figures, and a protest against the mythology of 'great people'.

17   Carlyle, op. cit., p.207.

18   Vasily Rozanov, *Opavshie list'ia* (Izdanie t-va A.S. Suvorina, St Petersburg, 1913), p.20.

19   A. Reitblat, *Ot Bovy k Bal'montu: Ocherki po istorii chteniia v Rossii vo vtoroi polovine XIX veka* (MPI, Moscow, 1991), p.72.

20   *Repin: Perepiska s P.M. Tretiakovym, 1873–1898*, ed. M.N. Grigoreva and A.N. Shchekotova (Iskusstvo, Moscow and Leningrad, 1946), p.120.

THE STATE TRETYAKOV GALLERY

Founded by the Russian textile merchant and businessman Pavel Tretyakov, the State Tretyakov Gallery is the major museum of Russian art in Moscow. Its founder began to collect Russian paintings in the 1850s and donated his collection to the city of Moscow in 1892. Today it possesses a unique collection of more than 170,000 works, which range from early religious icons to modern art and span a period of a thousand years.

The Gallery's main building is on Lavrushinsky Pereulok in the Zamoskvoreche district of Moscow, where merchants congregated in the nineteenth century. In late 1851, the Tretyakov family bought a property there, which is where Pavel's gallery of painting and sculpture was first housed. Special outbuildings were erected to accommodate the expanding collection, and the architect Viktor Vasnetsov redesigned the entire complex on Tretyakov's death in 1898, creating the Gallery's iconic façade (Fig. 6.10). A major new extension, the Engineering Building, was then added in the late twentieth century, providing accommodation for conservation and maintenance services, as well as a conference hall and temporary exhibition space.

The Tretyakov also occupies a separate building on Krymsky Val, which hosts major exhibitions of Russian and foreign art and houses the twentieth- and twenty-first-century collections. These include works by avant-garde artists such as Kazimir Malevich and Marc Chagall, Socialist Realist painting and sculpture of the 1930s, 1940s and 1950s, Nonconformist art of the later Soviet period, and contemporary art.

The galleries at both sites are open to the public every day apart from Mondays and stage a wealth of exhibitions, conferences, lectures and other events. For further information, please visit the website (www.tretyakovgallery.ru).

Fig. 6.10
Original design of the façade
of the Tretyakov Gallery
Viktor Vasnetsov, 1900

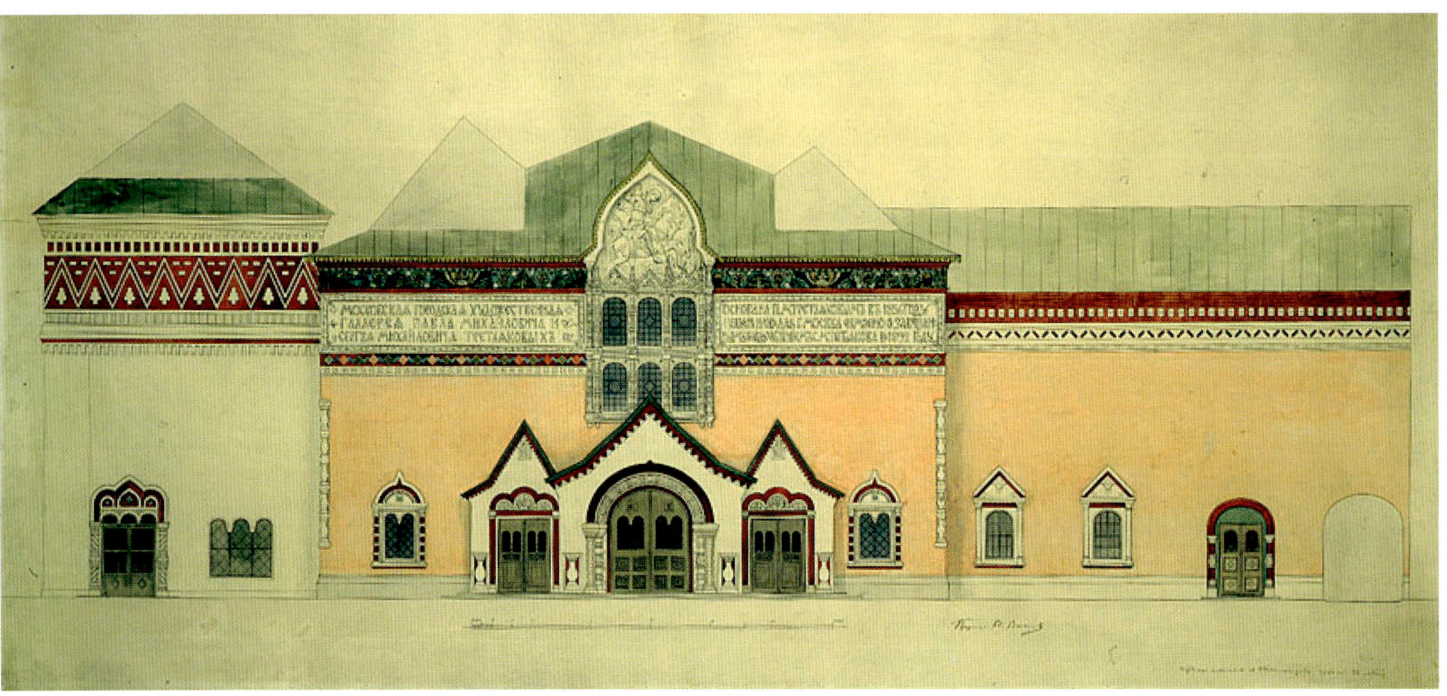

ACKNOWLEDGEMENTS

This project emerged from conversations with Sandy Nairne, former director of the National Portrait Gallery, whose excitement about the subject proved infectious. It has been championed with equal enthusiasm by his successor, Nicholas Cullinan who, together with Pim Baxter, Sarah Tinsley, Tarnya Cooper and Peter Funnell, has offered unflagging support and sage advice. I am grateful to them all for their expertise, and perhaps most of all for the pleasure of their company on trips to Russia that were unfailingly rich in incident.

The warmth of the welcome that we met at the State Tretyakov Gallery in Moscow was extraordinary. My sincere thanks to Zelfira Tregulova, the director, and to Tatiana Gubanova, Maria Shelkova and other members of staff there, who greeted our proposal with such interest and proved to be outstandingly resourceful and congenial collaborators. I owe particular gratitude to Tatiana Karpova, a dedicated advocate of this project, who has become a much-valued colleague and friend.

There are a number of people to thank for the creative interpretation and display of the Tretyakov paintings at the National Portrait Gallery, among them Jude Simmons, Rosie Wilson, Michelle Greaves, Ulrike Wachsmann, Liz Smith and Andrea Easey. Naomi Conway, Sarah Harwood, Jane Chambers and Catherine Yexley were tireless in their fundraising activities; Denise Vogelsang, Neil Evans and Nick Budden brought their characteristic flair to communications and marketing; and Helen Hillman and Eleanor Darton-Moore mastered the complexities of visa applications with aplomb. I am also grateful to the ever-cheerful Publications and Trading team, among them Robert Carr-Archer, Nicola Saunders, Christopher Tinker, Ruth Müller-Wirth, Kathleen Bloomfield and especially Andrew Roff, a sensitive editor and cake-maker extraordinaire. The National Portrait Gallery nurtures talented and dedicated staff, and has been an inspirational place to work.

Closer to home, I am grateful to Galina Mardilovich and Andrey Shabanov for their excellent translations, and Emma Widdis for her helpful comments on the catalogue text. My mother, Mavis Gray, and mother-in-law, Rosemary Blakesley, have held the fort at home while I've been cavorting in Russia, and are a fount of knowledge and support in countless ways. Finally, as ever, my thanks and love to Patrick, Samuel and Caitlin Blakesley, those irrepressible experts in laughter and life.

BIBLIOGRAPHY

Robert Auty and Dimitri Obolensky (eds), *An Introduction to Russian Art and Architecture* (Cambridge University Press, Cambridge, 1980)

Adele Barker and Bruce Grant (eds), *The Russia Reader: History, Culture, Politics* (Duke University Press, Durham, NC, and London, 2010)

Alan Bird, *A History of Russian Painting* (Phaidon Press, Oxford, 1987)

Rosalind P. Blakesley, *The Russian Canvas: Painting in Imperial Russia, 1757–1881* (Yale University Press, New Haven and London, 2016)

Rosalind P. Blakesley and Susan E. Reid (eds), *Russian Art and the West: A Century of Dialogue in Painting, Architecture and the Decorative Arts* (Northern Illinois University Press, DeKalb, 2007)

Rosalind P. Blakesley and Margaret Samu (eds), *From Realism to the Silver Age: New Studies in Russian Artistic Culture* (Northern Illinois University Press, DeKalb, 2014)

John E. Bowlt, *Russia's Silver Age: Moscow and St Petersburg, 1900–1920* (Thames & Hudson, London, 2010)

Caryl Emerson, *The Cambridge Introduction to Russian Literature* (Cambridge University Press, Cambridge, 2008)

Catherine Evtuhov, David Goldfrank, Lindsey Hughes and Richard Stites, *A History of Russia: Peoples, Legends, Events, Forces* (Houghton Mifflin Company, Boston and New York, 2004)

Simon Franklin and Emma Widdis (eds), *National Identity in Russian Culture: An Introduction* (Cambridge University Press, Cambridge, 2004)

Marina Frolova-Walker, *Russian Music and Nationalism from Glinka to Stalin* (Yale University Press, New Haven and London, 2008)

From Russia: French and Russian Master Paintings 1870–1925 (Royal Academy of Arts, London, 2007)

Lynn Garafola and Nancy Van Norman Baer (eds), *The Ballets Russes and Its World* (Yale University Press, New Haven and London, 1999)

Camilla Gray, *The Russian Experiment in Art 1863–1922*, third edn (revised and enlarged by Marion Burleigh-Motley, Thames & Hudson, London, 1986)

George Heard Hamilton, *The Art and Architecture of Russia* (Penguin Books, Harmondsworth, 1954)

Richard Hare, *The Art and Artists of Russia* (Methuen, London, 1965)

Jeremy Howard, *East European Art* (Oxford University Press, Oxford, 2006)

Lindsey Hughes, *The Romanovs: Ruling Russia 1613–1917* (Hambledon Continuum, London, 2008)

Aline Isdebsky-Pritchard, *The Art of Mikhail Vrubel 1856–1910* (UMI Research Press, Ann Arbor, 1982)

David Jackson, *The Russian Vision: The Art of Ilya Repin* (BAI, Schoten, 2006)

David Jackson, *The Wanderers and Critical Realism in Nineteenth-Century Russian Painting* (Manchester University Press, Manchester, 2006)

Beverly Whitney Kean, *French Painters, Russian Collectors*, 2nd edn (Hodder and Stoughton, London, 1994) (first published as *All the Empty Palaces: the Merchant Patrons of Modern Art in Pre-Revolutionary Russia*, New York, 1983)

Catriona Kelly, *Russian Literature: A Very Short Introduction* (Oxford University Press, Oxford, 2001)

Janet Kennedy, *The 'Mir Iskusstva' Group and Russian Art 1898–1912* (Garland Publications, New York, 1977)

W. Bruce Lincoln, *Between Heaven and Hell: The Story of a Thousand Years of Artistic Life in Russia* (Viking, New York, 1998)

W. Bruce Lincoln, *Sunlight at Midnight: St Petersburg and the Rise of Modern Russia* (Basic Books, New York, 2002)

Francis Maes, *A History of Russian Music: From Kamarinskaya to Babi Yar*, trans. Arnold J. Pomerans and Erica Pomerans (University of California Press, Berkeley, Los Angeles and London, 2002)

John Milner, *A Dictionary of Russian and Soviet Artists, 1420–1970* (Antique Collectors' Club, Woodbridge, 1993)

Robin Milner-Gulland, *The Russians* (Blackwell, Oxford, 1997)

Michael Raeburn (ed.), *The Twilight of the Tsars: Russian Art at the Turn of the Century* (Hayward Gallery, London, 1991)

Tamara Talbot Rice, *A Concise History of Russian Art*, second edn (Thames & Hudson, London, 1974)

Hans Rogger, *Russia in the Age of Modernisation and Revolution 1881–1917* (Longman, London and New York, 1983)

Russia! Nine Hundred Years of Masterpieces and Master Collections (Guggenheim Museum, New York, 2005)

Nicholas Rzhevsky (ed.), *The Cambridge Companion to Modern Russian Culture* (Cambridge University Press, Cambridge, 1998)

Dmitry V. Sarabianov, *Russian Art from Neoclassicism to the Avant-Garde* (Thames & Hudson, London, 1990)

David Saunders, *Russia in the Age of Reaction and Reform 1801–1881* (Longman, London and New York, 1992)

Theofanis George Stavrou (ed.), *Art and Culture in Nineteenth-Century Russia* (Indiana University Press, Bloomington, 1983)

Elizabeth Kridl Valkenier (ed.), *The Wanderers, Masters of 19th-Century Russian Painting* (Dallas Museum of Art, Dallas, 1990)

Elizabeth Kridl Valkenier, *Russian Realist Art, the State and Society: The Peredvizhniki and Their Tradition* (Columbia University Press, New York, 1989)

Elizabeth Kridl Valkenier, *Ilya Repin and the World of Russian Art* (Columbia University Press, New York, 1990)

Elizabeth Kridl Valkenier, *Valentin Serov: Portraits of Russia's Silver Age* (Northwestern University Press, Evanston, 2001)

PICTURE CREDITS

The National Portrait Gallery would like to thank the copyright holders for granting permission to reproduce works illustrated in this book. Every effort has been made to contact the holders of copyright material, and any omission will be corrected in future editions if the publisher is notified in writing. Dimensions are given height by width. The National Portrait Gallery would like to thank the State Tretyakov Gallery, Moscow, who loaned all of the works to the exhibition *Russia and the Arts: The Age of Tolstoy and Tchaikovsky*.

PLATES

1 *Alexander Herzen*
Nikolai Ge, 1867
Oil on canvas
795 x 630mm

2 *Alexander Ostrovsky*
Vasily Perov, 1871
Oil on canvas
1035 x 807mm

3 *Vladimir Dal*
Vasily Perov, 1872
Oil on canvas
940 x 805mm

4 *Fedor Dostoevsky*
Vasily Perov, 1872
Oil on canvas
996 x 810mm

5 *Ivan Turgenev*
Ilia Repin, 1874
Oil on canvas
1165 x 890mm

6 *Alexei Pisemsky*
Ilia Repin, 1880
Oil on canvas
895 x 715mm

7 *Modest Mussorgsky*
Ilia Repin, 1881
Oil on canvas
718 x 585mm

8 *Anton Rubinstein*
Ilia Repin, 1881
Oil on canvas
800 x 623mm

9 *The Actor Alexander Lensky as Petruchio in Shakespeare's* The Taming of the Shrew
Ivan Kramskoy, 1883
Oil on canvas
620 x 535mm

10 *Pelageia Strepetova*
Nikolai Iaroshenko, 1884
Oil on canvas
1213 x 790mm

11 *Leo Tolstoy*
Nikolai Ge, 1884
Oil on canvas
962 x 717mm

12 *Vladimir Stasov at His Dacha in the Village of Starozhilovka near Pargolovo*
Ilia Repin, 1889–90
Oil on canvas
400 x 376mm

13 *Sophie Menter*
Ilia Repin, 1887
Oil on canvas
1215 x 1245mm

14 *Baroness Varvara Ikskul von Hildenbandt*
Ilia Repin, 1889
Oil on canvas
1965 x 717mm

15 *Petr Tchaikovsky*
Nikolai Kuznetsov, 1893
Oil on canvas
960 x 740mm

16 *In the Summer*
Valentin Serov, 1895
Oil on canvas
740 x 940mm

17 *Nikolai Rimsky-Korsakov*
Valentin Serov, 1898
Oil on canvas
965 x 1132mm

18 *Anton Chekhov*
Iosif Braz, 1898
Oil on canvas
1020 x 800mm

19 *Pavel Tretyakov*
Ilia Repin, 1901
Oil on canvas
1110 x 1340mm

20 *Savva Mamontov*
Mikhail Vrubel, 1897
Oil on canvas
1890 x 1435mm

21 *Nadezhda Zabela-Vrubel*
Mikhail Vrubel, 1898
Oil on canvas
1253 x 765mm

22 *Fedor Shaliapin*
Konstantin Korovin, 1905
Oil on canvas
650 x 461mm

23 *Maria Ermolova*
Valentin Serov, 1905
Oil on canvas
2240 x 1200mm

24 *Ivan Morozov*
Valentin Serov, 1910
Tempera on cardboard
635 x 770mm

25 *Nikolai Gumilev*
Olga Della-Vos-Kardovskaia, 1909
Oil on canvas
1045 x 795mm

26 *Anna Akhmatova*
Olga Della-Vos-Kardovskaia, 1914
Oil on canvas
860 x 825mm

FIGURES

Fig. 1.1
Peter the Great, Tsar of Russia
Sir Godfrey Kneller, 1698
Oil on canvas
2417 x 1456mm
Royal Collection Trust
Royal Collection Trust/© Her Majesty
Queen Elizabeth II 2015

Fig. 1.2
Peter I (Peter the Great)
John Smith after Sir Godfrey Kneller, 1698
Mezzotint
415 x 290mm (406 x 279mm plate size)
© National Portrait Gallery, London
(NPG D11575)

Fig. 1.3
Tsarevna Anna Petrovna
Louis Caravaque, 1725
Oil on canvas
912 x 734mm
State Tretyakov Gallery, Moscow

Fig. 1.4
Gavriil Golovkin
Ivan Nikitin, 1720s
Oil on canvas
909 x 734mm
State Tretyakov Gallery, Moscow

Fig. 1.5
Empress Elizabeth
Georg Caspar von Prenner, 1754
Oil on canvas
2028 x 1572mm
State Tretyakov Gallery, Moscow

Fig. 1.6
Peter III
Aleksei Antropov, 1762
Oil on canvas
250 x 179mm
State Tretyakov Gallery, Moscow

Fig. 1.7
Imperial Academy of Arts, St Petersburg
(Jean-Baptiste Michel Vallin de la Mothe
with the assistance of Alexander Kokorinov),
1765–88

Fig. 1.8
Prince Alexander Golitsyn
Dmitry Levitsky, 1772
Oil on canvas
1266 x 1025mm
State Tretyakov Gallery, Moscow

Fig. 1.9
Prokofy Demidov
Dmitry Levitsky, 1773
Oil on canvas
2226 x 1660mm
State Tretyakov Gallery, Moscow

Fig. 1.10
Catherine II
Fedor Rokotov, 1763
Oil on canvas
1555 x 1390mm
State Tretyakov Gallery, Moscow

Fig. 2.1
Paul I, Emperor of Russia
(The Magnanimous Ally)
James Gillray, 1799
Hand-coloured etching
328 x 253mm
© National Portrait Gallery, London
(NPG D12707)

Fig. 2.2
Self-portrait
Orest Kiprensky, 1828
Oil on canvas
485 x 423mm
State Tretyakov Gallery, Moscow

Fig. 2.3
Alexander Pushkin
Orest Kiprensky, 1827
Oil on canvas
630 x 540mm
State Tretyakov Gallery, Moscow

Fig. 2.4
Nicholas I, Emperor of Russia
John Henry Robinson after George Dawe,
1826
Engraving
286 x 206mm
© National Portrait Gallery, London
(NPG D13720)

Fig. 2.5
Self-portrait
Ivan Kramskoy, 1867
Oil on canvas
527 x 440mm
State Tretyakov Gallery, Moscow

Fig. 2.6
Fedor Vasilev
Ivan Kramskoy, 1871
Oil on canvas
883 x 683mm
State Tretyakov Gallery, Moscow

Fig. 2.7
The Second Peredvizhnik
Exhibition at the Academy of Arts
World Illustration, 1873

Fig. 2.8
Barge Haulers on the Volga
Ilia Repin, 1870–3
Oil on canvas
1315 x 2810mm
State Russian Museum, St Petersburg
© 2015, State Russian Museum,
St Petersburg

Fig. 2.9
Ilia Repin
Photographed by I. Diagovchenko, 1884
State Tretyakov Gallery, Moscow

Fig. 2.10
The Village Religious Procession at Easter
Vasily Perov, 1861
Oil on canvas
715 x 890mm
State Tretyakov Gallery, Moscow

Fig. 2.11
Fedor Dostoevsky
Photographed by Constantin Chapiro, 1871
Archives Larousse, Paris, France/Bridgeman
Images

Fig. 2.12
Ivan Turgenev
Photographed by Nadar (Gaspard-Félix
Tournachon), 1877
© Corbis

Fig. 3.1
Nikolai Ge
Ilia Repin, 1880
Oil on canvas
825 x 662mm
State Tretyakov Gallery, Moscow

Fig. 3.2
Holiday
Nikolai Kuznetsov, 1879
Oil on canvas
550 x 980mm
State Tretyakov Gallery, Moscow

Fig. 3.3
Thickets
Ivan Shishkin, 1881
Oil on canvas
1420 x 930mm
State Tretyakov Gallery, Moscow

Fig. 3.4
The Morning of the Execution of the Streltsy
Vasily Surikov, 1881
Oil on canvas
2230 x 3835mm
State Tretyakov Gallery, Moscow

Fig. 3.5
Alexander II on His Deathbed
Konstantin Makovsky, 1881
Oil on canvas
610 x 855mm
State Tretyakov Gallery, Moscow

Fig. 3.6
Leo Tolstoy
Ivan Kramskoy, 1873
Oil on canvas
980 x 795mm
State Tretyakov Gallery, Moscow

Fig. 3.7
Count Leo Tolstoy
Unknown photographer, *c.*1894
Albumen print
145 x 99mm
© National Portrait Gallery, London
(NPG P1700(12a))

Fig. 3.8
The Ploughman. Leo Tolstoy ploughing
Ilia Repin, 1887
Oil on cardboard
278 x 403mm
State Tretyakov Gallery, Moscow

Fig. 3.9
Leo Tolstoy
Ilia Repin, 1887
Oil on canvas
1240 x 880mm
State Tretyakov Gallery, Moscow

Fig. 3.10
Vladimir Stasov
Ilia Repin, 1873
Oil on canvas
809 x 653mm
State Tretyakov Gallery, Moscow

Fig. 3.11
Modest Mussorgsky
Unknown photographer, 1870s
Private Collection/© Look and Learn/Elgar
Collection/Bridgeman Images

Fig. 3.12
Anton Rubinstein
Unknown photographer, 1880s
State Tretyakov Gallery, Moscow

Fig. 4.1
Certificate naming Pavel Tretyakov an
Honourable Citizen of Moscow, 1896
State Tretyakov Gallery, Moscow

Fig. 4.2
Savva Mamontov
Ilia Repin, 1878
Oil on canvas
710 x 580mm
Abramtsevo State Museum Reserve,
Abramtsevo

Fig. 4.3
Elizaveta Mamontova
Ilia Repin, 1874–9
Oil on canvas
730 x 590mm
Abramtsevo State Museum Reserve,
Abramtsevo

Fig. 4.4
Abramtsevo
Ilia Repin, 1880
Oil on canvas
522 x 490mm
V. D. Polenov State Museum Reserve

Fig. 4.5
Girl with Peaches
(Vera Mamontova)
Valentin Serov, 1887
Oil on canvas
910 x 850mm
State Tretyakov Gallery, Moscow

Fig. 4.6
Nadezhda Derviz
with Her Child (unfinished)
Valentin Serov, 1888–9
Oil on iron plate
1420 x 710mm
State Tretyakov Gallery, Moscow

Fig. 4.7
Coronation: the Anointing of Nicholas II in
the Cathedral of the Dormition
Valentin Serov, 1896
Oil on canvas
430 x 640mm
State Tretyakov Gallery, Moscow

Fig. 4.8
Petr Tchaikovsky
Unknown photographer, 1880s
© Corbis

Fig. 4.9
Bogatyrs
Viktor Vasnetsov, 1881–98
Oil on canvas
2953 x 4460mm
State Tretyakov Gallery, Moscow

Fig. 5.1
Royal group at Balmoral
Photographed by Robert Milne, 1896
Albumen print
137 x 97mm
National Portrait Gallery, London
(NPG P1700(24d))

Fig. 5.2
The Tsar and his family
Published by Rotary Photographic Co Ltd,
*c.*1906
Postcard print
73 x 130mm
National Portrait Gallery, London
(NPG x131654)

Fig. 5.3
Seated Demon
Mikhail Vrubel, 1890
Oil on canvas, 1165 x 2138mm
State Tretyakov Gallery, Moscow

Fig. 5.4
Mika Morozov
Valentin Serov, 1901
Oil on canvas
623 x 706mm
State Tretyakov Gallery, Moscow

Fig. 5.5
Mikhail Morozov
Valentin Serov, 1902
Oil on canvas
2155 x 808mm
State Tretyakov Gallery, Moscow

Fig. 5.6
Self-portrait
Kazimir Malevich, 1910
Watercolour and gouache on paper
270 x 268mm
State Tretyakov Gallery, Moscow

Fig. 5.7
Savva Mamontov
Unknown photographer, 1880s
Abramtsevo State Museum Reserve,
Abramtsevo © Fine Art Images

Fig. 5.8
The Swan Princess
Mikhail Vrubel, 1900
Oil on canvas
1425 x 935mm
State Tretyakov Gallery, Moscow

Fig. 5.9
Fedor Shaliapin in the Role of Holofernes
Alexander Golovin, 1908
Tempera and pastel on canvas
1685 x 2120mm
State Tretyakov Gallery, Moscow

Fig. 5.10
Nikolai Gumilev
Unknown photographer, 1900s
State Central Literary Museum, Moscow
© Fine Art Images

Fig. 5.11
Anna Akhmatova
Unknown photographer, *c.*1925
© Fine Art Images

Fig. 6.1
Pavel Tretyakov
Unknown photographer, 1871
State Tretyakov Gallery, Moscow

Fig. 6.2
Nikolai Gogol
Fedor Moller, early 1840s
Oil on canvas
590 x 470mm
State Tretyakov Gallery, Moscow

Fig. 6.3
Pavel Tretyakov and his family
Photographed by I. Diagovchenko, 1884
State Tretyakov Gallery, Moscow

Fig. 6.4
Study of Actress Pelageia Strepetova
Ilia Repin, 1882
Oil on canvas
647 x 535mm
State Tretyakov Gallery, Moscow

Fig. 6.5
At the Dressing-Table. Self-portrait
Zinaida Serebriakova, 1909
Oil on canvas attached to cardboard
750 x 650mm
State Tretyakov Gallery, Moscow

Fig. 6.6
Nikolai Karamzin
Vasily Tropinin, 1818
Oil on canvas
626 x 483mm
State Tretyakov Gallery, Moscow

Fig. 6.7
Dmitry Mendeleev
Ilia Repin, 1885
Watercolour on paper
575 x 460mm
State Tretyakov Gallery, Moscow

Fig. 6.8
Sergei Rachmaninov
Leonid Pasternak, 1916
Oil on canvas
565 x 412mm
State Tretyakov Gallery, Moscow

Fig. 6.9
The State Tretyakov Gallery, Moscow
State Tretyakov Gallery, Moscow

Fig. 6.10
Original design of the façade
of the Tretyakov Gallery
Viktor Vasnetsov, 1900
Watercolour, pen and India ink on paper
905 x 1940mm
State Tretyakov Gallery, Moscow

INDEX

References to illustrations are indicated in italic (e.g. *101* and *Plate 26*);
'*n*' refers to where an entry is mentioned in Notes.

A

Abramtsevo (country estate)
100–2, *101*, 116, 122, 130
Academy of Arts, St Petersburg
25–9, *28–9*, 32, 39, 43, 97, 127, 140
Acmeism 140
Akhmatova, Anna 127, 129, 140,
142–3, *142*, 149, *Plate 26*
Aksakov, Sergei 153
Alexander I, Tsar 37–9
Alexander II, Tsar 41, *68*
assassination 64, 69, 80, 142
Alexander III, Tsar 97, 108, 121
Alexandra Fedorovna, Empress
120, 121, *122*
Alexei I, Tsar 21
Alexei Nikolaevich, Tsarevich 121,
122
All-Russian Exhibition (1896) 130,
132
Anastasia Nikolaevna, Grand
Duchess 121, *122*
Anna Ioannovna, Empress 22
Anna Petrovna, Tsarevna *16–17*,
22, *23*
Antropov, Aleksei *27*
Apollon (magazine) 140
Art Nouveau 124
Association of Travelling Art
Exhibitions (Peredvizhnik
exhibitions) 43–4, *44*, 63–4, 69,
86, 105

B

Bakst, Lev 102
Balakirev, Mily 69, 70, 92,
112
Ballets Russes 102
Balmoral *120*, 121
Barbizon school 100, 124
Bastien-Lepage, Jules 100

Belinsky, Vissarion 155
Bell, The (almanac) 51
biography: and national identity
156
Bloody Sunday (1905) 127
Bolshoy Theatre, Moscow 124,
134
Bonnard, Pierre 138
Bonnat, Léon 48
Borodin, Alexander 69, 112, 123
Braque, Georges 129
Braz, Iosif 114, 140
Anton Chekhov 102, 114,
Plate 18
Britain *see* Great Britain
Byzantine art 122, 130

C

Caravaque, Louis *16–17*, 22, *23*
Carlyle, Thomas 156
Catherine I, Empress 22
Catherine II (the Great), Empress
25–32, *33*
Cézanne, Paul 138
Chagall, Marc 129, 138, 162
Chapiro, Constantin *56*
Chekhov, Anton 102, 114, 123, 136,
149, *Plate 18*
Chopin, Frédéric 70
Citizen, The (newspaper) 153
collecting, developments in 153–5
Constitution (1906) 127
country estates 102, 153
Abramtsevo 100–2, *101*, 116,
122, 130
Domotkanovo 102, 111,
Plate 16
Yasnaya Polyana 73, 89
Cui, César 69, 112

D

Dal, Vladimir 43, 54, 114, 159,
Plate 3
Dante Alighieri 156
Dargomyzhsky, Alexander 69
Dashkov, Vasily 155, 161*n*16
Dawe, George 37, 41
Decembrist Revolt (1825) 39
Degas, Edgar 124
Della-Vos-Kardovskaia, Olga 140
Anna Akhmatova 142, 149,
Plate 26
Nikolai Gumilev 6, 140,
Plate 25
Demidov, Prokofy 28–9, *31*
Denis, Maurice 124
Derain, André 129
Derviz, Nadezhda 102, *104*
Derviz, Vladimir 102, 111, 130
Diaghilev, Sergei 102, 123, 134
Diderot, Denis 25
Domotkanovo (country estate) 102,
111, *Plate 16*
Dostoevsky, Fedor 44, 56, *56*, 149,
153, 156, 159, *Plate 4*

E

Edward VII, King *120*
Elena Pavlovna, Grand Duchess 70,
97
Elizabeth, Empress 22, 25, *26*
Elizaveta Alekseevna, Empress
39
Emancipation of the Serfs (1861)
39–41
England *see* Great Britain
Enlightenment 25
Ermolova, Maria 124, 136, *Plate 23*
estates *see* country estates
Evelyn, John 19
Exposition Universelle (1889) 100

F

family portrait galleries 153
First World War 140
Five, The (composers) 69, 70, 90,
102, 108, 112
Florence 51
Uffizi Gallery 39
France:
art 22, 48–9, 97, 100, 124–5,
129, 138
relations with Russia 37
see also Paris
Free Music School 70, 92
Free Russian Press 51

G

Gainsborough, Thomas 155
Gandhi, Mahatma 89
Gauguin, Paul 125, 129, 138
Ge, Nikolai 51, *62*, 63, 132, 155
Alexander Herzen 51, 63,
Plate 1
Leo Tolstoy 73, 89, 112, 159,
Plate 11
George IV, King 37
Gillray, James: *The Magnanimous
Ally 36*, 37
Ginzburg, Ilya 159
Glinka, Mikhail 69, 149, 153
Gogol, Nikolai *148*, 149
Golden Fleece Exhibition (1908)
129
Golitsyn, Prince Alexander 28, *30*
Golovin, Alexander: *Fedor Shaliapin
in the Role of Holofernes* 134, *134*
Golovkin, Gavriil 22, *24*
Golubkina, Anna 124
Goncharova, Natalia 129, 138, 149
Gorky, Maxim 124
Grand Embassy of Peter the Great
(1697–8) 19, 21

Great Britain:
portraiture 37, 155
relations with Russia 37
see also London
Great Exhibition (1851) 73
Crystal Palace 155
Griboedov, Alexander 149, 153
Gumilev, Lev 142, 143
Gumilev, Nikolai *6*, 127, 140, *140*,
142, *Plate 25*

H

Hals, Frans 21
Hartmann, Viktor 70
Hermitage Museum, St Petersburg
39, 56, 138
Herzen, Alexander 41, 51, 63, *Plate 1*
Hildenbandt, Baroness Varvara
Ikskul von *9*, 97, 106, *Plate 14*
history painting 25, 43, 63, *66–7*,
116
Holbein, Hans, the Younger 155

I

Iaroshenko, Nikolai 86, 159
Pelageia Streptova 86, 149,
Plate 10
Ibsen, Henrik 123
icons 21, 52, 90
Imperial Academy of Arts, St
Petersburg *see* Academy of Arts
Impressionism 97, 100–2, 105,
124–5, 134, 138
Itter Castle 92

J

Janáček, Leoš 52
Japan: Russo-Japanese War
(1904–5) 127

K

Karamzin, Nikolai 153, *154*
Karatygin, Petr 153
Kardovsky, Dmitry 140
Kharlamov, Alexei 48–9
Khodynka Field tragedy (1896)
121–2
Kiev 28
Church of St Cyril 130
College for Women 142
St Sophia Cathedral 130
Kiprensky, Orest 39
Alexander Pushkin 39, *40*, 155
Self-portrait 38
Kneller, Sir Godfrey *18*, 19–21
Kokorinov, Alexander 28
Korovin, Konstantin 134, 138
Fedor Shaliapin 134, *Plate 22*
Kramskoy, Ivan 43, 48, 56, 86, 153
*The Actor Alexander Lensky as
Petruchio in Shakespeare's*
The Taming of the Shrew
14, 85, *Plate 9*
Christ in the Wilderness 159
Fedor Vasilev 43, *45*
Leo Tolstoy 71, 73
Self-portrait 42
Kuznetsov, Nikolai 100
Holiday 63, *64*, 100
Petr Tchaikovsky 108, *Plate 15*

L

landscape painting 63, *64*, *65*, *101*
Larionov, Mikhail 129, 138
Lavrov, Petr 156
Lawrence, Sir Thomas 37
Lensky, Alexander *14*, 85,
Plate 9
Lermontov, Mikhail 132, 153
Leskov, Nikolai 149, 159
Levitsky, Dmitry 28–9, *30*, *31*

Liszt, Franz 70, 82, 92

lithographs 155

Lomonosov, Mikhail 25

London:

    Great Exhibition (1851) 73, 155

    Herzen's exile in 41, 51

    Hyde Park 155

    International Exhibition (1862) 76

    National Portrait Gallery 155, 156

    Peter the Great visits 19

Lope de Vega 136

M

Maillol, Aristide 138

Makovsky, Konstantin: *Alexander II on His Deathbed* 64, *68*

Malevich, Kazimir 129, 162

    Self-portrait 128, 129

Maly Theatre, Moscow 85, 124, 136

Mamontov, Savva 100–1, 122–3, 130, *130*, 132, 134

    Savva Mamontov (Repin) *98*, 100

    Savva Mamontov (Vrubel) 122, 130, *Plate 20*

Mamontova, Elizaveta *99*, 100

Mamontova, Vera 101–2, *103*

Manet, Édouard 48, 125

    Olympia 92, 97

Maria Nikolaevna, Grand Duchess 121, *122*

Mariinsky Theatre, St Petersburg 70, 132, 134

Matisse, Henri 129, 138

Menter, Sophie *11*, 73, 92, *Plate 13*

Meshchersky, Vladimir 153

Mighty Handful, The (composers) *see* Five, The

Mikhail Pavlovich, Grand Duke 97

Milan: La Scala 134

Miunster, Alexander 155

Modigliani, Amedeo 142

Moller, Fedor (*né* Otto Friedrich Theodor von Möller): *Nikolai Gogol 148*, 149

Momontova, Elizaveta *99*

Monet, Claude 138

Morozov, Arseny 124

Morozov, Ivan *118–19*, 124–5, 138, *Plate 24*

Morozov, Mika 125, *125*

Morozov, Mikhail 124–5, *126*, 138

Morozov, Savva 124

Morozov, Sergei 124

Moscow:

    Bolshoy Theatre 124, 134

    Cathedral of the Dormition 102, *105*

    Foundling Hospital 28

    Golden Fleece Exhibition (1908) 129

    Maly Theatre 85, 124, 136

    Novodevichy Cemetery 134

    Novodevichy Convent 21

    Pushkin Museum of Fine Arts 138, 161*n*11

    Rumiantsev Museum 155

    St Basil's Cathedral 63

    see also Tretyakov Gallery

Moscow Art Theatre 114, 123–4

Moscow Conservatoire 70, 108

Moscow Literary and Artistic Circle 136

Moscow Society of Art Lovers 155

Moscow University 25

Mussorgsky, Modest 69–70, 80, *80*, 102, 112, 123, 134, 149

    Modest Mussorgsky (Repin) *10*, 69, 70, 80, 159–60, *Plate 7*

N

Nadar (Gaspard-Félix Tournachon) *58*

Napoleon Bonaparte 37

national identity, concepts of 155–6

National Portrait Gallery, London 155, 156

Nekrasov, Nikolai 149

Nemirovich-Danchenko, Vladimir 123, 124

Nesterov, Mikhail 149

Nevrev, Nikolai 149

New Society of Artists 140

New Time (journal) 149

New York: Carnegie Hall 108

Nicholas I, Tsar 39, *41*, 56, 70

Nicholas II, Tsar *120*, 121–2, *122*, 127

    coronation 102, *105*, 121–2

Nikitin, Ivan 22, *24*

Nizhny Novogorod: All-Russian Exhibition (1896) 130, 132

O

October Manifesto (1905) 127

Olga Nikolaevna, Grand Duchess *120*, 121, *122*

Orlov, Count Grigory 25

Orthodox Church 22, 52, 73

Ostrovsky, Alexander *34–5*, 52, 86, 124, 125, 149, *Plate 2*

Oxford University 44, 143

P

Panin, L.N. 155

Paris 44, 48, 51, 58, 97

    Exposition Universelle (1889) 100

    Sorbonne 140

parsuna portraiture 21
Pasternak, Leonid: *Sergei Rachmaninov 158*
Paul I, Tsar *36, 37,* 97
Paxton, Sir Joseph 155
Peredvizhniki *see* Association of Travelling Art Exhibitions
Perov, Vasily 43–4, 52, 149, 153
    Alexander Ostrovsky 34–5, 43, 52, *Plate 2*
    Fedor Dostoevsky 44, 56, 70, 159, *Plate 4*
    The Village Religious Procession at Easter 52, 52
    Vladimir Dal 43, 54, 70, 114, 159, *Plate 3*
Peter I (the Great), Tsar *18,* 19–22, *20,* 63
Peter III, Tsar 25, *27*
Petrashevsky Circle 56
photography 43, 153
Pisemsky, Alexei *2,* 63, 78, 86, 124, 149, 159, *Plate 6*
Pitt, William, the Younger 37
Pogodin, Mikhail 149, 156
Poland 21
Polar Star (almanac) 51
Polenov, Vasily 127
Popper, David 92
portrait galleries, developments in 153–60
Post-Impressionism 124–5, 138
Prakhov, Adrian 156
Prenner, Georg Caspar 25, *26*
prints and printmaking *20,* 21, 32, *36, 41,* 155
Private Opera Society *see* Russian Private Opera
Punin, Nikolai 142
Pushkin, Alexander 39, *40,* 149, 153, 155

Pushkin Museum of Fine Arts, Moscow 138, 161*n*11

R

Rachmaninov, Sergei 123, 134, *158*
Rasputin, Grigory 121
Realism, Russian 44, *46–7,* 90, 160
religion 22, 52, 73
    icons 21, 52, 90
Rembrandt van Rijn 21, 51
Renoir, Pierre-Auguste 124, 138
Repin, Ilia 44–9, *48,* 89, 100, 111, 116, 149, 153
    Abramtsevo 100, *101*
    Alexei Pisemsky 2, 63, 78, *Plate 6*
    Anton Rubinstein 12, 70, 82, *Plate 8*
    Barge Haulers on the Volga 44, 46, *46–7*
    Baroness Varvara Ikskul von Hildenbandt 9, 97, 106, *Plate 14*
    Dmitry Mendeleev 157
    Elizaveta Mamontova 99, 100
    Ivan Turgenev 44, 47–9, 58, 114, *Plate 5*
    Leo Tolstoy 73, 76, 159
    Leo Tolstoy Barefoot 159
    Modest Mussorgsky 10, 69, 70, 80, 159–60, *Plate 7*
    Nikolai Ge 62, 63
    Pavel Tretyakov 4–5, 102, 116, *Plate 19*
    The Ploughman, Leo Tolstoy ploughing 73, 74–5, 159
    Savva Mamontov 98, 100
    Sophie Menter 11, 73, 92, *Plate 13*
    Study of actress Pelageia Strepetova 86, 149, *151*

Vladimir Stasov 73, 77
Vladimir Stasov at His Dacha in the Village of Starozhilovka near Pargolovo 60–1, 73, 90, 106, *Plate 12*
Revolt of the Fourteen (1863) 43
Revolution (1905) 127
Revolution (1917) 106, 121, 138
Reynolds, Sir Joshua 155
Rimsky-Korsakov, Nikolai 69, 70, *94–5,* 102, 112, 123, 127, 132, 134, 149, *Plate 17*
Robinson, John Henry (engraver) *41*
Rokotov, Fedor 29, 32, *33*
Rostov Veliky 32
Rovinsky, Dmitry 155
Royal Philharmonic Society 92
Rozanov, Vasily 156
Rubinstein, Anton *12,* 70, 82, *82,* 92, 97, 108, 149, *Plate 8*
Rubinstein, Nikolai 70, 82, 108, 149
Rumiantsev Museum, Moscow 155
Russian Musical Society 70
Russian Philharmonic Society 108
Russian Private Opera 122–3, 130, 132, 134
Russo-Japanese War (1904–5) 127

S

St Petersburg, foundation and development 21–2, 77*n*2
St Petersburg:
    Academy of Arts 25–9, *28–9,* 32, 39, 43, 97, 127, 140
    Academy of Sciences 22, 90
    Hermitage Museum 39, 56, 138
    Imperial Public Library 90
    Kunstkamera 22

Mariinsky Theatre 70, 132, 134
Mikhailovsky Palace 97
Nikolaevsky Military Hospital
80
State Russian Museum 97
Summer Garden 22
Winter Palace 22, 37–9, 64,
121, 127
St Petersburg Conservatoire 70, 92,
108, 112, 127
salons (literary and musical) 97,
106
Schiller, Friedrich 136
Serebriakova, Zinaida 149, *152*
serfdom 29, 78
Emancipation of the Serfs
(1861) 39–41
Serov, Alexander 100, 134,
149
Serov, Valentin 100–5, 111, 122, 127
*Coronation: the Anointing of
Nicholas II in the Cathedral
of the Dormition* 102, *105*
*Girl with Peaches (Vera
Mamontova)* 101–2, *103*
In the Summer 102, 111,
Plate 16
Ivan Morozov 118–19, 138,
Plate 24
Maria Ermolova 124, 136,
Plate 23
Mika Morozov 125, *125*
Mikhail Morozov 125, *126*
*Nadezhda Derviz with Her
Child* 102, *104*
Nikolai Rimsky-Korsakov
94–5, 102, 112, 149, *Plate 17*
Serova, Olga 102, 111, *Plate 16*
Serova, Valentina 100, 101
Shakespeare, William 85, 123, 156
Shaliapin, Fedor 123, 134, *134, Plate
22*

Shaw, George Bernard 92
Shchepkin, Mikhail 149
Shchukin, Sergei 138
Shekhtel, Fedor 124
Shevchenko, Taras 153
Shishkin, Ivan: *Thickets* 63,
65
Shuvalov, Count Ivan 25
Sirius (journal) 142
Slavophile Society 149
Smith, John (engraver) *20*
Sophia Alekseyevna, Tsarevna
21
Soviet Union 129, 140, 142–3
Stalin, Joseph 129, 142
Stanislavsky, Konstantin 114,
123–4, 136
Stasov, Vladimir 47, 48–9, 69, 70,
73, 76, 90, 108
*Vladimir Stasov at His
Dacha in the Village of
Starozhilovka near
Pargolovo* (Repin) *60–1*,
73, 90, 106, *Plate 12*
Vladimir Stasov (Repin)
73, *77*
State Duma 127
State Russian Museum,
St Petersburg 97
State Tretyakov Gallery, Moscow
see Tretyakov Gallery
Streltsy Uprising (1698) 21, 63,
64, *66–7*
Strepetova, Pelageia (Polina) 86,
149, *151, Plate 10*
Surikov, Vasily: *The Morning of
the Execution of the Streltsy*
63, 64, *66–7*
Suvorin, Alexei 86
Symbolism 122, 130, 140

T

Tatiana Nikolaevna, Grand Duchess
121, *122*
Tatlin, Vladimir 129
Tchaikovsky, Petr 92, 108, *108*, 123,
149, *Plate 15*
Tolstaya, Countess Sophia 89
Tolstoy, Count Leo *72*, 73, 89, 90,
149, 156, 159, 161*n*16
Leo Tolstoy (Ge) 73, 89, 112,
159, *Plate 11*
Leo Tolstoy (Kramskoy) *71*, 73
Leo Tolstoy (Repin) 73, *76*, 159
Leo Tolstoy Barefoot (Repin)
159
*The Ploughman, Leo Tolstoy
ploughing* (Repin) 73,
74–5, 159
Toscanini, Arturo 134
Tretyakov, Pavel *146*
collection 51, 52, 58, 63, 69,
70, 73, 78, 97, 102, 116,
147–60
family, life and career 44, 82,
97, 102, *144–5*, 149, *150*
Pavel Tretyakov (Repin) *4–5*,
102, 116, *Plate 19*
Tretyakov, Sergei 97, 149
Tretyakov Gallery, Moscow:
buildings *160*, 162, *162*
collections 92, 147, 155, 156,
160, 162
history 44, 97, 162
Tretyakova, Liubov 102
Tretyakova, Vera 82
Tropinin, Vasily 149
Nikolai Karamzin 153, *154*
Trubetskoy, Pavel 159
Tsarskoe Selo 140
Turgenev, Ivan 43–4, 47–9, 58,
58, 114, 124, 149, *Plate 5*

U

Ukraine 21, 28, 44
   see also Kiev

V

Vallin de la Mothe, Jean-Baptiste
   Michel 28
Van Dyck, Sir Anthony 21, 56,
   155
Van Gogh, Vincent 124, 129, 138
Vasilev, Fedor 43, *45*
Vasnetsov, Viktor 162
   Bogatyrs 116, *116*
Vega, Lope de 136
Velázquez, Diego 49, 56
Vereshchagin, Vasily 161*n*16
Viardot, Louis 47
Viardot, Pauline 47–8, 58
Victoria, Queen *120*, 121
Vienna: International Exhibition
   (1873) 46
Vladimir Aleksandrovich,
   Grand Duke 46, 127
Vogüé, Eugène-Melchior de 156
Voltaire 25
Vrubel, Mikhail 122–3, 124, 130,
   132, 138, 149
    Nadezhda Zabela-Vrubel 122,
     132, *Plate 21*
    Savva Mamontov 122, 130,
     Plate 20
    Seated Demon 122, *123*
    The Swan Princess 132, *132*

W

William III, King 19
Windsor Castle: Waterloo Chamber
   37
women: and portraiture 149
World of Art (journal) 102, 123

Y

Yasnaya Polyana (country estate)
   73, 89

Z

Zabela-Vrubel, Nadezhda 122, 132,
   132, *Plate 21*
Zabolotsky, Petr 153

Published in Great Britain by
National Portrait Gallery Publications
St Martin's Place, London WC2H 0HE

Published to accompany the exhibition
*Russia and the Arts: The Age of Tolstoy
and Tchaikovsky* at the National Portrait
Gallery, London, from 17 March to 26 June 2016.

This exhibition has been made possible by the provision of insurance
through the Government Indemnity Scheme. The National Portrait
Gallery, London, would like to thank HM Government for providing
Government Indemnity and the Department for Culture, Media and
Sport and Arts Council England for arranging the indemnity.

Generously supported by the Blavatnik Family Foundation

Supported by the *Russia and the Arts* Exhibition Supporters Group

The National Portrait Gallery's Spring Season 2016 is sponsored by
Herbert Smith Freehills.

Every purchase supports the National Portrait Gallery, London. For
a complete catalogue of current publications, please write to the
National Portrait Gallery at the address above, or visit our website at
www.npg.org/publications

ISBN 978 1 85514 537 5

A catalogue record for this book is available from the British Library.

10 9 8 7 6 5 4 3 2

Managing Editor: Christopher Tinker
Editor: Andrew Roff
Copy-editor: Patricia Burgess
Picture research: Kathleen Bloomfield
Production Manager: Ruth Müller-Wirth
Designer: Will Webb

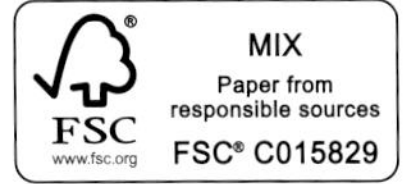

Printed in Italy

Page 2: *Alexei Pisemsky* by Ilia Repin, 1880
(detail of plate 6, page 79)

Pages 4–5: *Pavel Tretyakov* by Ilia Repin, 1901
(detail of plate 19, page 117)

Page 6: *Nikolai Gumilev* by Olga Della-Vos-Kardovskaia, 1909
(detail of plate 25, page 141)

Page 9: *Baroness Varvara Ikskul von Hildenbandt* by Ilia Repin, 1889
(detail of plate 14, page 107)

Page 10: *Modest Mussorgsky* by Ilia Repin, 1881
(detail of plate 7, page 81)

Page 11: *Sophie Menter* by Ilia Repin, 1887
(detail of plate 13, page 93)

Page 12: *Anton Rubinstein* by Ilia Repin, 1881
(detail of plate 8, page 83)

Page 14: *The Actor Alexander Lensky as Petruchio in Shakespeare's
The Taming of the Screw* by Ivan Kramskoy, 1883
(detail of plate 9, page 84)

Pages 16–17: *Tsarevna Anna Petrovna* by Louis Caravaque, 1725
(detail of Fig. 1.3, page 23)

Pages 34–5: *Alexander Ostrovsky* by Vasily Perov, 1871
(detail of plate 2, page 53)

Pages 60–1: *Vladimir Stasov at His Dacha in the Village of
Starozhilovka near Pargolovo* by Ilia Repin, 1889–90
(detail of plate 12, page 91)

Pages 94–5: *Nikolai Rimsky-Korsakov* by Valentin Serov, 1898
(detail of plate 17, page 113)

Pages 118–19: *Ivan Morozov* by Valentin Serov, 1910
(detail of plate 24, page 139)

Pages 144–5: Pavel Tretyakov and his family photographed by
I. Diagovchenko, 1884
(detail of Fig. 6.3, page 150)

This book uses a modified form of the Library of Congress system of
transliteration. For readability, it omits diacritical marks from proper
nouns (Gogol, rather than Gogol'), and uses 'y' rather than 'ii' and 'oy'
rather than 'oi' for the end of proper names (Dostoevsky rather than
Dostoevskii and Tolstoy rather than Tolstoi). The names of rulers are
given in their familiar English form, hence Peter, Catherine and Paul,
rather than Petr, Ekaterina and Pavel. The same is true of first names
such as Natalia and Maria, and of well known figures such as
Tchaikovsky and Shaliapin.